MW01488373

EARLY GREEK PHILOSOPHY

II

LCL 525

EARLY GREEK PHILOSOPHY

VOLUME II

BEGINNINGS AND EARLY IONIAN THINKERS

PART 1

EDITED AND TRANSLATED BY

ANDRÉ LAKS AND GLENN W. MOST

IN COLLABORATION WITH
GÉRARD JOURNÉE

AND ASSISTED BY
LEOPOLDO IRIBARREN

HARVARD UNIVERSITY PRESS
CAMBRIDGE, MASSACHUSETTS
LONDON, ENGLAND
2016

First published 2016

LOEB CLASSICAL LIBRARY® is a registered trademark
of the President and Fellows of Harvard College

Library of Congress Control Number 2015957358
CIP data available from the Library of Congress

ISBN 978-0-674-99689-2

*Composed in ZephGreek and ZephText by
Technologies 'N Typography, Merrimac, Massachusetts.
Printed on acid-free paper and bound by
The Maple-Vail Book Manufacturing Group*

CONTENTS

PRELIMINARIES

1. ANCIENT WAYS OF ORGANIZING AND PRESENTING EARLY GREEK THOUGHT: DOXOGRAPHY AND SUCCESSIONS [DOX.]

In this preliminary chapter, we present a series of texts intended to clarify the way in which the summaries of doctrine and the doxographic manuals, to which we owe a large part of our information on the doctrines of the archaic philosophers, were produced during the course of the history of Greek philosophy and how some of them have been reconstructed by modern philologists. Although doxographical literature goes back to pre-Aristotelian sources, notably the sophist Hippias and Plato, the systematic investigation of the 'opinions' (*doxai*) of predecessors arises with Aristotle and Theophrastus, who are the ultimate source—beyond the compressions, transformations, and additions that accumulated in the course of time—of a handbook of which the most ancient version probably dates to the third century BC and which scholars customarily refer to as the manual of Aëtius. **T17** illustrates how a version of that manual is hypothetically reconstructed on the basis of the various ancient authors who made use of it, **T18** the way in which the summaries scattered through-

out the different chapters of our anthology may have originally been presented in it. In this chapter, the critical apparatus is reduced to a very small number of indications, and references to parallels with texts that appear in other chapters are given only exceptionally.

BIBLIOGRAPHY

Editions of Doxographic Sources

H. Daiber. *Aetius Arabus. Die Vorsokratiker in arabischer Überlieferung* (Wiesbaden, 1980).

H. Diels. *Doxographi Graeci* (Berlin, 1879; repr., 1963).

J. Mansfeld and D. T. Runia. *Aëtiana. The Method and Intellectual Context of a Doxographer.* Vols. I–II: *The Sources* (vol. I), *The Compendium* (vol. II) (Leiden-New York-Cologne, 1997–2009).

General Studies

J. Mansfeld and D. T. Runia. *Aëtiana. The Method and Intellectual Context of a Doxographer.* Vol. III, *Studies in the Doxographical Traditions of Ancient Philosophy* (Leiden, New York, Cologne, 2009).

Particular Studies

J. Mansfeld. *Heresiography in Context: Hippolytus' 'Elenchos' as a Source for Greek Philosophy* (Leiden, New York, Cologne, 1992).

J. Mejer. *Diogenes Laertius and His Hellenistic Background* (Wiesbaden, 1978).

———. "Diogenes Laertius and The Transmission of Greek Philosophy," *ANRW* II.36.5 (1992): 3556–602.

A. Patzer. *Der Sophist Hippias als Philosophiehistoriker* (Munich, 1986).

OUTLINE OF THE CHAPTER

DOXOGRAPHY AND
SUCCESSIONS

By Topics ("Doxography") (T1–T19)
Pre-Aristotelian Schemes (T1–T7)

T1 (86 B6) Hippias in Clem. Alex. *Strom.* 6.15.2 [=
HIPPIAS D22]

τούτων ἴσως εἴρηται τὰ μὲν Ὀρφεῖ, τὰ δὲ Μουσαίῳ,
κατὰ βραχὺ ἄλλῳ ἀλλαχοῦ, τὰ δὲ Ἡσιόδῳ, τὰ δὲ
Ὁμήρῳ, τὰ δὲ τοῖς ἄλλοις τῶν ποιητῶν, τὰ δὲ ἐν συγ-
γραφαῖς τὰ μὲν Ἕλλησι, τὰ δὲ βαρβάροις· ἐγὼ δὲ ἐκ
πάντων τούτων τὰ μέγιστα καὶ ὁμόφυλα συνθεὶς τοῦτον καινὸν καὶ πολυειδῆ τὸν λόγον ποιήσομαι.

T2 (> 23 A6) Plat. *Theaet.* 152e

[ΣΩ.] καὶ περὶ τούτου πάντες ἑξῆς οἱ σοφοὶ πλὴν
Παρμενίδου συμφερέσθων, Πρωταγόρας τε καὶ Ἡράκλειτος καὶ Ἐμπεδοκλῆς, καὶ τῶν ποιητῶν οἱ ἄκροι
τῆς ποιήσεως ἑκατέρας, κωμῳδίας μὲν Ἐπίχαρμος,
τραγῳδίας δὲ Ὅμηρος, ὃς εἰπών,

DOXOGRAPHY AND SUCCESSIONS

By Topics ("Doxography") (T1–T19)
Pre-Aristotelian Schemes (T1–T7)

T1 (86 B6) Hippias in Clement of Alexandria, *Stromata*
[= **HIPPIAS D22**]

Of these [scil. probably: ancient opinions] some have doubtless been expressed by Orpheus, others by Musaeus, to put it briefly, by each one in a different place, others by Hesiod, others by Homer, others by the other poets; others in treatises; some by Greeks, others by non-Greeks. But I myself have put together from out of all these the ones that are most important and are akin to one another, and on their basis I shall compose the following new and variegated discourse.

T2 (> 23 A6) Plato, *Theaetetus*

[Socrates:] And on this point [i.e. that nothing exists but everything is always changing] let us admit that all the sages except Parmenides in sequence were in agreement—Protagoras, Heraclitus, and Empedocles, and among the poets the greatest representatives of both kinds of poetry, Epicharmus for comedy and Homer for tragedy, who when he says

Ὠκεανόν τε θεῶν γένεσιν καὶ μητέρα Τηθύν,

πάντα εἴρηκεν ἔκγονα ῥοῆς τε καὶ κινήσεως.

T3 (> 22 A6) Plat. *Crat.* 402a–c

[ΣΩ.] λέγει που Ἡράκλειτος ὅτι "πάντα χωρεῖ καὶ οὐδὲν μένει," καὶ ποταμοῦ ῥοῇ ἀπεικάζων τὰ ὄντα λέγει
ὡς "δὶς ἐς τὸν αὐτὸν ποταμὸν οὐκ ἂν ἐμβαίης." [. . .]
τί οὖν; δοκεῖ σοι ἀλλοιότερον Ἡρακλείτου νοεῖν ὁ
τιθέμενος τοῖς τῶν ἄλλων θεῶν προγόνοις ῾Ρέαν᾽ τε
καὶ ῾Κρόνον᾽; ἆρα οἴει ἀπὸ τοῦ αὐτομάτου αὐτὸν ἀμ-
φοτέροις ῥευμάτων ὀνόματα θέσθαι; ὥσπερ αὖ Ὅμηρος

Ὠκεανόν τε θεῶν γένεσίν, φησιν, καὶ μητέρα
    Τηθύν·

οἶμαι δὲ καὶ Ἡσίοδος. λέγει δέ που καὶ Ὀρφεὺς ὅτι

Ὠκεανὸς πρῶτος καλλίρροος ἦρξε γάμοιο,
ὅς ῥα κασιγνήτην ὁμομήτορα Τηθὺν ὄπυιεν.

ταῦτ᾽ οὖν σκόπει ὅτι καὶ ἀλλήλοις συμφωνεῖ καὶ πρὸς
τὰ τοῦ Ἡρακλείτου πάντα τείνει.

Ocean, the origin of the gods, and mother Tethys
[= **COSM. T10a**],

is stating that all things are born from flux and movement.

T3 (> 22 A6) Plato, *Cratylus*

[Socrates:] Heraclitus says something like this: that all things flow and nothing remains; and comparing the things that are to the flowing of a river, he says that you could not step twice into the same river [cf. **HER. D65c**]. [. . .] Well then, do you think that the man who gave the names 'Rhea' and 'Cronus' to the ancestors of the other gods had something different in mind from Heraclitus? Do you suppose that it is by chance that he gave to both of them the names of flowing things (*rheumata*)?[1] So too, Homer says,

Ocean, the origin of the gods, and their mother Tethys, [= **COSM. T10a**]

and I think Hesiod too [cf. *Th.* 776–77; **COSM. T7,** lines 789, 805–6]. And Orpheus too says somewhere that

Fair-flowing Ocean was the first to make a beginning of marriage,
He who wedded his sister Tethys, born of the same mother. [= **COSM. T15**]

Just look how these all agree with one another and tend toward Heraclitus' doctrines.

[1] The sound of the Greek term can be taken to refer both to *Rhea* and to *Kronos* (cf. *krênê, krounos*).

T4 (cf. 21 A29, 22 A10, 31 A29) Plat. *Soph.* 242c–243a

[ΞΕ.] μῦθόν τινα ἕκαστος φαίνεταί μοι διηγεῖσθαι παισὶν ὡς οὖσιν ἡμῖν, ὁ μὲν ὡς τρία ὄντα, πολεμεῖ δὲ ἀλλήλοις ἐνίοτε αὐτῶν ἄττα πῃ, τοτὲ δὲ καὶ φίλα γιγνόμενα γάμους τε καὶ τόκους καὶ τροφὰς τῶν ἐκγόνων παρέχεται· δύο δὲ ἕτερος εἰπών, ὑγρὸν καὶ ξηρὸν ἢ θερμὸν καὶ ψυχρόν, συνοικίζει τε αὐτὰ καὶ ἐκδίδωσι· τὸ δὲ παρ' ἡμῖν Ἐλεατικὸν ἔθνος, ἀπὸ Ξενοφάνους τε καὶ ἔτι πρόσθεν ἀρξάμενον, ὡς ἑνὸς ὄντος τῶν πάντων καλουμένων οὕτω διεξέρχεται τοῖς μύθοις. Ἰάδες δὲ καὶ Σικελαί τινες ὕστερον Μοῦσαι συνενόησαν ὅτι συμπλέκειν ἀσφαλέστατον ἀμφότερα καὶ λέγειν ὡς τὸ ὂν πολλά τε καὶ ἕν ἐστιν, ἔχθρᾳ δὲ καὶ φιλίᾳ συνέχεται. διαφερόμενον γὰρ ἀεὶ συμφέρεται, φασὶν αἱ συντονώτεραι τῶν Μουσῶν· αἱ δὲ μαλακώτεραι τὸ μὲν ἀεὶ ταῦτα οὕτως ἔχειν ἐχάλασαν, ἐν μέρει δὲ τοτὲ μὲν ἓν εἶναί φασι τὸ πᾶν καὶ φίλον ὑπ' Ἀφροδίτης, τοτὲ δὲ πολλὰ καὶ πολέμιον αὐτὸ αὑτῷ διὰ νεῖκός τι.

10

T4 (cf. 21 A29, 22 A10, 31 A29) Plato, *Sophist*

[The stranger from Elea:] Every one of them [scil. the early philosophers] seems to me to tell some kind of story to us as though we were children. One says that there are three beings, that at one time some of them wage war against each other, and that another they become friends, get married, give birth, and raise their offspring [= **PHER. R2**]; another, speaking of two [scil. beings], the moist and the dry or the hot and the cold, makes them live together and gives them to each other in marriage;[1] our Eleatic tribe, which begins with Xenophanes and even earlier, explain in their stories that what are called "all things" is one [= **XEN. R1**]. Certain Ionian Muses [i.e. Heraclitus], and later some Sicilian ones [i.e. Empedocles],[2] recognized that it would be safest to weave together both positions [i.e. monist and pluralist] and to say that being is at the same time many and one, and that it is held together by discord and friendship. For what is separated is always brought together, as the more tense of these Muses say [cf. **HER. R31**]. The other ones, more relaxed, have softened the idea that this is always how things are, and say that it is in alternation that at one time the whole is one and friendly under the dominion of Aphrodite, at another time many and hostile to itself because of a certain strife [= **EMP. D78**].

[1] The opposites function as principles for various natural philosophers, but no precise identification is required here.

[2] Plato is presumably referring to the title of Heraclitus' book [**HER. R3c**] and is extending it to Empedocles' poem.

11

T5 (≠ DK) Xen. *Mem.* 1.1.13–14

[. . .] τῶν τε περὶ τῆς τῶν πάντων φύσεως μεριμνών-
των τοῖς μὲν δοκεῖν ἓν μόνον τὸ ὂν εἶναι, τοῖς δ'
ἄπειρα τὸ πλῆθος, καὶ τοῖς μὲν ἀεὶ πάντα κινεῖσθαι,
τοῖς δ' οὐδὲν ἄν ποτε κινηθῆναι, καὶ τοῖς μὲν πάντα
γίγνεσθαί τε καὶ ἀπόλλυσθαι, τοῖς δὲ οὔτ' ἂν γενέσθαι ποτὲ οὐδὲν οὔτε ἀπολέσαι.

T6 (> 24 A3, > 36 A6, > 82 B1) Isocr. *Ant.* 268–69

διατρῖψαι μὲν οὖν περὶ τὰς παιδείας ταύτας χρόνον
τινὰ συμβουλεύσαιμ' ἂν τοῖς νεωτέροις, μὴ μέντοι
περιιδεῖν τὴν φύσιν τὴν αὑτῶν κατασκελετευθεῖσαν
ἐπὶ τούτοις μηδ' ἐξοκείλασαν εἰς τοὺς λόγους τοὺς
τῶν παλαιῶν σοφιστῶν, ὧν ὁ μὲν ἄπειρον τὸ πλῆθος
ἔφησεν εἶναι τῶν ὄντων, Ἐμπεδοκλῆς δὲ τέτταρα καὶ
νεῖκος καὶ φιλίαν ἐν αὐτοῖς, Ἴων δ' οὐ πλείω τριῶν,
Ἀλκμέων δὲ δύο μόνα, Παρμενίδης δὲ καὶ Μέλισσος
ἕν, Γοργίας δὲ παντελῶς οὐδέν. ἡγοῦμαι γὰρ τὰς μὲν
τοιαύτας τερατολογίας ὁμοίας εἶναι ταῖς θαυματο-
ποιίαις ταῖς οὐδὲν μὲν ὠφελούσαις, ὑπὸ δὲ τῶν ἀνοή-
των περιστάτοις γιγνομέναις.

T7 (≠ DK) Isocr. *Hel.* 3

πῶς γὰρ ἄν τις ὑπερβάλοιτο Γοργίαν τὸν τολμήσαντα
λέγειν ὡς οὐδὲν τῶν ὄντων ἔστιν ἢ Ζήνωνα τὸν ταὐτὰ
δυνατὰ καὶ πάλιν ἀδύνατα πειρώμενον ἀποφαίνειν ἢ

12

T5 (≠ DK) Xenophon, *Memorabilia*

[. . .] [Scil. Socrates was astonished that] among those who are preoccupied with the nature of all things, some think that what is is only one, others that it is infinite in number; the ones that all things are always in motion, the others that nothing could ever be in motion; and the ones that all things come into being and are destroyed, the others that nothing could ever either come into being or be destroyed.

T6 (> 24 A3, > 36 A6, > 82 B1) Isocrates, *Antidosis*

I would advise young men to spend some time on these kinds of study [i.e. philosophy] but not to allow their nature to become desiccated by them nor to run aground on the arguments of the ancient wise men (*sophistai*), of whom one said that the number of the things that are is unlimited [cf. **ATOM. D45–D47**]; Empedocles that there are four, and strife and love among them [cf. **EMP. D56**]; Ion that there are not more than three; Alcmaeon only two [cf. **ALCM. D3**]; Parmenides and Melissus that it is one [cf. **PARM. D8.11, R22; MEL. D6–D7**]; and Gorgias that it is none at all [cf. **GORG. D26a[1]**]. For I think that these kinds of marvelous tales are similar to magicians' tricks, which are of no use whatsoever but are admired by mindless people.

T7 (≠ DK) Isocrates, *Encomium of Helen*

For how could one surpass Gorgias, who dared to say that nothing exists of the things that exist [cf. **GORG. D26a[1], D26b[65]**], or Zeno, who tries to demonstrate that the same things are possible and then again impossible [cf.

Μέλισσον ὃς ἀπείρων τὸ πλῆθος πεφυκότων τῶν πρα-
γμάτων ὡς ἑνὸς ὄντος τοῦ παντὸς ἐπεχείρησεν ἀποδεί-
ξεις εὑρίσκειν;

Peripatetic Doxography (T8–T16)
Aristotle (T8–T12)
Reasons for Studying Ancient Opinions (T8–T10)

T8 (≠ DK) Arist. *Top.* 1.14 105a34–b18

τὰς μὲν οὖν προτάσεις ἐκλεκτέον ὁσαχῶς διωρίσθη
περὶ προτάσεως, ἢ τὰς πάντων δόξας προχειριζόμε-
νον ἢ τὰς τῶν πλείστων ἢ τὰς τῶν σοφῶν, καὶ τούτων
ἢ πάντων ἢ τῶν πλείστων ἢ τῶν γνωριμωτάτων, μὴ¹
ἐναντίας ταῖς φαινομέναις, καὶ ὅσαι δόξαι κατὰ τέχνας εἰσίν [. . .]. ἐκλέγειν δὲ χρὴ καὶ ἐκ τῶν γεγραμ-
μένων λόγων, τὰς δὲ διαγραφὰς ποιεῖσθαι περὶ ἑκάστου γένους ὑποτιθέντας χωρίς, οἷον περὶ ἀγαθοῦ ἢ
περὶ ζώου, καὶ περὶ ἀγαθοῦ παντός, ἀρξάμενον ἀπὸ
τοῦ τί ἐστιν. παρασημαίνεσθαι δὲ καὶ τὰς ἑκάστων
δόξας, οἷον ὅτι Ἐμπεδοκλῆς τέτταρα ἔφησε τῶν σωμάτων στοιχεῖα εἶναι· θείη γὰρ ἄν τις τὸ ὑπό τινος
εἰρημένον ἐνδόξου.

¹ μὴ Brunschwig (post Waitz): ἢ τὰς vel ἢ καὶ τὰς mss.

T9 (≠ DK) Arist. *Metaph.* A3 983a33–b6

τεθεώρηται μὲν οὖν ἱκανῶς περὶ αὐτῶν ἡμῖν ἐν τοῖς

ZEN. D4–D11], or Melissus, who, although things are by nature infinite in number, tried to find proofs that the whole is one [cf. **MEL. D6–D7, R24c**]?

Peripatetic Doxography (T8–T16)
Aristotle (T8–T12)
Reasons for Studying Ancient Opinions (T8–T10)

T8 (≠ DK) Aristotle, *Topics*

The premises should be chosen in just as many ways as the distinction we made regarding a premise [cf. 104a8–16], either selecting the opinions of all or those of the majority or those of the experts (*sophoi*), and of these latter either those of all or of the majority or of the most celebrated, when they are ‹not› opposite to the manifest ones [. . .]. One should also collect them [i.e. the premises] from written books, and make lists about every subject, setting them out under separate headings, for example "about the good" or "about the animal," (and "on every [scil. type] of good"), beginning with the essence.[1] And one should also mark in the margins the opinions of each author, for example that Empedocles said that the elements of bodies are four [cf. **EMP. D56**]; for what is said by someone reputable (*endoxos*) is likely to be accepted.

[1] For a list deriving ultimately from this program, see **T17**.

T9 (≠ DK) Aristotle, *Metaphysics*

Although we have examined them [i.e. the four causes]

περὶ φύσεως, ὅμως δὲ παραλάβωμεν καὶ τοὺς πρότερον ἡμῶν εἰς ἐπίσκεψιν τῶν ὄντων ἐλθόντας καὶ φιλοσοφήσαντας περὶ τῆς ἀληθείας. δῆλον γὰρ ὅτι
κἀκεῖνοι λέγουσιν ἀρχάς τινας καὶ αἰτίας· ἐπελθοῦσιν
οὖν ἔσται τι προὔργου τῇ μεθόδῳ τῇ νῦν· ἢ γὰρ
ἕτερόν τι γένος εὑρήσομεν αἰτίας ἢ ταῖς νῦν λεγομέ-
ναις μᾶλλον πιστεύσομεν.

T10 (≠ DK) Arist. *An.* 1.2 403b20–25

ἐπισκοποῦντας δὲ περὶ ψυχῆς ἀναγκαῖον, ἅμα διαπο-
ροῦντας περὶ ὧν εὐπορεῖν δεῖ προελθόντας, τὰς τῶν
προτέρων δόξας συμπαραλαμβάνειν ὅσοι τι περὶ αὐτῆς ἀπεφήναντο, ὅπως τὰ μὲν καλῶς εἰρημένα λάβω-
μεν, εἰ δέ τι μὴ καλῶς, τοῦτ᾽ εὐλαβηθῶμεν [. . . cf. **T12**].

Some Examples (T11–T13)

T11 (> 68 A135) Arist. *Phys.* 1.2 184b14–24

ἀνάγκη δ᾽ ἤτοι μίαν εἶναι τὴν ἀρχὴν ἢ πλείους, καὶ
εἰ μίαν, ἤτοι ἀκίνητον, ὥς φησι Παρμενίδης καὶ Μέλισσος, ἢ κινουμένην, ὥσπερ οἱ φυσικοί, οἱ μὲν ἀέρα
φάσκοντες εἶναι οἱ δ᾽ ὕδωρ τὴν πρώτην ἀρχήν· εἰ δὲ
πλείους, ἢ πεπερασμένας ἢ ἀπείρους, καὶ εἰ πεπερασμένας πλείους δὲ μιᾶς, ἢ δύο ἢ τρεῖς ἢ τέτταρας ἢ
ἄλλον τινὰ ἀριθμόν, καὶ εἰ ἀπείρους, ἢ οὕτως ὥσπερ
Δημόκριτος, τὸ γένος ἕν, σχήματι δὲ <διαφερούσας>,[1]

[1] add. Torstrick

sufficiently in our *Physics* [cf. *Phys.* 2.3], all the same let us also call upon those who, before us, proceeded to study beings and philosophized about the truth. For it is clear that they too speak of certain principles and causes; so it will be useful for the present investigation [scil. to consider them], for either we shall discover some different kind of cause, or else we shall have more confidence about the ones that we are speaking about now.

T10 (≠ DK) Aristotle, *On the Soul*

It is necessary, when we investigate about the soul, at the same time to consider the difficulties for which a solution is found as further progress is made, and to call upon the opinions of all of our predecessors who stated something about it, so that we can accept what has been said well, while if something has not been said well we can be wary of it [. . .].

Some Examples (T11–T13)

T11 (> 68 A135) Aristotle, *Physics*

It is necessary that the principle be either one or several, and if it is one, then either motionless, as Parmenides and Melissus say, or in motion, as the natural philosophers [scil. say], some saying that the first principle is air, others water; if it is more than one, then either limited [scil. in number] or unlimited, and if limited but more than one, either two or three, or four or some other number, and if unlimited then either as Democritus [scil. says], one in kind, but ⟨differing⟩ in shape [cf. e.g. **ATOM. D31–D32**], or else different in kind or even contrary. Those too

ἢ εἴδει διαφερούσας ἢ καὶ ἐναντίας. ὁμοίως δὲ ζητοῦσι καὶ οἱ τὰ ὄντα ζητοῦντες πόσα· ἐξ ὧν γὰρ τὰ
ὄντα ἐστὶ πρώτων, ζητοῦσι ταῦτα πότερον ἓν ἢ πολλά,
καὶ εἰ πολλά, πεπερασμένα ἢ ἄπειρα, ὥστε τὴν ἀρχὴν καὶ τὸ στοιχεῖον ζητοῦσι πότερον ἓν ἢ πολλά.

T12 (cf. ad 31 B109) Arist. *An.* 1.2 403b27–31, 404b8–11

παρειλήφαμεν δὲ καὶ παρὰ τῶν προγενεστέρων σχεδὸν δύο ταῦτα περὶ ψυχῆς· φασὶ γὰρ ἔνιοι καὶ μάλιστα καὶ πρώτως ψυχὴν εἶναι τὸ κινοῦν. οἰηθέντες δὲ
τὸ μὴ κινούμενον αὐτὸ μὴ ἐνδέχεσθαι κινεῖν ἕτερον,
τῶν κινουμένων τι τὴν ψυχὴν ὑπέλαβον εἶναι [. . .]
ὅσοι δ᾽ ἐπὶ τὸ γινώσκειν καὶ τὸ αἰσθάνεσθαι τῶν
ὄντων, οὗτοι δὲ λέγουσι τὴν ψυχὴν τὰς ἀρχάς, οἱ μὲν
πλείους ποιοῦντες, ταύτας, οἱ δὲ μίαν, ταύτην [. . .].

T13 (cf. 42.5) Arist. *Meteor.* 1.6 342b25–343a4

περὶ δὲ τῶν κομητῶν καὶ τοῦ καλουμένου γάλακτος
λέγωμεν, διαπορήσαντες πρὸς τὰ παρὰ τῶν ἄλλων
εἰρημένα πρῶτον. Ἀναξαγόρας μὲν οὖν καὶ Δημόκριτός φασιν εἶναι τοὺς κομήτας σύμφασιν τῶν πλανή-
των ἀστέρων, ὅταν διὰ τὸ πλησίον ἐλθεῖν δόξωσι
θιγγάνειν ἀλλήλων· τῶν δ᾽ Ἰταλικῶν τινες καλουμένων Πυθαγορείων ἕνα λέγουσιν αὐτὸν εἶναι τῶν πλα-
νήτων ἀστέρων, ἀλλὰ διὰ πολλοῦ τε χρόνου τὴν φαντασίαν αὐτοῦ εἶναι καὶ τὴν ὑπερβολὴν ἐπὶ μικρόν,

who inquire into how many beings there are inquire in a similar way: for they inquire whether the first things out of which beings derive are one or many, and if they are many, whether they are limited or unlimited, so that they inquire whether the principle and the element is one or many.

T12 (cf. ad 31 B109) Aristotle, *On the Soul*

We have received from our predecessors roughly speaking the following two [scil. opinions] regarding soul. For some say that what imparts motion is especially and first of all soul. Believing that what is not itself moved is not capable of moving something else, they assumed that the soul is one of the things that are moved [. . .] But all those who [scil. considered] the fact of knowing and perceiving the things that are say that the soul is [scil. constituted out of] principles, those who posit several, those principles, those who posit only one, that principle, [. . .].

T13 (cf. 42.5) Aristotle, *Meteorology*

Let us speak about comets and what is called the "milk" [i.e. the "Milky Way"] after we have first examined the difficulties regarding what others have said. Anaxagoras and Democritus say that comets are a simultaneous flashing of the planets, when by reason of coming closer they seem to touch each other [**ANAXAG. D50; ATOM. D99**], while some of the Italians called Pythagoreans say that it [i.e. a comet] is one of the wandering heavenly bodies [i.e. a planet] but that it only becomes visible at great intervals and that it only rises a little [scil above the hori-

19

ὅπερ συμβαίνει καὶ περὶ τὸν τοῦ Ἑρμοῦ ἀστέρα· διὰ
γὰρ τὸ μικρὸν ἐπαναβαίνειν πολλὰς ἐκλείπει φάσεις,
ὥστε διὰ χρόνου φαίνεσθαι πολλοῦ. παραπλησίως δὲ
τούτοις καὶ οἱ περὶ Ἱπποκράτην τὸν Χῖον καὶ τὸν
μαθητὴν αὐτοῦ Αἰσχύλον ἀπεφήναντο [42 A5 DK],
πλὴν τήν γε κόμην οὐκ ἐξ αὐτοῦ φασιν ἔχειν, ἀλλὰ
πλανώμενον διὰ τὸν τόπον ἐνίοτε λαμβάνειν ἀνακλω-
μένης τῆς ἡμετέρας ὄψεως ἀπὸ τῆς ἑλκομένης ὑγρότητος ὑπ᾽ αὐτοῦ πρὸς τὸν ἥλιον.

Theophrastus (T14–T16)

T14 (11 A13, 3ε A4, 11 B1, 18.7, 22 A5, 12 A9) Simpl. *In
Phys.*, p. 23.21–24.6 (< Theophr. Frag. 225 FHS&G)

τῶν δὲ μίαν καὶ κινουμένην λεγόντων τὴν ἀρχήν, οὓς
καὶ φυσικοὺς ἰδίως καλεῖ, οἱ μὲν πεπερασμένην αὐτήν
φασιν, ὥσπερ Θαλῆς μὲν Ἐξαμύους Μιλήσιος καὶ
Ἵππων, ὃς δοκεῖ καὶ ἄθεος γεγονέναι, ὕδωρ ἔλεγον
τὴν ἀρχὴν ἐκ τῶν φαινομένων κατὰ τὴν αἴσθησιν εἰς
τοῦτο προαχθέντες. καὶ γὰρ τὸ θερμὸν τῷ ὑγρῷ ζῇ
καὶ τὰ νεκρούμενα ξηραίνεται καὶ τὰ σπέρματα πάντων ὑγρὰ καὶ ἡ τροφὴ πᾶσα χυλώδης· ἐξ οὗ δέ ἐστιν
ἕκαστα, τούτῳ καὶ τρέφεσθαι πέφυκεν· τὸ δὲ ὕδωρ
ἀρχὴ τῆς ὑγρᾶς φύσεώς ἐστι καὶ συνεκτικὸν πάντων.
διὸ πάντων ἀρχὴν ὑπέλαβον εἶναι τὸ ὕδωρ καὶ τὴν
γῆν ἐφ᾽ ὕδατος ἀπεφήναντο κεῖσθαι. Θαλῆς δὲ πρῶτος
παραδέδοται τὴν περὶ φύσεως ἱστορίαν τοῖς Ἕλλη-

zon]—this happens also with Mercury [**PYTHS. ANON. D43**], which because it only rises a little often is not seen, so that it becomes visible at great intervals. Hippocrates of Chios and his pupil Aeschylus[1] express a view very similar to these, except that they say that the tail is not an intrinsic part of it but that it sometimes becomes attached to it while it is wandering through that area, when our sight is reflected toward the sun by the moisture that is attracted by it.

[1] Not the tragedian.

Theophrastus (T14–T16)

T14 (11 A13, 38 A4, 11 B1, 18.7, 22 A5, 12 A9) Theophrastus in Simplicius, *Commentary on Aristotle's* Physics

Among those who say that the principle is one and in motion, whom he [i.e. Aristotle] calls natural philosophers in the proper sense, some say that it is limited—as Thales of Miletus, son of Examyes, and Hippo, who is considered to have been an atheist, said that the principle is water, an opinion to which they were led by perceptible appearances. For what is warm lives by what is moist, and corpses dry out, and the seeds of all things are moist, and all nourishment is juicy; and that from which each thing comes is also that by which it is nourished by nature. And water is the principle of moist nature and is what holds all things together. And this is why they supposed that water is the principle of all things and declared that the earth rests upon water [cf. **THAL. D7; HIPPO D20**]. Thales is reported to have been the first to reveal the study of nature

21

σιν ἐκφῆναι, πολλῶν μὲν καὶ ἄλλων προγεγονότων, ὡς καὶ τῷ Θεοφράστῳ δοκεῖ, αὐτὸς δὲ πολὺ διενεγκὼν ἐκείνων, ὡς ἀποκρύψαι πάντας τοὺς πρὸ αὐτοῦ· λέγεται δὲ ἐν γραφαῖς μηδὲν καταλιπεῖν πλὴν τῆς καλουμένης Ναυτικῆς ἀστρολογίας.

Ἵππασος δὲ ὁ Μεταποντῖνος καὶ Ἡράκλειτος ὁ Ἐφέσιος ἓν καὶ οὗτοι καὶ κινούμενον καὶ πεπερασμένον, ἀλλὰ [24] πῦρ ἐποίησαν τὴν ἀρχὴν καὶ ἐκ πυρὸς ποιοῦσι τὰ ὄντα πυκνώσει καὶ μανώσει καὶ διαλύουσι πάλιν εἰς πῦρ, ὡς ταύτης μιᾶς οὔσης φύσεως τῆς ὑποκειμένης· πυρὸς γὰρ ἀμοιβὴν εἶναί φησιν Ἡράκλειτος πάντα. ποιεῖ δὲ καὶ τάξιν τινὰ καὶ χρόνον ὡρισμένον τῆς τοῦ κόσμου μεταβολῆς κατά τινα εἱμαρμένην ἀνάγκην.

T15 (cf. 31 A86, 24 B1a, 59 A92, 62.2, 64 A19, 68 A135)
Theophr. *Sens.* 1, 2, 3, 5, 7, 25, 27, 38, 39, 49

[1] περὶ δ᾽ αἰσθήσεως αἱ μὲν πολλαὶ καὶ καθόλου δόξαι δύ᾽ εἰσίν· οἱ μὲν γὰρ τῷ ὁμοίῳ ποιοῦσιν, οἱ δὲ τῷ ἐναντίῳ. Παρμενίδης μὲν καὶ Ἐμπεδοκλῆς καὶ Πλάτων τῷ ὁμοίῳ, οἱ δὲ περὶ Ἀναξαγόραν καὶ Ἡράκλειτον τῷ ἐναντίῳ [. . .].
[2] [. . .] καθόλου μὲν οὖν περὶ αἰσθήσεως αὗται παραδέδονται δόξαι. περὶ ἑκάστης δὲ τῶν κατὰ μέρος οἱ μὲν ἄλλοι σχεδὸν ἀπολείπουσιν, Ἐμπεδοκλῆς δὲ πειρᾶται καὶ ταύτας ἀνάγειν εἰς τὴν ὁμοιότητα.

to the Greeks. Many others had preceded him, as is the view of Theophrastus too, but he was far superior to them so that he eclipsed all his predecessors [cf. **THAL. R10**]. He is said to have left behind nothing in writing except for the so-called *Nautical Astronomy* [cf. **THAL. R6–R8**].

Hippasus of Metapontum [cf. **HIPPAS. D4**] and Heraclitus of Ephesus too [scil. said] that it is one, in motion, and limited, but [24] they established fire as the principle and make beings come to be out of fire by condensation and rarefaction and dissolve them again into fire, on the idea that this is the one nature that is a substrate. For Heraclitus says that all things are an exchange of fire [cf. **D87**]; and he establishes a certain order and a determinate period for the transformation of the world in conformity with a certain necessity that is fixed by destiny [cf. **D85**].

T15 (cf. 31 A86, 24 B1a, 59 A92, 62.2, 64 A19, 68 A135) Theophrastus, *On Sensations*

[1] Concerning sensation, most of the general opinions are of two kinds: for some explain it by the similar, others by the contrary: Parmenides, Empedocles, and Plato by the similar, the followers of Anaxagoras and Heraclitus by the contrary. [. . .]

[2] [. . .] These are in general the opinions concerning sensation that have been transmitted. Concerning each of the particular sensations, the others almost entirely neglect them, but Empedocles tries to reduce them too to similarity.

EARLY GREEK PHILOSOPHY II

[3] Παρμενίδης μὲν γὰρ ὅλως οὐδὲν ἀφώρικεν ἀλλὰ μόνον ὅτι [. . .].
[5] Πλάτων δὲ ἐπὶ πλέον μὲν ἦπται τῶν κατὰ μέρος [. . .].
[7] Ἐμπεδοκλῆς δὲ περὶ ἁπασῶν ὁμοίως λέγει [. . .].
[25] τῶν δὲ μὴ τῷ ὁμοίῳ ποιούντων τὴν αἴσθησιν Ἀλκμαίων μὲν πρῶτον [. . .].
[27] Ἀναξαγόρας δὲ γίνεσθαι μὲν τοῖς ἐναντίοις· [. . .].
[38] Κλείδημος δὲ μόνος ἰδίως εἴρηκε περὶ τῆς ὄψεως [. . .].
[39] Διογένης δ' [. . .] τῷ ἀέρι καὶ τὰς αἰσθήσεις ἀνά- πτει· διὸ καὶ δόξειεν ἂν τῷ ὁμοίῳ ποιεῖν [. . .].
[49] Δημόκριτος δὲ περὶ μὲν αἰσθήσεως οὐ διορίζει, πότερα τοῖς ἐναντίοις ἢ τοῖς ὁμοίοις ἐστίν.

T16 (cf. 59 A117, 62.3, 64 A32) Theophr. HP 3.1.4

[. . .] καὶ ἔτι τὰς αὐτομάτους, ἃς καὶ οἱ φυσιολόγοι λέγουσιν· Ἀναξαγόρας μὲν τὸν ἀέρα πάντων φάσκων ἔχειν σπέρματα καὶ ταῦτα συγκαταφερόμενα τῷ ὕδατι γεννᾶν τὰ φυτά· Διογένης δὲ σηπομένου τοῦ ὕδατος καὶ μίξιν τινὰ λαμβάνοντος πρὸς τὴν γῆν· Κλείδημος δὲ συνεστάναι μὲν ἐκ τῶν αὐτῶν τοῖς ζῴοις, ὅσῳ δὲ θολερωτέρων καὶ ψυχροτέρων τοσοῦτον ἀπέχειν τοῦ ζῷα εἶναι. λέγουσι δέ τινες καὶ ἄλλοι περὶ τῆς γενέσεως.

24

[3] Parmenides has not defined absolutely anything, but only that [. . .].

[5] Plato has approached the particular [scil. sensations] to a greater extent [. . .].

[7] Empedocles speaks about all the sensations in the same way [. . .].

[25] Among those who do not explain sensation by the similar, Alcmaeon begins by [. . .].

[27] Anaxagoras: sensation comes about by the contraries [. . .].

[38] Cleidemus is the only one to have spoken differently from the others about vision [. . .].

[39] Diogenes [. . .] connects sensations too to air. And that is why one might think that he explains them by the similar [. . .].

[49] Democritus does not define, concerning sensation, whether it is produced by the contraries or by the similar.

T16 (cf. 59 A117, 62.3, 64 A32) Theophrastus, *History of Plants*

[. . .] and also the spontaneous [scil. modes of generation of trees], about which the natural philosophers speak too: Anaxagoras, when he says that air contains the seeds of all things and that these descend together with rainwater and generate plants; Diogenes, when water decomposes and takes on some kind of mixture with earth; Cleidemus, that they [i.e. plants] are composed of the same things as animals are, but that they are more removed from being animals, the murkier and colder they are [62.3 DK]; and some others too speak about their generation.

Aëtius' Doxographic Manual (T17–T19)
An Example Showing the Sources for Its
Reconstitution (T17)

T17 (*Dox. Gr.*, pp. 327–29) Aët. 2.1 [περὶ κόσμου]

Theod. *Cur.*	Ps.-Plut. *Plac.*	Stob.
1		1.21.6c: Πυθαγόρας φησὶ γενητὸν κατ᾽ ἐπίνοιαν τὸν κόσμον, οὐ κατὰ χρόνον.—ὃς καὶ πρῶτος ὠνόμασε τὴν τῶν ὅλων περιοχὴν κόσμον ἐκ τῆς ἐν αὐτῷ τάξεως.—ἄρξασθαι δὲ τὴν γένεσιν τοῦ κόσμου ἀπὸ πυρὸς καὶ τοῦ πέμπτου στοιχείου.—πέντε δὲ σχημάτων ὄντων στερεῶν, ἅπερ καλεῖται καὶ μαθηματικά, ἐκ μὲν τοῦ κύβου φησὶ γεγονέναι τὴν γῆν, ἐκ δὲ τῆς πυραμίδος τὸ πῦρ, ἐκ δὲ τοῦ ὀκταέδρου τὸν ἀέρα, ἐκ δὲ τοῦ εἰκοσαέδρου <τὸ ὕδωρ, ἐκ δὲ τοῦ δωδεκαέδρου> τὴν τοῦ παντὸς σφαῖραν.
	2.1.1: Πυθαγόρας πρῶτος ὠνόμασε τὴν τῶν ὅλων περιοχὴν κόσμον ἐκ τῆς ἐν αὐτῷ τάξεως.	

Aëtius' Doxographic Manual (T17–T19)
An Example Showing the Sources for Its
Reconstitution (T17)

T17 (≠ DK) Aëtius, Chapter "On the World"[1]

Theodoret, *Cure of the Greek Maladies*	Ps.-Plutarch, *Opinions of the Philosophers*	Stobaeus, *Anthology*
1		1.21.6c: Pythagoras *says that the cosmos is created in concept, not in time.*—He was also the first to call what surrounds everything the "world" (*kosmos*) because of the order in it.—*The creation of the cosmos began out of fire and the fifth element.—There being five solid figures, which are also called mathematical, he says that out of the cube comes earth, out of the pyramid fire, out of the octahedron air, out of the icosahedron <water, out of the dodecahedron> the sphere of the whole.*
	2.1.1: Pythagoras was the first to name what surrounds everything "world" (*kosmos*) because of the order in it.	

[1] The portions of the translations in italics correspond to additions in Stobaeus regarding Pythagoras that derive from the pseudepigraphic tradition, to rearrangements of the notices about the Stoics in Stobaeus that are due to Stobaeus himself, and to an introductory phrase that has been added by Theodoret.

	Theod. *Cur.*	᾿s.-Plut. *Plac.*	Stob.
2	4.15: οὐ μόνον δὲ ἐν τούτοις διαφωνίᾳ γε πλείστῃ, ἀλλὰ κἀν τοῖς ἄλλοις ἐχρήσαντο. καὶ γὰρ δὴ τὸν κόσμον Θαλῆς μὲν καὶ Πυθαγόρας καὶ Ἀναξαγόρας καὶ Παρμενίδης καὶ Μέλισσος καὶ Ἡράκλειτος καὶ Πλάτων καὶ Ἀριστοτέλης καὶ Ζήνων ἕνα εἶναι ξυνωμολόγησαν.	2.1.2: Θαλῆς καὶ οἱ ἀπ᾿ αὐτοῦ ἕνα τὸν κόσμον.	1.22.3b (1): Θαλῆς, Πυθαγόρας, Ἐμπεδοκλῆς, Ἔκφαντος, Παρμενίδης, Μέλισσος, Ἡράκλειτος, Ἀναξαγόρας, Πλάτων, Ἀριστοτέλης, Ζήνων ἕνα τὸν κόσμον.
3	4.15: Ἀναξίμανδρος δὲ καὶ Ἀναξιμένης καὶ Ἀρχέλαος καὶ Ξενοφάνης καὶ Διογένης καὶ Λεύκιππος καὶ Δημόκριτος καὶ Ἐπίκουρος πολλοὺς εἶναι καὶ ἀπείρους ἐδόξασαν.	2.1.3: Δημόκριτος καὶ Ἐπίκουρος καὶ ὁ τούτου καθηγητὴς Μητρόδωρος ἀπείρους κόσμους ἐν τῷ ἀπείρῳ κατὰ πᾶσαν περίστασιν.	1.22.3b (2): Ἀναξίμανδρος, Ἀναξιμένης, Ἀρχέλαος, Ξενοφάνης, Διογένης, Λεύκιππος, Δημόκριτος, Ἐπίκουρος ἀπείρους κόσμους ἐν τῷ ἀπείρῳ κατὰ πᾶσαν περιαγωγήν.
4		2.1.4: Ἐμπεδοκλῆς τὸν τοῦ ἡλίου περίδρομον εἶναι περιγραφὴν τοῦ κόσμου καὶ τοῦ πέρατος αὐτοῦ.	1.21.3a (1): Ἐμπεδοκλῆς τὸν τοῦ ἡλίου περίδρομον εἶναι περιγραφὴν τοῦ πέρατος τοῦ κόσμου.
5		2.1.5: Σέλευκος ἄπειρον τὸν κόσμον.	1.21.3a (2): Σέλευκος ὁ Ἐρυθραῖος καὶ Ἡρακλείδης ὁ Ποντικὸς ἄπειρον τὸν κόσμον.
6		2.1.6: Διογένης τὸ μὲν πᾶν ἄπειρον, τὸν δὲ κόσμον πεπεράνθαι.	1.21.3a (3): Διογένης καὶ Μέλισσος τὸ μὲν πᾶν ἄπειρον, τὸν δὲ κόσμον πεπεράνθαι.

28

	Theodoret, *Cure of the Greek Maladies*	Ps.-Plutarch, *Opinions of the Philosophers*	Stobaeus, *Anthology*
2	4.15: *Not only in these matters was there the greatest difference of opinion among them, but also in others.* For in fact Thales, Pythagoras, Anaxagoras, Parmenides, Melissus, Heraclitus, Plato, Aristotle, and Zeno agreed that the world is one. [see 3]	2.1.2: Thales and his followers: the world [scil. is] one.	1.22.3b (1): Thales, Pythagoras, Empedocles, Ecphantus, Parmenides, Melissus, Anaxagoras, Plato, Aristotle, Zeno: the world [scil. is] one.
3	4.15: Anaximander, Anaximenes, Archelaus, Xenophanes, Diogenes, Leucippus, Democritus, and Epicurus had the opinion that they are many and infinite.	2.1.3: Democritus, Epicurus, and his teacher Metrodorus: worlds unlimited [scil. in number] in the unlimited, throughout the entire surrounding area (*peristasis*).	1.22.3b (2): Anaximander, Anaximenes, Archelaus, Xenophanes, Diogenes, Leucippus, Democritus, Epicurus: worlds unlimited [scil. in number] in the unlimited, throughout the entire circumference (*periagôgê*).
4		2.1.4: Empedocles: the circular course of the sun is the outline of the world and of its limit.	1.21.3a (1): Empedocles: the circular course of the sun is the outline of the limit of the world.
5		2.1.5: Seleucus: the world [scil. is] unlimited.	1.21.3a (2): Seleucus of Erythrae and Heraclides of Pontus: the world [scil. is] unlimited.
6		2.1.6: Diogenes: the universe [scil. is] unlimited, but the world is limited.	1.21.3a (3): Diogenes and Melissus: the universe is unlimited, but the world is limited.

Theod. *Cur.*	Ps.-Plut. *Plac.*	Stob.
7	2.1.7: οἱ Στωικοὶ δια-φέρειν τὸ πᾶν καὶ τὸ ὅλον· πᾶν μὲν γὰρ εἶναι τὸ σὺν κενῷ ἄπειρον, ὅλον δὲ χω-ρὶς τοῦ κενοῦ τὸν κόσμον· ὥστε [οὐ] τὸ αὐτὸ εἶναι τὸ ὅλον καὶ τὸν κόσμον.	1.21.3b: οἱ Στωικοὶ διαφέρειν τὸ πᾶν καὶ τὸ ὅλον· πᾶν μὲν γὰρ εἶναι σὺν τῷ κενῷ τῷ ἀπείρῳ, ὅλον δὲ χωρὶς τοῦ κενοῦ τὸν κό-σμον.—μήτε αὔξεσθαι δὲ μήτε μειοῦσθαι τὸν κόσμον, τοῖς δὲ μέρε-σιν ὁτὲ μὲν παρεκτείνε-σθαι πρὸς πλείονα τόπον, ὁτὲ δὲ συστέλ-λεσθαι.—ἀπὸ γῆς δὲ ἄρξασθαι τὴν γένεσιν τοῦ κόσμου, καθάπερ ἀπὸ κέντρου, ἀρχὴ δὲ σφαίρας τὸ κέντρον.
8		1.22.3c: τῶν ἀπείρους ἀποφηναμένων τοὺς κόσμους. Ἀναξίμανδρος τὸ ἴσον αὐτοὺς ἀπέχειν ἀλλήλων, Ἐπίκουρος ἄνισον εἶναι τὸ μεταξὺ τῶν κόσμων διάστημα.

Some Examples Showing the Structure of the
Chapters (T18)

T18

a (*Dox. Gr.*, pp. 364–66) Aët. 3.1 (Ps.-Plut., Stob., cf. Gal.) [περὶ τοῦ γαλαξίου κύκλου]

1. κύκλος ἐστὶ νεφελοειδὴς ἐν μὲν τῷ ἀέρι διὰ παντὸς φαινόμενος, διὰ δὲ τὴν λευκόχροιαν ὀνομαζόμενος γαλαξίας.

Theodoret, *Cure of the Greek Maladies*	Ps.-Plutarch, *Opinions of the Philosophers*	Stobaeus, *Anthology*
7	2.1.7: The Stoics: the universe and the whole differ; for the universe is the unlimited together with the void, while the whole is the world without the void. So that the whole and the world are [not] the same.	1.21.3b: The Stoics: the universe and the whole differ; for the universe is with the unlimited void, while the whole is the world without the void.—*The world neither increases nor decreases, but sometimes it extends in its parts farther in a greater space, and at other times it contracts.—The generation of the world started from the earth, as from a center, and the starting point of a sphere is the center.*
8		1.22.3c: Among those who assert that the worlds are infinite, Anaximander: they are equally distant from one another. Epicurus: the distance between the worlds is unequal.

Some Examples Showing the Structure of the Chapters (T18)

T18

a (≠ DK) Aëtius, Chapter "On the Milky Way"

1. It is a cloud-like circle which is visible everywhere in the air and is called "galaxy" (i.e. milky) because of its white color.

---

1 ὀνομαζόμενος γαλαξίας Stob. Gal.: γαλ- ὀν- Plut

2. τῶν Πυθαγορείων οἱ μὲν ἔφασαν ἀστέρος εἶναι διά-
καυσιν, ἐκπεσόντος μὲν ἀπὸ τῆς ἰδίας ἕδρας, δι᾽ οὗ δὲ
περιέδραμε χωρίου κυκλοτερῶς αὐτὸ περιφλέξαντος
ἐπὶ τοῦ κατὰ Φαέθοντα ἐμπρησμοῦ· οἱ δὲ τὸν ἡλιακὸν
ταύτῃ φασὶ κα᾽ ἀρχὰς γεγονέναι δρόμον. τινὲς δὲ
κατοπρικὴν εἶναι φαντασίαν τοῦ ἡλίου τὰς αὐγὰς
πρὸς τὸν οὐρανὸν ἀνακλῶντος, ὅπερ κἀπὶ τῆς ἴριδος
ἐπὶ τῶν νεφῶν συμβαίνει.

3. Μητρόδωρος διὰ τὴν πάροδον τοῦ ἡλίου, τοῦτον
γὰρ εἶναι τὸν ἡλιακὸν κύκλον.

4. Παρμενίδης τὸ τοῦ πυκνοῦ καὶ ἀραιοῦ μῖγμα γαλα-
κτοειδὲς ἀποτελέσαι χρῶμα.

5. Ἀναξαγόρας τὴν σκιὰν τῆς γῆς κατὰ τόδε τὸ μέρος
ἵστασθαι τοῦ οὐρανοῦ, ὅταν ὑπὸ τὴν γῆν ὁ ἥλιος γενόμενος μὴ πάντα περιφωτίζῃ.

6. Δημόκριτος πολλῶν καὶ μικρῶν καὶ συνεχῶν ἀστέρων συμφω᾽ιζομένων ἀλλήλοις συναυγασμὸν διὰ τὴν
πύκνωσιν.

7. Ἀριστοτέλης ἀναθυμιάσεως ξηρᾶς ἔξαψιν πολλῆς
τε καὶ συνεχοῦς· καὶ οὕτω κόμην πυρὸς ὑπὸ τὸν
αἰθέρα κατωτέρω τῶν πλανητῶν.

8. Ποσειδώνιος πυρὸς σύστασιν ἄστρου μὲν μανο-
τέραν αὐγῆς δὲ πυκνοτέραν.

2 περιέδραμε Stob. Gal.: ἐπέδραμε Plut.   4 καὶ τὸ τοῦ
ἀραιοῦ Stob.   5 κατὰ τόδε Stob. Gal.: κατὰ τοῦτο Plut.
περιφωτίζῃ Stob. Gal.: φωτίζῃ   7 καὶ οὕτω κτλ. non hab.
Stob.   8 ἄστρου κτλ. om. Gal., sed ante Ποσειδώνιος hab.
οἱ Στωικοὶ τοῦ αἰθερίου πυρὸς ἀραιότητα ἀνώτερον τῶν πλανητῶν.

2. Among the Pythagoreans, some said that it is the burned-up remains of a heavenly body that fell from its proper place and burned up the area that it moved around in a circle, at the time of the conflagration caused by Phaethon; others say that the course of the sun went there at the beginning. Some too [scil. say] that it is the mirror image of the sun reflecting its rays against the heavens, which also happens with the rainbow on the clouds.

3. Metrodorus: because of the passage of the sun, for this is the solar orbit.

4. Parmenides: the mixture of dense and rarefied makes a milk-like color.

5. Anaxagoras: the shadow of the earth is projected onto this part of the heavens when the sun passes under the earth and does not illuminate everything all around it.

6. Democritus: the combined illumination of many small adjacent stars illuminating one another simultaneously because of their crowding together.

7. Aristotle: the igniting of a dry exhalation that is both abundant and continuous; and in this way a tail of fire under the region of the aether below the planets.

8. Posidonius: an accumulation of fire more rarefied than a heavenly body but denser than a sunbeam.

b (*Dox. Gr.*, pp. 381–82) Aët. 3.16 (Ps.-Plut.) [περὶ θαλάσσης πῶς συνέστη καὶ πῶς ἐστι πικρά]

1. Ἀναξίμανδρος τὴν θάλασσάν φησιν εἶναι τῆς πρώτης ὑγρασίας λείψανον, ἧς τὸ μὲν πλεῖον μέρος ἀν-
εξήρανε τὸ πῦρ, τὸ δ᾽ ὑπολειφθὲν διὰ τὴν ἔκκαυσιν
μετέβαλεν.

2. Ἀναξαγόρας τοῦ κατ᾽ ἀρχὴν λιμνάζοντος ὑγροῦ
περικαέντος ὑπὸ τῆς ἡλιακῆς περιφορᾶς καὶ τοῦ λι-
παροῦ ἐξατμισθέντος εἰς ἁλυκίδα καὶ πικρίαν τὸ λοιπὸν ὑποστῆναι.

3. Ἐμπεδοκλῆς ἱδρῶτα τῆς γῆς ἐκκαιομένης ὑπὸ τοῦ
ἡλίου διὰ τὴν ἐπὶ τὸ πλεῖον πίλησιν.

4. Ἀντιφῶν ἱδρῶτα θερμοῦ, ἐξ οὗ τὸ περιληφθὲν
ὑγρὸν ἀπεκρίθη, τῷ καθεψηθῆναι παραλυκίσαντα
ὅπερ ἐπὶ παντὸς ἱδρῶτος συμβαίνει.

5. Μητρόδωρος διὰ τὸ διηθεῖσθαι διὰ τῆς γῆς μετει-
ληφέναι τοῦ περὶ αὐτὴν πάχους, καθάπερ τὰ διὰ τῆς
τέφρας ὑλιζόμενα.

6. οἱ ἀπὸ Πλάτωνος τοῦ στοιχειώδους ὕδατος τὸ μὲν
ἐξ ἀέρος κατὰ περίψυξιν συνιστάμενον γλυκὺ γίνεσθαι, τὸ δ᾽ ἀπὸ γῆς κατὰ περίκαυσιν καὶ ἐκπύρωσιν
ἀναθυμιώμενον ἁλμυρόν.

b (≠ DK) Aëtius, Chapter "On the sea, how it was formed and why it is salty"

1. Anaximander says that the sea is a residue of the original moisture, of which the fire dried up the greater part, while what remained was transformed by the heat.

2. Anaxagoras: the moisture that formed stagnant pools at the beginning was heated by the sun's revolution, and when the fatty part evaporated the rest turned toward saltiness and bitterness.

3. Empedocles: it is the sweat of the earth that has been completely burned up by the sun because of an ever greater compression.

4. Antiphon: it is the sweat of heat, from which the residue of humidity has separated out, becoming salty by being boiled down—which happens with every kind of sweat.

5. Metrodorus: by being strained through the earth it takes on a portion of the latter's density, like what is filtered through ash.

6. The followers of Plato: one part of the elementary water, condensing from air by being cooled, becomes sweet, while the other part rising up from the earth by combustion and burning [scil. becomes] salty.[1]

[1] Cf. Aristotle, *Meteorology* 2.3 357b24–358a27.

c (*Dox. Gr.*, pp. 406–7) Aët. 4.16 (Ps.-Plut., Stob. = Johan. Damas.)[1] [περὶ ἀκοῆς]

1. Ἐμπεδοκλῆς τὴν ἀκοὴν γίνεσθαι κατὰ πρόσπτωσιν πνεύματος τῷ χονδρώδει, ὅπερ φησὶν ἐξηρτῆσθαι ἐντὸς τοῦ ὠτὸς κώδωνος δίκην αἰωρούμενον καὶ τυπτόμενον.

2. Ἀλκμαίων ἀκούειν ἡμᾶς τῷ κενῷ τῷ ἐντὸς τοῦ ὠτός· τοῦτο γὰρ εἶναι τὸ διηχοῦν κατὰ τὴν τοῦ πνεύματος ἐμβολήν· πάντα γὰρ τὰ κενὰ ἠχεῖ.

3. Διογένης τοῦ ἐν τῇ κεφαλῇ ἀέρος ὑπὸ τῆς φωνῆς τυπτομένου καὶ κινουμένου.

4. Πλάτων καὶ οἱ ἀπ᾽ αὐτοῦ πλήττεσθαι τὸν ἐν τῇ κεφαλῇ ἀέρα· τοῦτον δ᾽ ἀνακλᾶσθαι εἰς τὰ ἡγεμονικὰ καὶ γίνεσθαι τῆς ἀκοῆς τὴν αἴσθησιν.

[1] Stobaeus 1.53 (p. 491 Wachsmuth) supplies only the final *doxa* (with a slight variant), which is completed by a citation of Plato, *Timaeus* 67a–c. His text is restituted on the basis of the florilegium attributed to John of Damascus.

An Example Showing the Effects of Abridgement (T19)

T19 (*Dox. Gr.*, p. 327) Aët. 2.1.2–3 [περὶ κόσμου]

a (Stob., Theod.)

2. Θαλῆς, Πυθαγόρας, Ἐμπεδοκλῆς, Ἔκφαντος, Παρ-

c (≠ DK) Aëtius, Chapter "On hearing"

1. Empedocles: hearing comes about when air strikes cartilage, which, he says, hanging suspended inside the ear, oscillates and is struck like a bell.

2. Alcmaeon: we hear by means of the void inside the ear; for this is what resounds when air strikes it. For all empty things resound.

3. Diogenes: when the air located in the head is struck and set in motion by a sound.

4. Plato and his followers: the air located in the head is struck; this rebounds toward the governing parts and the sensation of hearing is produced.

An Example Showing the Effects of
Abridgment (T19)

T19 (≠ DK) Aëtius, Chapter "On the world"

a (Stobaeus, Theodoret)

2. Thales, Pythagoras, Empedocles, Ecphantus, Par-

μενίδης, Μέλισσος, Ἡράκλειτος, Ἀναξαγόρας, Πλάτων, Ἀριστοτέλης, Ζήνων ἕνα τὸν κόσμον.
3. Ἀναξίμανδρος, Ἀναξιμένης, Ἀρχέλαος, Ξενοφάνης,
Διογένης, Λεύκιππος, Δημόκριτος, Ἐπίκουρος ἀπείρους κόσμους ἐν τῷ ἀπείρῳ κατὰ πᾶσαν περιαγωγήν.

b (Ps.-Plut.)

2. Θαλῆς καὶ οἱ ἀπ᾽ αὐτοῦ ἕνα τὸν κόσμον.
3. Δημόκριτος καὶ Ἐπίκουρος καὶ ὁ τούτου καθηγη-
τὴς Μητρόδωρος ἀπείρους κόσμους ἐν τῷ ἀπείρῳ
κατὰ πᾶσαν περίστασιν.

By Schools and Successions (T20–T22)
Two Lines of Descent (T20)

T20 (≠ DK) Diog. Laert. 1.13–15

[13] φιλοσοφίας δὲ δύο γεγόνασιν ἀρχαί, ἥ τε ἀπὸ
Ἀναξιμάνδρου καὶ ἡ ἀπὸ Πυθαγόρου· τοῦ μὲν Θαλοῦ
διακηκοότος, Πυθαγόρου δὲ Φερεκύδης καθηγήσατο.
καὶ ἐκαλεῖτο ἡ μὲν Ἰωνική, ὅτι Θαλῆς Ἴων ὤν, Μιλήσιος γάρ, καθηγήσατο Ἀναξιμάνδρου· ἡ δὲ Ἰταλικὴ ἀπὸ Πυθαγόρου, ὅτι τὰ πλεῖστα κατὰ τὴν
Ἰταλίαν ἐφιλοσόφησεν. [14] καταλήγει δὲ ἡ μὲν εἰς
Κλειτόμαχον καὶ Χρύσιππον καὶ Θεόφραστον· ἡ δὲ
Ἰταλικὴ εἰς Ἐπίκουρον. Θαλοῦ μὲν γὰρ Ἀναξίμανδρος, οὗ Ἀναξιμένης, οὗ Ἀναξαγόρας, οὗ Ἀρχέλαος,
οὗ Σωκράτης ὁ τὴν ἠθικὴν εἰσαγαγών· οὗ οἵ τε ἄλλοι

menides, Melissus, Heraclitus, Anaxagoras, Plato, Aristotle, Zeno: the world is one.

3. Anaximander, Anaximenes, Archelaus, Xenophanes, Diogenes, Leucippus, Democritus, Epicurus: worlds unlimited in the unlimited throughout the entire circumference.

b (Ps.-Plutarch)

2. Thales and his followers: the world is one.

3. Democritus, Epicurus, and his teacher Metrodorus: worlds unlimited in the unlimited throughout the entire surrounding area.

By Schools and Successions (T20–T22)
Two Lines of Descent (T20)

T20 (≠ DK) Diogenes Laertius

[13] There were two starting points of philosophy, one from Anaximander and the other from Pythagoras. The former had studied with Thales, while Pherecydes taught Pythagoras. And the one [scil. line of descent] is called Ionian, because Thales was an Ionian (for he was from Miletus) and taught Anaximander; the Italian one is [scil. named] from Pythagoras, for he did most of his philosophizing in Italy. [14] And the one [i.e. the Ionian one] comes to an end with Cleitomachus, Chrysippus, and Theophrastus, and the Italian one with Epicurus. For of Thales [scil. the disciple was] Anaximander; of him, Anaximenes; of him, Anaxagoras; of him, Archelaus; of him, Socrates, who introduced ethics; of him, the other Socrat-

Σωκρατικοὶ καὶ Πλάτων ὁ τὴν ἀρχαίαν Ἀκαδημίαν
συστησάμενος· οὗ Σπεύσιππος καὶ Ξενοκράτης, οὗ
Πολέμων, οὗ Κράντωρ καὶ Κράτης, οὗ Ἀρκεσίλαος ὁ
τὴν μέσην Ἀκαδημίαν εἰσηγησάμενος· οὗ Λακύδης
ὁ τὴν νέαν Ἀκαδημίαν φιλοσοφήσας· οὗ Καρνεάδης,
οὗ Κλειτόμαχος. καὶ ὧδε μὲν εἰς Κλειτόμαχον. [15] εἰς
δὲ Χρύσιππον οὕτω καταλήγει· Σωκράτους Ἀντισθένης, οὗ Διογένης ὁ κύων, οὗ Κράτης ὁ Θηβαῖος, οὗ
Ζήνων ὁ Κιτιεύς, οὗ Κλεάνθης, οὗ Χρύσιππος. εἰς δὲ
Θεόφραστον οὕτως· Πλάτωνος Ἀριστοτέλης, οὗ Θεόφραστος. καὶ ἡ μὲν Ἰωνικὴ τοῦτον καταλήγει τὸν
τρόπον.

ἡ δὲ Ἰταλικὴ οὕτω· Φερεκύδους Πυθαγόρας, οὗ
Τηλαύγης ὁ υἱός, οὗ Ξενοφάνης, οὗ Παρμενίδης, οὗ
Ζήνων ὁ Ἐλεάτης, οὗ Λεύκιππος, οὗ Δημόκριτος, οὗ
πολλοὶ μέν, ἐπ᾽ ὀνόματος δὲ Ναυσιφάνης καὶ Ναυκύ-
δης, ὧν Ἐπίκουρος.

Three Lines of Descent (T21)

T21 (≠ DK) Clem. Alex. *Strom.* 1.62.1–64.5

[62.1] φιλοσοφίας τοίνυν μετὰ τοὺς προειρημένους
ἄνδρας τρεῖς γεγόνασι διαδοχαὶ ἐπώνυμοι τῶν τόπων

ics, and Plato, who founded the Old Academy; of him, Speusippus and Xenocrates; of him, Polemon; of him, Crantor and Crates; of him, Arcesilaus, who introduced the Middle Academy; of him, Lacydes who [scil. introduced] the New Academy; of him, Carneades; of him, Cleitomachus. And in this way [scil. it came to an end] with Cleitomachus. [15] It came to an end with Chrysippus in the following way: of Socrates [scil. the disciple was] Antisthenes; of him, Diogenes the Cynic; of him, Crates of Thebes; of him, Zeno of Citium; of him, Cleanthes; of him, Chrysippus. [Scil. It came to an end] with Theophrastus in the following way: of Plato [scil. the disciple was] Aristotle; of him, Theophrastus. And the Ionian one [scil. line of descent] comes to an end in this way.

The Italian one [scil. line of descent] in the following way: of Pherecydes [scil. the disciple was] Pythagoras; of him, his son Telauges; of him, Xenophanes; of him, Parmenides; of him, Zeno of Elea; of him, Leucippus; of him, Democritus; of him, many, but by name Nausiphanes and Naucydes; of them, Epicurus.

Three Lines of Descent (T21)

T21 (≠ DK) Clement of Alexandria, *Stromata*

[62.1] After the men about whom I have just spoken [scil. the Seven Sages], there were three successions of philoso-

---

1 Plato at *Sophist* 242c [= **T4**] derives the Eleatic School from Xenophanes. Aristotle identifies the Italian philosophers with the Pythagoreans (cf. **PYTHS ANON. D2, D36**). Combining these two indications produces, for the Ionian line of descent, three successions.

περὶ οὓς διέτριψαν, Ἰταλικὴ μὲν ἡ ἀπὸ Πυθαγόρου,
Ἰωνικὴ δὲ ἡ ἀπὸ Θαλοῦ, Ἐλεατικὴ δὲ ἡ ἀπὸ Ξενοφάνους. [2] Πυθαγόρας μὲν οὖν Μνησάρχου Σάμιος, ὥς
φησιν Ἱππόβοτος, ὡς δὲ Ἀριστόξενος ἐν τῷ Πυθαγόρου βίῳ καὶ Ἀριστοτέλης[1] καὶ Θεόπομπος Τυρρη-
νὸς ἦν, ὡς δὲ Νεάνθης, Σύριος ἢ Τύριος, ὥστε εἶναι
κατὰ τοὺς πλείστους τὸν Πυθαγόραν βάρβαρον τὸ
γένος. [3] ἀλλὰ καὶ Θαλῆς, ὡς Λέανδρος καὶ Ἡρόδοτος ἱστοροῦσι, Φοῖνιξ ἦν, ὡς δέ τινες ὑπειλήφασι,
Μιλήσιος. [4] μόνος οὗτος δοκεῖ τοῖς τῶν Αἰγυπτίων
προφήταις συμβεβληκέναι, διδάσκαλος δὲ αὐτοῦ οὐδεὶς ἀναγράφεται, ὥσπερ οὐδὲ Φερεκύδου τοῦ Συρίου,
ᾧ Πυθαγόρας ἐμαθήτευσεν. [63.1] ἀλλ’ ἡ μὲν ἐν Με-
ταποντίῳ τῆς Ἰταλίας ἡ κατὰ Πυθαγόραν φιλοσοφία
ἡ Ἰταλικὴ κατεγήρασεν. [2] Ἀναξίμανδρος δὲ Πραξιάδου Μιλήσιος Θαλῆν διαδέχεται, τοῦτον δὲ Ἀναξιμένης Εὐρυστράτου Μιλήσιος, μεθ’ ὃν Ἀναξαγόρας
Ἡγησιβούλου Κλαζομένιος. οὗτος μετήγαγεν ἀπὸ
τῆς Ἰωνίας Ἀθήναζε τὴν διατριβήν. [3] τοῦτον διαδέχεται Ἀρχέλαος, οὗ Σωκράτης διήκουσεν.

ἐκ δ’ ἄρα τῶν ἀπέκλινεν ⟨ὁ⟩ λαξόος,[2]
    ἐννομολέσχης,
Ἑλλήνων ἐπαοιδός.

ὁ Τίμων φησὶν ἐν τοῖς Σίλλοις [Frag. 25.1–2a Di

---

[1] Ἀριστοτέλης Preller: Ἀρίσταρχος mss.

phy, named after the places in which they were active: the Italian one from Pythagoras, the Ionian one from Thales, and the Eleatic one from Xenophanes. [2] Pythagoras, the son of Mnesarchus, was from Samos, as Hippobotus says, but as Aristoxenus [scil. says] in his *Life of Pythagoras,* Aristotle and Theopompus, from Tyrrhenia, or as Neanthes [scil. says], Syrian or Tyrian, so that Pythagoras was, according to most people, a barbarian by descent. [3] But Thales, as Leander and Herodotus report, was a Phoenician, although some people suppose that he was from Miletus. [4] He is thought to have been the only one to have met with the priests of the Egyptians, but no teacher of his is recorded, just as little as for Pherecydes of Syros too, with whom Pythagoras studied. [63.1] But the Italian philosophy of Pythagoras grew old in Metapontium in Italy. [2] Anaximander of Miletus, son of Praxiades, followed in succession after Thales, and he was followed by Anaximenes of Miletus, son of Eurystratus, after whom [scil. came] Anaxagoras of Clazomenae, son of Hegesiboulus. He transferred the discipline from Ionia to Athens. [3] He was followed in succession by Archelaus, with whom Socrates studied.

> From them then the sculptor turned aside, the lawchatterer, Enchanter of the Greeks,

says Timon in his *Mockeries,* because he turned aside from

---

² ⟨ὁ⟩ λαξόος Meineke: λαξόος Diog. Laert. 2.19: λαοξόος Clem.

Marco] διὰ τὸ ἀποκεκλικέναι ἀπὸ τῶν φυσικῶν ἐπὶ τὰ
ἠθικά. [4] Σωκράτους δὲ ἀκούσας Ἀντισθένης μὲν
ἐκύνισε, Πλάτων δὲ εἰς τὴν Ἀκαδημίαν ἀνεχώρησε.
[5] παρὰ Πλάτωνι Ἀριστοτέλης φιλοσοφήσας μετελ-
θὼν εἰς τὸ Λύκειον κτίζει τὴν Περιπατητικὴν αἵρεσιν.
τοῦτον δὲ διαδέχεται Θεόφραστος, ὃν Στράτων, ὃν
Λύκων, εἶτα Κριτόλαος, εἶτα Διόδωρος. [6] Σπεύσιππος δὲ Πλάτωνα διαδέχεται, τοῦτον δὲ Ξενοκράτης,
ὃν Πολέμων. Πολέμωνος δὲ ἀκουσταὶ Κράτης τε καὶ
Κράντωρ, εἰς οὓς ἡ ἀπὸ Πλάτωνος κατέληξεν ἀρχαία
Ἀκαδημία.

   Κράντορος δὲ μετέσχεν Ἀρκεσίλαος, ἀφ' οὗ μέχρι
Ἡγησίνου ἤνθησεν Ἀκαδημία ἡ μέση. [64.1] εἶτα
Καρνεάδης διαδέχεται Ἡγησίνουν καὶ οἱ ἐφεξῆς·
Κράτητος δὲ Ζήνων ὁ Κιτιεὺς ὁ τῆς Στωικῆς ἄρξας
αἱρέσεως γίνεται μαθητής. τοῦτον δὲ διαδέχεται Κλε-
άνθης, ὃν Χρύσιππος καὶ οἱ μετ' αὐτόν.

   [2] τῆς δὲ Ἐλεατικῆς ἀγωγῆς Ξενοφάνης ὁ Κολο-
φώνιος κατάρχει, ὅν φησι Τίμαιος κατὰ Ἱέρωνα τὸν
Σικελίας δυνάστην καὶ Ἐπίχαρμον τὸν ποιητὴν γεγο-
νέναι, Ἀπολλόδωρος δὲ κατὰ τὴν τεσσαρακοστὴν
Ὀλυμπιάδα γενόμενον παρατετακέναι ἄχρι τῶν Δα-
ρείου τε καὶ Κύρου χρόνων. [3] Παρμενίδης τοίνυν
Ξενοφάνους ἀκουστὴς γίνεται, τούτου δὲ Ζήνων, εἶτα
Λεύκιππος, εἶτα Δημόκριτος. [4] Δημοκρίτου δὲ ἀκου-
σταὶ Πρωταγόρας ὁ Ἀβδηρίτης καὶ Μητρόδωρος ὁ
Χῖος, οὗ Διογένης ὁ Σμυρναῖος, οὗ Ἀνάξαρχος, τού-

natural philosophy to ethics. [4] After they had studied with Socrates, Antisthenes became a Cynic and Plato withdrew to the Academy. [5] After Aristotle philosophized with Plato he moves to the Lyceum and founds the Peripatetic school. Theophrastus follows him in succession, Strato him, Lycon him, then Critolaus, then Diodorus. [6] Speusippus follows Plato in succession, Xenocrates him, Polemon him. Polemon's pupils [scil. were] Crates and Crantor, with whom the Old Academy, which had begun with Plato, came to an end.

Arcesilaus participated [scil. in the teaching of] Crantor; from him [i.e. Arcesilaus], the Middle Academy flourished until Hegesinus. [64.1] Then Carneades and those in sequence after him follow in succession Hegesinus. Zeno of Citium, the initiator of the Stoic school, was the pupil of Crates. Cleanthes followed him in succession, Chrysippus and those after him, him.

[2] Xenophanes of Colophon is the initiator of the Eleatic school; according to Timaeus he lived at the time of Hieron, the ruler of Sicily, and of the poet Epicharmus, while Apollodorus says he was born in the 40th Olympiad and lived until the times of Darius and Cyrus. [3] Parmenides then becomes Xenophanes' student; Zeno, his; then Leucippus, then Democritus. [4] Democritus' pupils [scil. were] Protagoras of Abdera and Metrodorus of Chios; Diogenes of Smyrna, his; Anaxagoras, his; Pyrrho,

του δὲ Πύρρων, οὗ Ναυσιφάνης· τούτου φασὶν ἔνιοι μαθητὴν Ἐπίκουρον γενέσθαι.

[5] καὶ ἡ μὲν διαδοχὴ τῶν παρ᾽ Ἕλλησι φιλοσόφων ὡς ἐν ἐπιτομῇ ἥδε, οἱ χρόνοι δὲ τῶν προκαταρξάντων τῆς φιλοσοφίας αὐτῶν ἑπομένως λεκτέοι, ἵνα δὴ ἐν συγκρίσει ἀποδείξωμεν πολλαῖς γενεαῖς πρεσβυτέραν τὴν κατὰ Ἑβραίους φιλοσοφίαν.

A Doxographic List Based on a Succession (T22)

T22 (*Dox. Gr.*, pp. 589–90) Epiph. 3.2.9

1. αὐτὸς γὰρ Θαλῆς ὁ Μιλήσιος εἷς ὢν τῶν ἑπτὰ σοφῶν ἀρχέγονον πάντων ἀπεφήνατο τὸ ὕδωρ· ἐξ ὕδατος γάρ φησι τὰ πάντα εἶναι καὶ εἰς ὕδωρ πάλιν ἀναλύεσθαι.

2. Ἀναξίμανδρος ὁ τοῦ Πραξιάδου καὶ αὐτὸς Μιλήσιος τὸ ἄπειρον ἀρχὴν ἁπάντων ἔφησεν εἶναι· ἐκ τούτου γὰρ τὰ πάντα γίνεσθαι καὶ εἰς αὐτὸ τὰ πάντα ἀναλύεσθαι.

3. Ἀναξιμένης ὁ τοῦ Εὐρυστράτου καὶ αὐτὸς Μιλήσιος τὸν ἀέρα τοῦ παντὸς ἀρχὴν εἶναι λέγει καὶ ἐκ τούτου τὰ πάντα.

4. Ἀναξαγόρας ὁ τοῦ Ἡγησιβούλου ὁ Κλαζομένιος ἀρχὰς τῶν πάντων τὰς ὁμοιομερείας ἔφησεν εἶναι.

5. Ἀρχέλαος ὁ Ἀπολλοδώρου, κατὰ δέ τινας Μίλτωνος, Ἀθηναῖος δὲ ἦν, φυσικός, ἐκ γῆς τὰ πάντα λέγει γεγενῆσθαι. αὕτη γὰρ ἀρχὴ τῶν ὅλων ἐστίν, ὥς φησι.

this man's; Nausiphanes, his; some say that Epicurus became the pupil of this last.

[5] And this is, in summary form, the succession of the philosophers among the Greeks; next we must state the dates of those among them who made a beginning of philosophy, so that we can demonstrate by comparison that philosophy among the Hebrews was older by many generations.

A *Doxographic List Based on a Succession (T22)*

T22 (≠ DK) Epiphanius, *Panarion (Against Heresies)*

1. For Thales of Miletus himself, who was one of the Seven Sages, declared that water is the origin of all things; for he says that all things come from water and in turn are dissolved into water.

2. Anaximander—from Miletus too, son of Praxiades,—said that the unlimited is the principle of all things; for out of this all things come to be and into it all things are dissolved.

3. Anaximenes—from Miletus too, son of Eurystratus—said that air is the principle of the whole and that all things come from it.

4. Anaxagoras—from Clazomenae, son of Hegesiboulus—said that the homoiomeries are the principles of all things.

5. Archelaus—son of Apollodorus (but according to some people, son of Milton), and he was an Athenian natural philosopher—says that all things have come to be out of earth. For this is the principle of all things, as he says.

6. Σωκράτης ὁ ἑρμογλύφου Σωφρονίσκου καὶ Φαιναρέτης τῆς μαίας ὁ ἠθικὸς τὰ καθ᾿ ἑαυτὸν ἔλεγε μόνον δεῖν περιεργάζεσθαι τὸν ἄνθρωπον, πλείονα δὲ μή.

7. Φερεκύδης καὶ αὐτὸς γῆν φησι πρὸ πάντων γεγενῆσθαι.

8. Πυθαγόρας ὁ Σάμιος Μνησάρχου υἱὸς θεὸν ἔφη εἶναι τὴν μονάδα καὶ δίχα ταύτης μηδὲν γεγενῆσθαι. ἔλεγε δὲ μὴ δεῖν θύειν τοῖς θεοῖς ζῷα μηδὲ μὴν ἐσθίειν τι τῶν ἐμψύχων μηδὲ κυάμους μηδὲ οἶνον πίνειν τοὺς σοφούς. ἔλεγε δὲ τὰ ἀπὸ σελήνης κάτω παθητὰ εἶναι πάντα, τὰ δὲ ὑπεράνω τῆς σελήνης ἀπαθῆ εἶναι. ἔλεγε δὲ καὶ μεταβαίνειν τὴν ψυχὴν εἰς πολλὰ ζῷα. ἐκέλευσε δὲ καὶ τοῖς μαθηταῖς αὐτοῦ σιωπᾶν ἐπὶ πενταετῆ χρόνον καὶ τὸ τελευταῖον θεὸν ἑαυτὸν ἐπωνόμασε.

9. Ξενοφάνης ὁ τοῦ Ὀρθομένους Κολοφώνιος ἐκ γῆς καὶ ὕδατος ἔφη τὰ πάντα γίνεσθαι. εἶναι δὲ τὰ πάντα ὡς ἔφη οὐδὲν ἀληθές. οὕτως τὸ ἀτρεκὲς ἄδηλον, δόκησις δὲ ἐπὶ πᾶσι τέτυκται μάλιστα τῶν ἀφανέων.

10. Παρμενίδης ὁ τοῦ Πύρητος τὸ γένος Ἐλεάτης καὶ αὐτὸς τὸ ἄπειρον ἔλεγεν ἀρχὴν τῶν πάντων.

11. Ζήνων ὁ Ἐλεάτης ὁ ἐριστικὸς ἴσα τῷ ἑτέρῳ Ζήνωνι καὶ τὴν γῆν ἀκίνητον λέγει καὶ μηδένα τόπον κενὸν εἶναι. καὶ λέγει οὕτως· τὸ κινούμενον ἤτοι ἐν ᾧ

6. Socrates—son of the sculptor Sophroniscus and the midwife Phaenarete—philosopher of ethics, said that a human being should only concern himself with himself, and with nothing more.

7. Pherecydes too says that earth came to be before all things [cf. **PHER. D5**].

8. Pythagoras—from Samos, son of Mnesarchus—said that the monad is god and that nothing has come to be without this. He said that wise men must not sacrifice animals to the gods, nor eat anything animate or beans, nor drink wine. He said that all the things below the moon are subject to affections while those above the moon are impassible. He also said that the soul passes into many animals. He also ordered his pupils to remain silent for a period of five years and in the end he proclaimed himself a god.

9. Xenophanes—son of Orthomenes, from Colophon—said that all things come from earth and water. And he said that the totality of things is not at all true; so what is certain is unclear, and opinion extends over all things, especially invisible ones.

10. Parmenides too—the son of Pyres, from Elea by family—said that the unlimited is the principle of all things.[1]

11. Zeno of Elea, the eristic philosopher, says like the other Zeno [scil. of Citium] both that the earth is immobile and that no place is empty. And he says the following: what is in motion is in motion either in the place in which it is

---

[1] This is an error, perhaps indirectly caused by a confusion with Melissus.

ἐστι τόπῳ κινεῖται ἢ ἐν ᾧ οὐκ ἔστι. καὶ οὔτε ἐν ᾧ ἐστι τόπῳ κινεῖται οὔτε ἐν ᾧ οὐκ ἔστιν· οὐκ ἄρα τι κινεῖται.

12. Μέλισσος ὁ τοῦ Ἰθαγένους Σάμιος τὸ γένος ἓν τὸ πᾶν ἔφη εἶναι, μηδὲν δὲ βέβαιον ὑπάρχειν τῇ φύσει, ἀλλὰ πάντα εἶναι φθαρτὰ ἐν δυνάμει.

13. Λεύκιππος ὁ Μιλήσιος, κατὰ δέ τινας Ἐλεάτης, καὶ οὗτος ἐριστικός· ἐν ἀπείρῳ καὶ οὗτος τὸ πᾶν ἔφη εἶναι, κατὰ φαντασίαν δὲ καὶ δόκησιν τὰ πάντα γίνεσθαι καὶ μηδὲν κατὰ ἀλήθειαν, ἀλλ᾽ οὕτω φαίνεσθαι κατὰ τὴν ἐν τῷ ὕδατι κώπην.

14. Δημόκριτος ὁ τοῦ Δαμασίππου Ἀβδηρίτης τὸν κόσμον ἄπειρον ἔφη καὶ ὑπὲρ κενοῦ κεῖσθαι. ἔφη δὲ καὶ ἓν τέλος εἶναι τῶν πάντων καὶ εὐθυμίαν τὸ κράτιστον εἶναι, τὰς δὲ λύπας ὅρους κακίας. καὶ τὸ δοκοῦν δίκαιον οὐκ εἶναι δίκαιον, ἄδικον δὲ τὸ ἐναντίον τῆς φύσεως. ἐπίνοιαν γὰρ κακὴν τοὺς νόμους ἔλεγε καὶ οὐ χρὴ νόμοις πειθαρχεῖν τὸν σοφόν, ἀλλὰ ἐλευθερίως ζῆν.

15. Μητρόδωρος ὁ Χῖος ἔφη μηδένα μηδὲν ἐπίστασθαι, ἀλλὰ ταῦτα ἃ δοκοῦμεν γινώσκειν, ἀκριβῶς οὐκ ἐπιστάμεθα, οὐδὲ ταῖς αἰσθήσεσι δεῖ προσέχειν· δοκήσει γάρ ἐστι τὰ πάντα.

16. Πρωταγόρας ὁ τοῦ Μενάνδρου Ἀβδηρίτης ἔφη μὴ θεοὺς εἶναι μηδὲ ὅλως θεὸν ὑπάρχειν.

17. Διογένης ὁ Σμυρναῖος, κατὰ δέ τινας Κυρηναῖος, τὰ αὐτὰ τῷ Πρωταγόρᾳ ἐδόξασε.

or in the one in which it is not. And neither is it in motion in the one in which it is nor in the one in which it is not. Therefore nothing is in motion.

12. Melissus—son of Ithagenes, from Samos by family— said that the whole is one, and that nothing stable comes about in nature, but that all things are potentially destructible.

13. Leucippus too—from Miletus (but according to some from Elea)—an eristic philosopher too, said too that the whole is in the unlimited, and that it is in appearance and opinion that all things come to be and that this is not true at all, but that it appears in the same way as an oar in water.

14. Democritus—son of Damasippus, from Abdera—said that the world is unlimited and rests upon the void. He also said that the end of all things is one and that contentment (*euthumia*) is the best thing, while sufferings are the limits of evil. And what is thought to be just is not just, while what is contrary to nature is unjust. For he said that the laws are a bad invention, and that the wise man should not obey the laws but live freely.

15. Metrodorus—from Chios—said that no one knows anything, but that what we think we know, we do not know exactly, nor should we pay attention to sense perception. For all things are by opinion.

16. Protagoras—son of Menander, from Abdera—said that the gods do not exist and that on the whole there is no god.

17. Diogenes—from Smyrna (but according to some from Cyrene)—had the same opinions as Protagoras.

18. Πύρρων ἀπὸ Ἤλιδος τῶν ἄλλων σοφῶν τὰ δό-
γματα συναγαγὼν πάντα ἀντιθέσεις αὐτοῖς ἔγραψεν
ἀνατρέπων τὰς δόξας αὐτῶν καὶ οὐδενὶ δόγματι ἠρέ-
σκετο.

19. Ἐμπεδοκλῆς ὁ τοῦ Μέτωνος Ἀκραγαντῖνος πῦρ
καὶ γῆν καὶ ὕδωρ καὶ ἀέρα τέτταρα πρωτόγονα εἰσ-
έφερε στοιχεῖα καὶ ἔλεγεν ἔχθραν ὑπάρχειν πρῶτον
τῶν στοιχείων. κεχώριστο γάρ, φησί, τὸ πρότερον,
νῦν δὲ συνήνωται, ὡς λέγει, φιλωθέντα ἀλλήλοις. δύο
οὖν εἰσι κατ᾽ αὐτὸν ἀρχαὶ καὶ δυνάμεις ἔχθρα καὶ
φιλία, ὧν ἡ μέν ἐστιν ἑνωτικὴ ἡ δὲ διαχωριστική.

20. Ἡράκλειτος ὁ τοῦ Βλέσωνος Ἐφέσιος ἐκ πυρὸς
ἔλεγε τὰ πάντα εἶναι καὶ εἰς πῦρ πάλιν ἀναλύεσθαι.

21. Πρόδικος τὰ τέσσαρα στοιχεῖα θεοὺς καλεῖ εἶτα
ἥλιον καὶ σελήνην. ἐκ γὰρ τούτων πᾶσι τὸ ζωτικὸν
ἔλεγεν ὑπάρχειν.

18. Pyrrho—from Elis—after having collected all the opinions of the other wise men, wrote antitheses to them, reversing their opinions; and he did not accept any opinion.
19. Empedocles—son of Meton, from Acragas—introduced fire, earth, water, and air as four firstborn elements and said that hatred exists before the elements. For, he said, earlier they had been separated, but now they are united, as he says, having become friends of one another. Thus there are two principles and powers according to him, hatred and love, of which the one unifies and the other separates.
20. Heraclitus—son of Bleson, from Ephesus—said that all things come from fire and in turn are dissolved into fire.
21. Prodicus calls the four elements gods, then the sun and moon. For he said that it is out of these that life comes for all things.[2]

---

[2] The list continues with the Socratic schools (Plato, the Cyrenaics, the Cynics) and their descendants (New Academy, Aristotle, and the Peripatetics), the Stoics, and concludes with Epicurus.

BACKGROUND

2. COSMOLOGICAL
SPECULATIONS [COSM.]

The thinkers traditionally identified as the first philosophers were not the first people in ancient Greece to have speculated about the origin and structure of the world: various traces of cosmological reflection are preserved in the earliest surviving Greek poetry. Aristotle distinguished terminologically between *theologoi,* the archaic poets who wrote about gods (cf. *Metaphysics* B4, 1000a9), and *phusiologoi,* the early philosophers who wrote about nature (cf. Λ6, 1071b27; Λ10, 1075b26); but he was also careful to indicate the continuities, indeed the similarities between the two groups (cf. N4, 1091a34; cf. also **THAL. R32**). Indeed, a number of 'philosophical' cosmologies only become fully comprehensible against the background of traditional representations, which they presuppose even on the level of specific expressions.

The present chapter brings together a number of cosmological passages drawn from archaic Greek poets and thereby presents one kind of background that is useful for contextualizing the thought of the early Greek philosophers. Some of these texts are of interest as surviving vestiges of kinds of speculation that must have been widespread in early Greek oral culture but have otherwise been lost; others are presupposed, in content or expression, by

various texts that are classified as philosophical and that are found in the following chapters.

In this chapter, as in those dedicated to ancient doxography (chap. 1), to the most ancient reflections on gods and men (chap. 3), and to the echoes of philosophical doctrines found among the Greek dramatists (chap. 43), the critical apparatus for the Greek texts is reduced to a minimum, indicating solely our divergences, if any, from the editions of reference listed in volume 1. We have also refrained from providing bibliographical indications, which would not have made much sense here.

OUTLINE OF THE CHAPTER

COSMOLOGICAL
SPECULATIONS

The Structure of the World (T1–T9)
Earth and Heavens (T1)

T1 (> 7 B2) Hom. *Il.* 18.483–89

ἐν μὲν γαῖαν ἔτευξ᾽, ἐν δ᾽ οὐρανόν, ἐν δὲ
  θάλασσαν,
ἠέλιόν τ᾽ ἀκάμαντα σελήνην τε πλήθουσαν,
485 ἐν δὲ τὰ τείρεα πάντα, τά τ᾽ οὐρανὸς
  ἐστεφάνωται,
Πληϊάδας θ᾽ Ὑάδας τε τό τε σθένος Ὠρίωνος
Ἄρκτόν θ᾽, ἣν καὶ Ἄμαξαν ἐπίκλησιν καλέουσιν,
ἥ τ᾽ αὐτοῦ στρέφεται καί τ᾽ Ὠρίωνα δοκεύει,
οἴη δ᾽ ἄμμορός ἐστι λοετρῶν Ὠκεανοῖο.

Ocean (T2–T3)

T2 Hom. *Il.*

a (> 1 B2, ad B10, B13; 3 B5; 11 A12; 70 A24) 14.200–201
≈ 14.301–2

εἶμι γὰρ ὀψομένη πολυφόρβου πείρατα γαίης,

COSMOLOGICAL
SPECULATIONS

The Structure of the World (T1–T9)
Earth and Heavens (T1)

T1 (> 7 B2) Homer, *Iliad*

He [i.e. Hephaestus] made the earth on it [i.e.
    Achilles' shield], and the heavens, and the sea,
And the tireless sun and the full moon,
And all the constellations with which the heavens are   485
    crowned,
The Pleiades and the Hyades and Orion's strength
And the Bear, which they also call the Wagon by
    name,
Which turns around in place and watches Orion,
And is the only one to have no share of Ocean's baths.

Ocean (T2–T3)

T2 Homer, *Iliad*

a (> 1 B2, ad B10, B13; 3 B5; 11 A12; 70 A2ε)

For I [i.e. Hera] am going to see the limits of the all-
    nourishing earth,

Ὠκεανόν τε [. . . = **T10a**].

b (> 7 B2) 18.607–8

ἐν δὲ τίθει ποταμοῖο μέγα σθένος Ὠκεανοῖο
ἄντυγα πὰρ πυμάτην σάκεος πύκα ποιητοῖο.

T3 (≠ DK) Hes. *Th.* 274–75

Γοργούς θ᾽, αἳ ναίουσι πέρην κλυτοῦ Ὠκεανοῖο
ἐσχατιῇ πρὸς νυκτός, ἵν᾽ Ἑσπερίδες λιγύφωνοι
[. . .].

Tartarus (T4–T5)

T4 (> 28 A44) Hom. *Il.* 8.13–16

ἤ μιν ἑλὼν ῥίψω ἐς Τάρταρον ἠερόεντα
τῆλε μάλ᾽, ἧχι βάθιστον ὑπὸ χθονός ἐστι
  βέρεθρον,
15 ἔνθα σιδήρειαί τε πύλαι καὶ χάλκεος οὐδός,
τόσσον ἔνερθ᾽ Ἀΐδεω ὅσον οὐρανός ἐστ᾽ ἀπὸ
  γαίης.

T5 (> ad 31 B39) Hes. *Th.* 717–45

[. . .] καὶ τοὺς μὲν ὑπὸ χθονὸς εὐρυοδείης
πέμψαν καὶ δεσμοῖσιν ἐν ἀργαλέοισιν ἔδησαν,
νικήσαντες χερσὶν ὑπερθύμους περ ἐόντας,

And Ocean [. . .].

b (> 7 B2) [Description of the shield of Achilles]

And he [i.e. Hephaestus] put on it [i.e. Achilles'
    shield] the great strength of river Ocean,
Along the outer rim of the very well made shield.

T3 (≠ DK) Hesiod, *Theogony*

And the Gorgons who dwell beyond glorious Ocean
At the edge toward the night, where the clear-voiced
    Hesperides are [. . .].

Tartarus (T4–T5)

T4 (> 28 A44) Homer, *Iliad*

Or I [i.e. Zeus] will seize him[1] and throw him into
    murky Tartarus,
Very far away, where there is the deepest gulf
    beneath the earth,
Where iron gates and a bronze threshold are,
As far below Hades as the sky is from the earth.

[1] Any god who defies Zeus' orders not to help the Greeks or
Trojans.

T5 (> ad 31 B39) Hesiod, *Theogony*

They [i.e. the Olympian gods] sent them [i.e. the
    Titans] down under the broad-pathed earth
And bound them in distressful bonds

61

720   τόσσον ἔνερθ᾽ ὑπὸ γῆς ὅσον οὐρανός ἐστ᾽ ἀπὸ
    γαίης
   τόσσον γάρ τ᾽ ἀπὸ γῆς ἐς Τάρταρον ἠερόεντα.
   ἐννέα γὰρ νύκτας τε καὶ ἤματα χάλκεος ἄκμων
   οὐρανόθεν κατιών, δεκάτῃ κ᾽ ἐς γαῖαν ἵκοιτο·
723a   [ἶσον δ᾽ αὖτ᾽ ἀπὸ γῆς ἐς Τάρταρον ἠερόεντα]
   ἐννέα δ᾽ αὖ νύκτας τε καὶ ἤματα χάλκεος ἄκμων
725   ἐκ γαίης κατιών, δεκάτῃ κ᾽ ἐς Τάρταρον ἵκοι.
   τὸν πέρι χάλκεον ἕρκος ἐλήλαται· ἀμφὶ δέ μιν
    νύξ
   τριστοιχὶ κέχυται περὶ δειρήν· αὐτὰρ ὕπερθε
   γῆς ῥίζαι πεφύασι καὶ ἀτρυγέτοιο θαλάσσης.

   ἔνθα θεοὶ Τιτῆνες ὑπὸ ζόφῳ ἠερόεντι
730   κεκρύφαται βουλῇσι Διὸς νεφεληγερέταο,
   χώρῳ ἐν εὐρώεντι, πελώρης ἔσχατα γαίης.
   τοῖς οὐκ ἐξιτόν ἐστι, θύρας δ᾽ ἐπέθηκε Ποσειδέων
   χαλκείας, τεῖχος δ᾽ ἐπελήλαται ἀμφοτέρωθεν.
   ἔνθα Γύγης Κόττος τε καὶ Ὀβριάρεως μεγάθυμος
735   ναίουσιν, φύλακες πιστοὶ Διὸς αἰγιόχοιο.
   ἔνθα δὲ γῆς δνοφερῆς καὶ Ταρτάρου ἠερόεντος

734–45 secl. West

After they had gained victory over them with their
    hands, high-spirited though they were,
As far down beneath the earth as the sky is above the   720
    earth:
For it is just as far from the earth to murky Tartarus.
For a bronze anvil, falling down from the sky for nine
    nights and days,
On the tenth day would arrive at the earth;
[And in turn it is the same distance from the earth to   723a
    murky Tartarus;][1]
And again, a bronze anvil, falling down from the
    earth for nine nights and days,
On the tenth would arrive at Tartarus.   725
Around this a bronze barricade is extended, and on
    both sides of it night
Is poured out threefold around its neck; and above it
Grow the roots of the earth and of the barren sea.
        That is where the Titan gods are hidden
    under murky gloom
By the plans of the cloud-gatherer Zeus,   730
In a dank place, at the farthest part of huge earth.
They cannot get out, for Poseidon has set bronze
    gates upon it,
And a wall is extended on both sides.
        That is where Gyges, Cottus, and great-
    spirited Obriareus[2]
Dwell, the trusted guards of aegis-holding Zeus.   735
That is where the sources and limits of the dark earth
    are, and of murky Tartarus,

[1] This line is rejected as an interpolation by many editors.
[2] The Hundred-Handers.

πόντου τ᾽ ἀτρυγέτοιο καὶ οὐρανοῦ ἀστερόεντος
ἑξείης πάντων πηγαὶ καὶ πείρατ᾽ ἔασιν,
ἀργαλέ᾽ εὐρώεντα, τά τε στυγέουσι θεοί περ·
740   χάσμα μέγ᾽, οὐδέ κε πάντα τελεσφόρον εἰς
      ἐνιαυτόν
οὖδας ἵκοιτ᾽, εἰ πρῶτα πυλέων ἔντοσθε γένοιτο,
ἀλλά κεν ἔνθα καὶ ἔνθα φέροι πρὸ θύελλα
    θυέλλης
ἀργαλέη· δεινὸν δὲ καὶ ἀθανάτοισι θεοῖσι
τοῦτο τέρας· καὶ Νυκτὸς ἐρεμνῆς οἰκία δεινά
745   ἕστηκεν νεφέλῃς κεκαλυμμένα κυανέῃσιν.

Styx (T6–T7)

T6 (> 11 A12) Hom. *Il.* 15.37–38

καὶ τὸ κατειβόμενον Στυγὸς ὕδωρ, ὅς τε μέγιστος
ὅρκος δεινότατός τε πέλει μακάρεσσι θεοῖσι [. . .]

T7 (ad 31 B115) Hes. *Th.* 782–95, 805–6

ὁππότ᾽ ἔρις καὶ νεῖκος ἐν ἀθανάτοισιν ὄρηται,
καί ῥ᾽ ὅστις ψεύδηται Ὀλύμπια δώματ᾽ ἐχόντων,
Ζεὺς δέ τε ῏Ιριν ἔπεμψε θεῶν μέγαν ὅρκον ἐνεῖκαι

Of the barren sea, and of the starry sky,
Of everything, one after another,
Distressful, dank, things which even the gods abhor:
A great chasm, whose bottom one would not reach in   740
    a whole long year,
Once one was inside the gates,
But one would be borne hither and thither by one
    distressful blast after another—
It is terrible for the immortal gods as well,
This monstrosity; and the terrible houses of dark
    Night
Stand here, shrouded in black clouds.   745

Styx (T6–T7)

T6 (> 11 A12) Homer, *Iliad*

[. . .] the downward-flowing water of the Styx, which
    is the greatest
and most dreadful oath for the blessed gods [. . .][1]

[1] For other Homeric references to the Styx as the gods' oath,
see *Il.* 2.755, 14.271 (= *Od.* 5.184–86, *Hymn to Apollo* 84–86);
Hymn to Demeter 259; *Hymn to Hermes* 518–19.

T7 (ad 31 B115) Hesiod, *Theogony*

Whenever strife and quarrel arise among the
    immortals
And one of those who have their mansions on
    Olympus tells a lie,
Zeus sends Iris to bring the great oath of the gods

785   τηλόθεν ἐν χρυσέῃ προχόῳ πολυώνυμον ὕδωρ,
    ψυχρόν, ὅ τ᾽ ἐκ πέτρης καταλείβεται ἠλιβάτοιο
    ὑψηλῆς· πολλὸν δὲ ὑπὸ χθονὸς εὐρυοδείης
    ἐξ ἱεροῦ ποταμοῖο ῥέει διὰ νύκτα μέλαιναν·
    Ὠκεανοῖο κέρας, δεκάτη δ᾽ ἐπὶ μοῖρα δέδασται·
790   ἐννέα μὲν περὶ γῆν τε καὶ εὐρέα νῶτα θαλάσσης
    δίνῃς ἀργυρέῃς εἱλιγμένος εἰς ἅλα πίπτει,
    ἡ δὲ μί᾽ ἐκ πέτρης προρέει, μέγα πῆμα θεοῖσιν.
    ὅς κεν τὴν ἐπίορκον ἀπολλείψας ἐπομόσσῃ
    ἀθανάτων οἳ ἔχουσι κάρη νιφόεντος Ὀλύμπου,
795   κεῖται νήυτμος τετελεσμένον εἰς ἐνιαυτόν.
    [. . .]
805   τοῖον ἄρ᾽ ὅρκον ἔθεντο θεοὶ Στυγὸς ἄφθιτον
       ὕδωρ,
    ὠγύγιον· τὸ δ᾽ ἵησι καταστυφέλου διὰ χώρου.

Night and Day (T8–T9)

T8 (≠ DK) Hes. *Th.* 746–57

    [. . . = **T5**] τῶν πρόσθ᾽ Ἰαπετοῖο πάις ἔχει
      οὐρανὸν εὐρύν
    ἑστηὼς κεφαλῇ τε καὶ ἀκαμάτῃσι χέρεσσιν
    ἀστεμφέως, ὅθι Νύξ τε καὶ Ἡμέρη ἆσσον ἰοῦσαι

From afar in a golden jug, the much-renowned water,   785
Icy, which pours down from a great, lofty crag.
It flows abundantly from under the broad-pathed
    earth,
From the holy river through the black night—
A branch of Ocean, and a tenth portion has been
    assigned to her.
For nine-fold around the earth and the broad back of   790
    the sea
He whirls in silver eddies and falls into the sea,
And she as one portion flows forth from the crag, a
    great woe for the gods.
For whoever of the immortals, who possess the peak
    of snowy Olympus,
Swears a false oath after having poured a libation
    from her,
He lies breathless for one full year [. . .]   795
It is this sort of oath that the gods have established   805
    the imperishable water of Styx,
Primeval; and it pours out through a rugged place.[1]

[1] For another Hesiodic reference to the Styx as the gods' oath,
see *Theogony* 400.

Night and Day (T8–T9)

T8 (≠ DK) Hesiod, *Theogony*

In front of these [i.e. the gates of Tartarus], Iapetus'
    son [scil. Atlas] holds the broad sky
With his head and tireless hands, standing
Immovable, where Night and Day passing near

ἀλλήλας προσέειπον ἀμειβόμεναι μέγαν οὐδόν
750   χάλκεον· ἡ μὲν ἔσω καταβήσεται, ἡ δὲ θύραζε
ἔρχεται, οὐδέ ποτ' ἀμφοτέρας δόμος ἐντὸς ἐέργει,
ἀλλ' αἰεὶ ἑτέρη γε δόμων ἔκτοσθεν ἐοῦσα
γαῖαν ἐπιστρέφεται, ἡ δ' αὖ δόμου ἐντὸς ἐοῦσα
μίμνει τὴν αὑτῆς ὥρην ὁδοῦ, ἔστ' ἂν ἵκηται·
755   ἡ μὲν ἐπιχθονίοισι φάος πολυδερκὲς ἔχουσα,
ἡ δ' Ὕπνον μετὰ χερσί, κασίγνητον Θανάτοιο,
Νὺξ ὀλοή, νεφέλῃ κεκαλυμμένη ἠεροειδεῖ.

T9 (≠ DK) Stesich. Frag. S17 = 185 *PMGF*

τᾶμος δ' Ὑπεριονίδα ἲς
δέπας ἐσκατέβα ⟨παγ⟩χρύσεον ὄ-
φρα δι' Ὠκεανοῖο περάσαις
ἀφίκοιθ' ἱαρᾶς ποτὶ βένθεα νυκτὸς ἐρεμνᾶς
ποτὶ ματέρα κουριδίαν τ' ἄλοχον
παῖδας τε φίλους [. . .]

textus valde incertus
    1 τᾶμος Barrett: ἅλιος mss.   Ὑπεριονίδα ἲς West:
-δας mss.

68

Greet one another as they cross the great bronze
Threshold. The one is about to go in and the other   750
Is going out the door, and never does the house hold
    them both inside,
But always the one, being outside of the house,
Passes over the earth, while the other in turn
    remaining inside the house
Waits for the time of her own departure, until it
    comes.[1]
The one holds much-seeing light for those on the   755
    earth,
But the other holds Sleep in her hands, the brother
    of Death—
Deadly Night, shrouded in murky cloud.

[1] Cf. Homer, *Od.* 10.82–86.

T9 (≠ DK) Stesichorus, Fragment of *Geryoneis*

Then the strength of Hyperion's son [i.e. Helios]
Went down into a cup of solid gold so
    That he could travel across Ocean
And arrive at the depths
    Of holy, gloomy night,
To see his mother, his wedded wife,
    And his dear children [. . .].

---

2 ἐσκατέβαινε χρύσεον mss., corr. West apud Führer
3 περάσας mss., corr Page
4 ἀφίκηθ’, corr.   Blomfield   ἱερᾶς mss., corr. Page

Forms of Cosmotheogony (T10–T22)
Homeric Traces (T10)

T10 *Il.*

a (> 1 B2, ad B10, B13; 3 B5; 11 A12; 70 A24) 14.201 = 14.302

    [. . . = **T2a**] Ὠκεανόν τε θεῶν γένεσιν καὶ μητέρα
    Τηθύν [. . .].

b (< 38 B1) 21.194–97

    τῷ οὐδὲ κρείων Ἀχελώϊος ἰσοφαρίζει,
    οὐδὲ βαθυρρείταο μέγα σθένος Ὠκεανοῖο,
    ἐξ οὗ περ πάντες ποταμοὶ καὶ πᾶσα θάλασσα
    καὶ πᾶσαι κρῆναι καὶ φρείατα μακρὰ νάουσιν.

c (≠ DK) 14.245–46

              [. . .] ποταμοῖο ῥέεθρα
    Ὠκεανοῦ, ὅς περ γένεσις πάντεσσι τέτυκται.

Hesiod (T11)

T11 (> 7 B1a, 9 B2, 30 A5, 31 B27) *Th.* 116–38

    ἤτοι μὲν πρώτιστα Χάος γένετ᾽· αὐτὰρ ἔπειτα
    Γαῖ᾽ εὐρύστερνος, πάντων ἕδος ἀσφαλὲς αἰεί
    ἀθανάτων οἳ ἔχουσι κάρη νιφόεντος Ὀλύμπου

Forms of Cosmotheogony (T10–T22)
Homeric Traces (T10)

T10 *Iliad*

a (> 1 B2, ad B10, B13; 3 B5; 11 A12; 70 A24)

[. . .] Ocean, the origin of the gods, and mother
Tethys [. . .]

b (< 38 B1)

Not even does mighty Achelous equal him [i.e. Zeus],
Nor even the great strength of deep-flowing Ocean,
From whom all the rivers and all the sea
And all springs and deep wells flow.

c (≠ DK)

[. . .] the streams of the river
Ocean, who is the origin of all [. . .]

Hesiod (T11)

T11 (> 7 B1a, 9 B2, 30 A5, 31 B27) *Theogony*

In truth, first of all Chaos [i.e. Chasm] came to be,
and then
Broad-breasted Earth, the ever immovable seat of all
The immortals who possess snowy Olympus' peak

71

Τάρταρά τ᾽ ἠερόεντα μυχῷ χθονὸς εὐρυοδείης,
120   ἠδ᾽ Ἔρος, ὃς κάλλιστος ἐν ἀθανάτοισι θεοῖσι,
λυσιμελής, πάντων τε θεῶν πάντων τ᾽ ἀνθρώπων
δάμναται ἐν στήθεσσι νόον καὶ ἐπίφρονα
βουλήν.

ἐκ Χάεος δ᾽ Ἔρεβός τε μέλαινά τε Νὺξ ἐγένοντο·
Νυκτὸς δ᾽ αὖτ᾽ Αἰθήρ τε καὶ Ἡμέρη ἐξεγένοντο,
125   οὓς τέκε κυσαμένη Ἐρέβει φιλότητι μιγεῖσα.

Γαῖα δέ τοι πρῶτον μὲν ἐγείνατο ἶσον ἑωυτῇ
Οὐρανὸν ἀστερόενθ᾽, ἵνα μιν περὶ πάντα
καλύπτοι,
ὄφρ᾽ εἴη μακάρεσσι θεοῖς ἕδος ἀσφαλὲς αἰεί,
γείνατο δ᾽ οὔρεα μακρά, θεᾶν χαρίεντας ἐναύλους
130   Νυμφέων, αἳ ναίουσιν ἀν᾽ οὔρεα βησσήεντα,
ἠδὲ καὶ ἀτρύγετον πέλαγος τέκεν οἴδματι θυῖον,
Πόντον, ἄτερ φιλότητος ἐφιμέρου· αὐτὰρ ἔπειτα
Οὐρανῷ εὐνηθεῖσα τέκ᾽ Ὠκεανὸν βαθυδίνην
Κοῖόν τε Κρεῖόν θ᾽ Ὑπερίονά τ᾽ Ἰαπετόν τε
135   Θείαν τε Ῥείαν τε Θέμιν τε Μνημοσύνην τε
Φοίβην τε χρυσοστέφανον Τηθύν τ᾽ ἐρατεινήν.
τοὺς δὲ μεθ᾽ ὁπλότατος γένετο Κρόνος
ἀγκυλομήτης,
δεινότατος παίδων, θαλερὸν δ᾽ ἤχθηρε τοκῆα.

And murky Tartarus in the depths of the broad-
  pathed earth,
And Eros, who is the most beautiful among the   120
  immortal gods,
The limb-melter—he overpowers the mind and the
  thoughtful counsel
Of all the gods and of all human beings in their
  breasts.
    From Chaos, Erebos and black Night came to be;
And then Aether and Day came forth from Night,
Who conceived and bore them after mingling in love   125
  with Erebos.
    Earth first of all bore starry Ouranus [i.e. Sky]
Equal to herself, to cover her on every side,
So that there would be an ever immovable seat for
  the blessed gods;
And she bore the high mountains, the graceful haunts
  of the goddesses,
Nymphs who dwell on the wooded mountains.   130
And she also bore the barren sea seething with its
  swell,
Pontus, without delightful love; and then,
Having bedded with Ouranos, she bore deep-eddying
  Ocean
And Coeus and Crius and Hyperion and Iapetus
And Theia and Rhea and Themis and Mnemosyne   135
And golden-crowned Phoebe and lovely Tethys.
After these, Cronus was born, the youngest of all,
  crooked-counseled,
The most terrible of her children; and he hated his
  vigorous father.

Orphic Texts (T12–T20)
In the Derveni Papyrus (T12)

T12 (≠ DK)

a (10F Bernabé = **DERV. Col. XIV.5–6** + **XV.6**)

ὃς μέγ᾽ ἔρεξεν . . .
Οὐρανὸς Εὐφρονίδης, ὃς πρώτιστος βασίλευσεν,
ἐκ τοῦ δὴ Κρόνος αὖτις, ἔπειτα δὲ μητίετα Ζεύς.

b (12F Bernabé = **DERV. Col. XVI.3–6**)

πρωτογόνου βασιλέως αἰδοίου· τῶι δ᾽ ἄρα πάντες
ἀθάνατοι προσέφυν μάκαρες θεοὶ ἠδὲ θέαιναι
καὶ ποταμοὶ καὶ κρῆναι ἐπήρατοι ἄλλα τε πάντα,
ἅσσα τότ᾽ ἦν γεγαῶτ᾽, αὐτὸς δ᾽ ἄρα μοῦνος
ἔγεντο.

c (14F Bernabé) (1 = 31.1F Bernabé + **DERV. Col. XVII.6**; 2 = **DERV. Col. XVII.12**; 3 = 31.5F Bernabé + **DERV. Col. XVIII.1**; 4 = **DERV. Col. XIX.10**)

Ζεὺς πρῶτος ‹γένετο, Ζεὺς› ὕστατος
  ‹ἀργικέραυνος›
Ζεὺς κεφα‹λή, Ζεὺς μέσ›σα, Διὸς δ᾽ ἐκ ‹π›άντα
  τέτ‹υκται,›
‹Ζεὺς πνοιὴ πάντων, Ζεὺς πάντων ἔπλετο› μοῖρα
Ζεὺς βασιλεύς, Ζεὺς δ᾽ ἀρχὸς ἁπάντων
  ἀργικέραυνος.

Orphic Texts (T12–T20)
In the Derveni Papyrus (T12)

T12 (≠ DK)

a

>   . . . he who did a great deed . . .
>
> Ouranos, son of Euphronê [i.e. Night], who was the
>   first of all to rule,
> From him in turn came Cronus and then prudent
>   Zeus.

b

> Of the firstborn king, the reverend one. And upon
>   him all
> The immortals grew, blessed gods and goddesses
> And rivers and lovely springs and everything else
> That was born then; and he himself was alone.

c

> Zeus ⟨was born⟩ first, ⟨Zeus with bright lightning⟩
>   last
> Zeus is the head, Zeus the middle, and by Zeus all
>   things ⟨are made⟩
> ⟨Zeus is the breath of all things, Zeus⟩ the fate ⟨of all
>   things⟩,
> Zeus the king, Zeus the ruler of all, god of the bright
>   bolt.[1]

[1] The sequence of verses and the supplements are due to the
editor A. Bernabé and are reproduced here *exempli gratia*. For
the way in which these verses are transmitted in the Derveni
Papyrus, see the corresponding columns in the chapter **DERV.**

d (16F Bernabé, cf. **DERV. Col. XXIII.4–6, 11**)

⟨μήσατο δ᾽ αὖ⟩ Γαῖάν ⟨τε καὶ⟩ Οὐρανὸν εὐρὺν
    ⟨ὕπερθεν,⟩
μήσατο δ᾽ Ὠκεανοῖο μέγα σθένος εὐρὺ ῥέοντος,
ἶνας δ᾽ ἐγκατέλεξ᾽ Ἀχελωίου ἀργυροδίνεω
ἐξ οὗ πᾶσα θάλασ⟨σα⟩

e (17F Bernabé = **DERV. Col. XXIV.2–3**)

    . . . ἰσομελὴς . . .
ἢ πολλοῖς φαίνει μερόπεσσι ἐπ᾽ ἀπείρονα γαῖαν.

In Orphic Theogonies Reported by
Later Authors (T13–T20)
Various Starting Points (T13–T18)

T13 (< 1 B12) Dam. *Princ.*124 (3.162.19–23 Westerink)

ἡ δὲ παρὰ τῷ περιπατητικῷ Εὐδήμῳ [Frag. 150 Wehrli]
ἀναγεγραμμένη ὡς τοῦ Ὀρφέως οὖσα θεολογία [. . .]
ἀπὸ δὲ τῆς Νυκτὸς ἐποιήσατο τὴν ἀρχήν [. . .].

T14 (20F, V Bernabé) Io. Lyd. *Mens.* 2.8 (26.1 Wünsch)

[. .] τρεῖς πρῶται κατ᾽ Ὀρφέα ἐξεβλάστησαν ἀρχαὶ
τῆς γενέσεως, Νὺξ καὶ Γῆ καὶ Οὐρανός [. . .].

COSMOLOGICAL SPECULATIONS

d

<And he [i.e. Zeus] devised> Earth <and> broad
  Ouranos <up above,>
And he devised the great strength of broadly flowing
  Ocean,
He placed in it the sinews of silver-eddying Achelous.
From which the whole sea . . .[1]

[1] The same applies here as in the preceding note

e

      . . . equal-limbed . . .
She [i.e. the moon] who shines for many mortals
  upon the boundless earth.

In Orphic Theogonies Reported by
Later Authors (T13–T20)
Various Starting Points (T13–T18)

T13 (< 1 B12) Damascius, *On the Principles*

The theogony recorded by the Peripatetic Eudemus as
being by Orpheus [. . .] it took Night as the starting point
[. . .].

T14 (≠ DK) John Lydus, *On the Months*

[. . .] according to Orpheus, three starting points of generation blossomed: Night, Earth, and Sky [. . .].

T15 (< 1 B2) Plat. *Crat.* 402b

Ὠκεανὸς πρῶτος καλλίρροος ἦρξε γάμοιο,
ὅς ῥα κασιγνήτην ὁμομήτορα Τηθὺν ὄπυιεν.

T16 (< 1 B13) Dam. *Princ.* 123 bis (3.160.17–20
Westerink)

ἡ δὲ κατὰ τὸν Ἱερώνυμον φερομένη καὶ Ἑλλάνικον
[. . .] οὕτως ἔχει. ὕδωρ ἦν, φησίν, ἐξ ἀρχῆς καὶ ὕλη
ἐξ ἧς ἐπάγη ἡ γῆ, δύο ταύτας ἀρχὰς ὑποτιθέμενος
πρώτας [. .].

T17 (109F, I Bernabé) Procl. *In Crat.* 59.17 Pasquali

[. . .] Ὀρφεὺς τὴν πρώτην πάντων αἰτίαν Χρόνον καλεῖ ὁμωνύμως σχεδὸν τῷ Κρόνῳ [. . .].

T18 (111F Bernabé) Procl. *In Remp.* 2.138.8 Kroll (v.
1–2), Simpl. *In Phys.* 528.14 (v. 3)

Αἰθέρα μὲν Χρόνος οὗτος ἀγήραος, ἀφθιτόμητις
γένατο καὶ μέγα Χάσμα πελώριον ἔνθα καὶ
   ἔνθα,
ο̄ δέ τι πεῖραρ ὑπῆν, οὐ πυθμήν, οὐδέ τις ἕδρα.

T15 (< 1 B2) Plato, *Cratylus*

> Fair-flowing Ocean was the first to make a beginning
>   of marriage,
> He who wedded his sister Tethys, born of the same
>   mother.[1]

[1] Cf. the testimonia collected as 23F Bernabé.

T16 (< 1 B13 DK) Damascius, *On the Principles*

The [scil. theogony] reported by Hieronymus and Hellanicus [. . .] goes as follows: there was from the beginning water and the matter out of which the earth was solidified, [scil. Orpheus?] establishing first of all these two principles [. . .].

T17 (≠ DK) Proclus, *Commentary on Plato's Cratylus*

Orpheus calls the first cause of all things Time [*Khronos*], almost identical in sound with Cronus [*Kronos*].

T18 (≠ DK) Proclus, *Commentary on Plato's* Republic (v. 1–2); Simplicius, *Commentary on Aristotle's* Physics (v. 3)

> This Time, unaging, eternal-counseled, begot Aether
> And great Chasm, immense here and immense there,
> And there was no limit, no bottom, nor any abode.

The Cosmic Egg (T19–T20)

T19 (103F, V; 104F, I; 115F; 117F Bernabé) Appio ap.
Ps.-Clem. Rom. *Homil.,* 6.3.4–4.3

[. . .] ὅπερ Ὀρφεὺς ᾠὸν λέγει γενητόν, ἐξ ἀπείρου τῆς
ὕλης προβεβλημένον, γεγονὸς δὲ οὕτω· τῆς τετραγε-
νοῦς ὕλης ἐμψύχου οὔσης, καὶ ὅλου ἀπείρου τινὸς
βυθοῦ ἀεὶ ῥέοντος, καὶ ἀκρίτως φερομένου, καὶ μυρίας ἀτελεῖς κράσεις ἄλλοτε ἄλλως ἐπαναχέοντος,
καὶ διὰ τοῦτο αὐτὰς ἀναλύοντος τῇ ἀταξίᾳ, καὶ κεχη-
νότος ὡς εἰς γένεσιν ζῴου δεθῆναι μὴ δυναμένου,
συνέβη ποτέ, αὐτοῦ τοῦ ἀπείρου πελάγους ὑπὸ ἰδίας
φύσεως περιωθουμένου, κινήσει φυσικῇ εὐτάκτως
ῥυῆναι ἀπὸ τοῦ αὐτοῦ εἰς τὸ αὐτὸ ὥσπερ ἴλιγγα καὶ
μῖξαι τὰς οὐσίας καὶ οὕτως ἐξ ἑκάστου τῶν πάντων
τὸ νοστιμώτατον, ὅπερ πρὸς γένεσιν ζῴου ἐπιτηδει-
ότατον ἦν, ὥσπερ ἐν χώνῃ κατὰ μέσου ῥυῆναι τοῦ
παντὸς καὶ ὑπὸ τῆς πάντα φερούσης ἴλιγγος χωρῆ-
σαι εἰς βάθος καὶ τὸ περικείμενον πνεῦμα ἐπισπάσα-
σθαι καὶ ὡς εἰς γονιμώτατον συλληφθὲν ποιεῖν κρι-
τικὴν σύστασιν. ὥσπερ γὰρ ἐν ὑγρῷ φιλεῖ γίνεσθαι
πομφόλυξ, οὕτως σφαιροειδὲς πανταχόθεν συνελή-
φθη κύτος. ἔπειτα αὐτὸ ἐν ἑαυτῷ κινηθὲν ὑπὸ τοῦ περι-
ειληφότος θειώδους πνεύματος ἀναφερόμενον προέκυ-
ψεν εἰς φῶς μέγιστόν τι τοῦτο ἀποκύημα, ὡς ἂν ἐκ
παντὸς τοῦ ἀπείρου βυθοῦ ἀποκεκυημένον ἔμψυχον
δημιούργημα, καὶ τῇ περιφερείᾳ τῷ ᾠῷ προσεοικὸς
καὶ τῷ τάχει τῆς πτήσεως.

The Cosmic Egg (T19–T20)

T19 (≠ DK) Appion in Ps.-Clement, *Homilies*

[. . .] the egg that Orpheus says was generated, sent forth from the infinity of matter, and born in the following way: the four-fold matter is animate and a whole infinite abyss is always flowing, which moves in a confused way, inundating each time differently innumerable imperfect mixtures, and for this reason, by reason of its disorder, it dissolves them, and it gapes open as though for the birth of an animal since it cannot be bound; in these circumstances, it happened once that, the infinite sea being impelled by its own nature, it flowed in an orderly manner with a natural motion from itself into itself like a whirlpool and mixed together the substances; and in this way, out of every thing in the universe, the element that was most nutritious and most suitable for the generation of an animal flowed toward the center of the universe, as in a funnel, and proceeded into the depths by the effect of the whirlpool that carries all things; and the surrounding wind was attracted by it and, when it had been assembled in the direction of the most perfect generative element, it produced an organism endowed with discernment. For just as a bubble tends to come about in a liquid, in the same way a spherical container was assembled from all sides. Then, when it had been procreated within itself and was lifted up by the surrounding divine wind, this greatest procreation emerged into the light, like an animate contrivance that emerged from the whole infinite abyss, similar to an egg in its round form and in the speed of its flight.

T20 (114F Bernabé) Dam. *Princ.* 55 (2.40.14 Westerink)

– ∪ ἔπειτα δ᾿ ἔτευξε μέγας Χρόνος Αἰθέρι δίῳ
ᾤεον ἀργύφεον.

*Musaeus, Acusilaus, and Other Authors of Archaic
Cosmotheogonies (T21–T22)*

T21 (< 2 B14, 9 B1) Philod. *Piet.* 137.3–5, pp. 61–62
Gomperz

ἐν μέν ǀ [τισι]ν ἐκ Νυκτὸς καὶ ǀ [Ταρ]τάρου λέγεται ǀ
[τὰ π]άντα, ἐν δέ τι[σιν ἐ]ξ Ἅιδου καὶ Αἰ[θέρ]ος· ὁ
δὲ τὴν Τι[τανο]μαχίαν γρά[ψας ἐξ] Αἰθέρος φη[σίν],
Ἀκουσίλαος ǀ [δ᾿ ἐκ] Χάους πρώτου ǀ [τἆλ]λα· ἐν δὲ
τοῖς ǀ [ἀνα]φερομένοις εἰς ǀ [Μο]υσαῖον γέγραπται ǀ
[Τάρτ]αρον πρῶτον ǀ [καὶ Ν]ύκτα.[1]

[1] [καὶ Ν]ύκτα Zeller, cett. Gomperz

T22 (< 9 B1) Dam. *Princ.* 124 (3.163.19–164.8 Westerink)

Ἀκουσίλαος δὲ Χάος μὲν ὑποτίθεσθαί μοι δοκεῖ τὴν
πρώτην ἀρχήν, ὡς πάντη ἄγνωστον, τὰς δὲ δύο μετὰ
τὴν μίαν, Ἔρεβος μὲν τὴν ἄρρενα, τὴν δὲ θήλειαν
Νύκτα [. . .] ἐκ δὲ τούτων φησὶ μιχθέντων Αἰθέρα
γενέσθαι καὶ Ἔρωτα καὶ Μῆτιν [. . .]. παράγει δὲ ἐπὶ
τούτοις ἐκ τῶν αὐτῶν καὶ ἄλλων θεῶν πολὺν ἀριθμὸν
κατὰ τὴν Εὐδήμου ἱστορίαν [< Frag. 150 Wehrli].

T20 (≠ DK) Damascius, *On the Principles*

> then great Time produced for divine Aether
> An egg shining like silver.

*Musaeus, Acusilaus, and Other Authors of Archaic
Cosmotheogonies (T21–T22)*

T21 (< 2 B14, 9 B1) Philodemus, *On Piety*

Among some it is said that all things come from Night and
Tartarus, among some from Hades and Aether. The author
of the *War of the Titans* [i.e. perhaps Eumelus of Corinth]
says [scil. that they came from] Aether, Acusilaus [scil. says
that] all other things [scil. came] first from Chaos. In the
writings attributed to Musaeus it is written that Tartarus
and Night were the first.

T22 (< 9 B1) Damascius, *On the Principles*

Acusilaus seems to me to establish Chaos as the first beginning, supposing that it is entirely unknown, and then
the two after the one: Erebus the male, and the female
Night [. . .]. He says that from these, when they were
united, were born Aether, Eros, and Metis [. . .]. And he
adds, besides these, also a large number of other gods
that came from the same ones, according to the history of
Eudemus.

3. REFLECTIONS ON GODS
AND MEN [MOR.]

Reflection on the similarities and, especially, the differences between the lives of gods and of human beings dominates Greek thought from the beginning. If the assertions of the early Greek philosophers about the gods and about men are to be understood fully, they need to be seen in relation with their predecessors', of whom (as, too, in the case of cosmological reflection) they take up some themes and formulas but also do not hesitate to distance themselves from other ones, criticizing and polemicizing, sometimes explicitly, against ideas endowed with a very strong cultural authority—just as their precursors themselves had often done.

The present chapter puts together a number of passages on the nature of human and divine life drawn from archaic and Classical Greek poets and traditional prose wisdom literature. It thereby presents one background to the thought of the early Greek philosophers. Some of these texts are of interest as surviving vestiges of kinds of popular thought that must have been widespread in early Greek oral culture but have otherwise been lost; others are presupposed specifically, in content or expression, by a number of the texts classified as belonging to early Greek philosophy and presented in the following chapters. The

presence of theological and political patterns is evident everywhere, but it must be emphasized that wisdom literature is echoed interestingly not only among philosophers even before the fifth century BC but also in the ways in which the later tradition depicts philosophers' character and behavior.

In this chapter, as in the ones dedicated to ancient doxography (chap. 1), to the most ancient reflections on the world (chap. 2), and to the echoes of philosophical doctrines found among the Greek dramatists (chap. 43), the critical apparatus for the Greek texts is reduced to a minimum, indicating solely our divergences, if any, from the editions of reference indicated in volume 1. In the case of the Orphic bone tablet and gold leaf (**T33–T34**), we have not reproduced the diacritical signs that appeared in the original edition. We have limited the bibliographical indications to the Seven Sages.

BIBLIOGRAPHY ON THE
SEVEN SAGES

A. Busine. *Les sept sages de la Grèce antique: Transmission et utilisation d'un patrimoine légendaire d'Hérodote à Plutarque* (Paris, 2002).

J. Engels. *Die sieben Weisen: Leben, Lehren und Legenden* (Munich, 2010).

L. Kurke. *Aesopic Conversations: Popular Tradition, Cultural Dialogue, and the Invention of Greek Prose* (Princeton, 2011).

B. Snell, ed. *Leben und Meinungen der Sieben Weisen: Griechische und lateinische Quellen aus 2000 Jahren* (Munich, 1938).

OUTLINE OF THE CHAPTER

REFLECTIONS ON
GODS AND MEN

The Condition of the Gods (T1–T6)
Zeus (T1–T3)

T1 (≠ DK) Aesch. Ag. 160–83

[χο.]   Ζεύς, ὅστις ποτ᾽ ἐστίν, εἰ τόδ᾽ αὐ-
            τῷ φίλον κεκλημένῳ,
        τοῦτό νιν προσεννέπω·
        οὐκ ἔχω προσεικάσαι
            πάντ᾽ ἐπισταθμώμενος
165   πλὴν Διός, εἰ τὸ μάταν ἀπὸ φροντίδος ἄχθος
        χρὴ βαλεῖν ἐτητύμως.

        οὐδ᾽ ὅστις πάροιθεν ἦν μέγας,
            παμμάχῳ θράσει βρύων,
170   οὐδὲ λέξεται πρὶν ὤν·
        ὃς δ᾽ ἔπειτ᾽ ἔφυ, τρια-
            κτῆρος οἴχεται τυχών.
        Ζῆνα δέ τις προφρόνως ἐπινίκια κλάζων
175   τεύξεται φρενῶν τὸ πᾶν,

        τὸν φρονεῖν βροτοὺς ὁδώ-
        σαντα, τὸν πάθει μάθος

88

REFLECTIONS ON
GODS AND MEN

The Condition of the Gods (T1–T5)
Zeus (T1–T3)

T1 (≠ DK) Aeschylus, *Agamemnon*

[CHORUS:]   Zeus, whoever he is, if this is what
        pleases him to be called,
    I call upon him as this.
    For I am not able to compare,
        pondering everything,
    Except for Zeus, if I am to cast truthfully   165
    The futile weight from my thought.

    Neither whoever earlier was great,
        bursting with all-battling force,
    Will be even spoken of as having existed formerly;   170
    And as for him who was born later, he is gone,
        having encountered a victor.
    That man will hit completely upon wisdom
        (*phrenes*)
    Who eagerly proclaims Zeus victorious—   175

    Zeus, who sets men on the path to wisdom (*phro-
        nein*),
    Who has established the law that learning

θέντα κυρίως ἔχειν.
στάζει δ' ἀνθ' ὕπνου πρὸ καρδίας
180   μνησιπήμων πόνος· καὶ παρ' ἄ-
κοντας ἦλθε σωφρονεῖν.
δαιμόνων δέ που χάρις βίαιος
σέλμα σεμνὸν ἡμένων.

182 δέ που T, δὲ ποῦ cett.   βίαιος Turnebus: βιαίως mss.

T2 (≠ DK) Aesch. *Heliad.* Frag. 70 R

Ζεύς ἐστιν αἰθήρ, Ζεὺς δὲ γῆ, Ζεὺς δ'οὐρανός,
Ζεύς τοι τὰ πάντα χὤ τι τῶνδ' ὑπέρτερον.

T3 (≠ DK) Soph. *Trach.* 1276–78

[ΤΛ.]   [. . . μεγάλους μὲν ἰδοῦσα νέους θανάτους,
πολλὰ δὲ πήματα καὶ καινοπαθῆ,
κοὐδὲν τούτων ὅ τι μὴ Ζεύς.

Aphrodite and Other Divinities (T4–T6)

T4 (ad 59 A112) Aesch. *Danaid.* Frag. 44 R

[ΑΦ.]   ἐρᾶ μὲν ἁγνὸς οὐρανὸς τρῶσαι χθόνα,
ἔρως δὲ γαῖαν λαμβάνει γάμου τυχεῖν·

Comes through suffering.
There drips down instead of sleep before the heart
Anguish, mindful of misery; wisdom   180
Arrives to the unwilling too.
From the deities throned on lofty seat
Comes somehow a grace, violent.

T2 (≠ DK) Aeschylus, Fragment from *Daughters of the Sun*

Zeus is the aether, Zeus the earth, Zeus the sky:
Indeed, Zeus is everything, and whatever is beyond
    that.

T3 (≠ DK) Sophocles, *Trachinian Women*

[HYLLUS TO THE CHORUS:] [. . .] seeing terrible recent
    deaths,
    And sufferings, many and unprecedented—
    And of these things, nothing that is not Zeus.

Aphrodite and Other Divinities (T4–T6)

T4 (ad 59 A112) Aeschylus, Fragment from *The Danaids*

[APHRODITE:] The pure sky desires to penetrate the
    earth,
    And desire seizes the earth to experience wedlock.

91

ὄμβρος δ᾽ ἀπ᾽ εὐνάεντος οὐρανοῦ πεσὼν
ἔκυσε γαῖαν· ἡ δὲ τίκτεται βροτοῖς
μήλων τε βοσκὰς καὶ βίον Δημήτριον
δένδρων τ᾽ ὀπώραν· ἐκ νοτίζοντος γάμου
τελεῖθ᾽ ὅσ᾽ ἔστι· τῶν δ᾽ ἐγὼ παραίτιος

3 verbi εὐνάεντος forma et significatio valde incertae

T5 (≠ DK) Soph. Frag. 941 R

ὦ παῖδες, ἤ τοι Κύπρις οὐ Κύπρις μόνον,
ἀλλ᾽ ἐστὶ πολλῶν ὀνομάτων ἐπώνυμος.
ἔστιν μὲν Ἅιδης, ἔστι δ᾽ ἄφθιτος βίος,
ἔστιν δὲ λύσσα μανιάς, ἔστι δ᾽ ἵμερος
5   ἄκρατος ἔστ᾽ οἰμωγμός. ἐν κείνῃ τὸ πᾶν
σπουδαῖον, ἡσυχαῖον, ἐς βίαν ἄγον.
ἐντήκεται γὰρ πλευμόνων ὅσοις ἔνι
ψυχή· τίς οὐχὶ τῆσδε τῆς θεοῦ πόρος;
εἰσέρχεται μὲν ἰχθύων πλωτῷ γένει,
10   ἔνεστι δ᾽ ἐν χέρσου τετρασκελεῖ γονῇ,
νωμᾷ δ᾽ ἐν οἰωνοῖσι τοὐκείνης πτερόν.
⟨. . .⟩
ἐν θηρσίν, ἐν βροτοῖσιν, ἐν θεοῖς ἄνω.
τίν᾽ οὐ παλαίουσ᾽ ἐς τρὶς ἐκβάλλει θεῶν;
εἴ μοι θέμις—θέμις δὲ τἀληθῆ λέγειν—
15   Διὸς τυραννεῖ πλευμόνων, ἄνευ δορός,
ἄνευ σιδήρου· πάντα τοι συντέμνεται
Κύπρις τὰ θνητῶν καὶ θεῶν βουλεύματα

Rain, falling from the well-flowing (?) sky,
Impregnates the earth; and she gives birth for mor-
   tals
To pastures for sheep, and Demeter's sustenance
   for life [i.e. grain],
And the fruit of trees: from moistening wedlock
Is fulfilled all that exists. Of these things I am part
   cause.

T5 (≠ DK) Sophocles, Fragment from an unidentified
play

Children, Cypris [i.e. Aphrodite] is not only Cypris,
But her name is equivalent to many names.
She is Hades, she is imperishable life,
She is insane frenzy, she is unmixed
Desire, is lamentation. In her resides all that is   5
Noble, calm, leading to violence.
For she melts into the lungs of all that are
Animate—what resource does not belong to this
   goddess?
She enters into the fishes' swimming tribe,
She is located within the land's four-legged offspring,   10
Her wing plies among birds.
⟨. . .⟩
Among animals, among mortals, among gods above.
Which of the gods does she not wrestle and
   overthrow three times?
If it is lawful for me—and it is lawful to say the
   truth—
She is tyrant over Zeus' lungs, without a spear,   15
Without iron. Cypris cuts short
All the plans of mortals and of gods.

T6 (≠ DK) Eur. Frag. 898 K

> τὴν Ἀφροδίτην οὐχ ὁρᾷς ὅση θεός;
> ἣν οὐδ' ἂν εἴποις οὐδὲ μετρήσειας ἂν
> ὅση πέφυκε κἀφ' ὅσον διέρχεται.
> αὕτη τρέφει σὲ κἀμὲ καὶ πάντας βροτούς.
> 5 τεκμήριον δέ, μὴ λόγῳ μόνον μάθῃς·
> ἐρᾷ μὲν ὄμβρου γαῖ', ὅταν ξηρὸν πέδον
> ἄκαρπον αὐχμῷ νοτίδος ἐνδεῶς ἔχῃ,
> ἐρᾷ δ' ὁ σεμνὸς οὐρανὸς πληρούμενος
> 10 ὄμβρου πεσεῖν εἰς γαῖαν Ἀφροδίτης ὕπο·
> ὅταν δὲ συμμιχθῆτον ἐς ταὐτὸν δύο,
> φύουσιν ἡμῖν πάντα καὶ τρέφουσ' ἅμα
> δι' ὧν βρότειον ζῇ τε καὶ θάλλει γένος.

5 post hunc versum hab. mss. ἔργῳ δὲ δείξω τὸ σθένος τὸ τῆς θεοῦ, del. Gomperz

The Human Condition (T7–T39)
Men in Their Difference from Gods (T7–T9)

T7 (≠ DK) Hom. *Il.* 24.525–33

> 525 ὡς γὰρ ἐπεκλώσαντο θεοὶ δειλοῖσι βροτοῖσιν,
> ζώειν ἀχνυμένους· αὐτοὶ δέ τ' ἀκηδέες εἰσίν.
> δοιοὶ γάρ τε πίθοι κατακείαται ἐν Διὸς οὔδει
> δώρων οἷα δίδωσι, κακῶν, ἕτερος δὲ ἑάων.
> ᾧ μέν κ' ἀμμείξας δώῃ Ζεὺς τερπικέραυνος,

T6 (≠ DK) Euripides, Fragment from an unidentified play

Do you not see how great a goddess Aphrodite is?
You could neither say nor measure
How great she is by nature, and how far she reaches.
She nurtures you and me and all mortals.
Here is evidence, so that you can learn it not only   5
   through words.
The earth desires rain when the dry soil,   7
Infertile because of drought, is in need of moisture,
And the majestic sky, when it is filled
With rain, desires to fall upon the earth—because of   10
   Aphrodite:
And when these two are commingled into one and
   the same,
They generate and nurture for us all the things
Through which the mortal race lives and flourishes.

The Human Condition (T7–T39)
Men in Their Difference from Gods (T7–T9)

T7 (≠ DK) Homer, *Iliad* [Achilles to Priam:]

For this is how the gods have spun matters for   525
   wretched mortals,
To live in grief, while they themselves are free of
   care.
For two urns are set on Zeus' floor,
Of gifts of the sort he gives, [scil. the one] of evils,
   the other of benefits.
To whomever thunder-delighting Zeus gives a
   mixture of these,

530   ἄλλοτε μέν τε κακῷ ὅ γε κύρεται, ἄλλοτε δ'
    ἐσθλῷ·
    ᾧ δέ κε τῶν λυγρῶν δώῃ, λωβητὸν ἔθηκεν,
    καί ἑ κακὴ βούβρωστις ἐπὶ χθόνα δῖαν ἐλαύνει,
    φοιτᾷ δ' οὔτε θεοῖσι τετιμένος οὔτε βροτοῖσιν.

T8 (≠ DK) Hom. *Od.*

a 1.31–34

    τοῦ ὅ γ' ἐπιμνησθεὶς ἔπε' ἀθανάτοισι μετηύδα·
    "ὦ πόποι, οἷον δή νυ θεοὺς βροτοὶ αἰτιόωνται.
    ἐξ ἡμέων γὰρ φασὶ κάκ' ἔμμεναι· οἱ δὲ καὶ αὐτοί
    σφῇσιν ἀτασθαλίῃσιν ὑπὲρ μόρον ἄλγε' ἔχουσιν
    [. . .]."

b 18.130–37

130   οὐδὲν ἀκιδνότερον γαῖα τρέφει ἀνθρώποιο
    πάντων, ὅσσα τε γαῖαν ἔπι πνείει τε καὶ ἕρπει.
    οὐ μὲν γάρ ποτέ φησι κακὸν πείσεσθαι ὀπίσσω,
    ὄφρ' ἀρετὴν παρέχωσι θεοὶ καὶ γούνατ' ὀρώρῃ·
    ἀλλ' ὅτε δὴ καὶ λυγρὰ θεοὶ μάκαρες τελέωσι,
135   καὶ τὰ φέρει ἀεκαζόμενος τετληότι θυμῷ.
    τοῖος γὰρ νόος ἐστὶν ἐπιχθονίων ἀνθρώπων,
    οἷον ἐπ' ἦμαρ ἄγῃσι πατὴρ ἀνδρῶν τε θεῶν τε.

That man sometimes meets with evil, and sometimes   530
    with good;
But to whomever he gives only of the evils, he treats
    that man outrageously,
And evil hunger drives him over the sacred earth,
And he wanders honored neither by gods nor by
    mortals.

T8 (≠ DK) Homer, *Odyssey*

a [Zeus to the gods:]

Thinking of him [i.e. Aegisthus] he [i.e. Zeus] spoke
    to the immortals:
"Oh for shame, how mortals blame the gods!
For they say that evils come from us, but it is they
    themselves too
Who by their own follies get sorrows beyond what is
    fated [. . .]."

b [Odysseus to Amphinomeus:]

Earth nourishes nothing weaker than man,   130
Of all the things that breathe and move on the earth;
For he says that he will never suffer evil in the future
So long as the gods give him manliness and his knees
    move.
But when the blessed gods fulfill misfortunes too for
    him,
These too he bears, sorrowing with an enduring   135
    spirit.
For the mind of men upon the earth is such
As the day that the father of gods and men brings
    upon them.

T9 (≠ DK) Aesch. *Choe.* 585–602

585 [χο.]   πολλὰ μὲν γᾶ τρέφει
            δεινὰ δειμάτων ἄχη,
          πόντιαι τ᾽ ἀγκάλαι
          κνωδάλων ἀνταίων
          βρύουσ᾽· βλαστοῦσι καὶ πεδαίχμιοι
590   λαμπάδες πεδάοροι·
          πτανὰ δὲ καὶ πεδοβάμονα κἀνεμόεντ᾽ ἄν
          αἰγίδων φράσαι κότον·

          ἀλλ᾽ ὑπέρτολμον ἀν-
595   δρὸς φρόνημα τίς λέγοι
          καὶ γυναικῶν φρεσίν
          τλαμόνων παντόλμους
          ἔρωτας, ἄταισι συννόμους βροτῶν;
          ξυζύγους δ᾽ ὁμαυλίας
600   θηλυκρατὴς ἀπέρωπος ἔρως παρανικᾷ
          κνωδάλων τε καὶ βροτῶν.

589 βλασ-οῦσι ΣΜ: βλάπτουσι Butler   591 πτανὰ δὲ
Hermann: πτανά τε mss.

Human Time (T10–T13)

T10 (≠ DK) Soph. *OC* 607–13, 617–18

[οι.]   [. . .] μόνοις οὐ γίγνεται
            θεοῖσι γῆρας οὐδὲ κατθανεῖν ποτε,

T9 (≠ DK) Aeschylus, *The Libation Bearers*

[CHORUS:] Many are the terrible sufferings of dread   585
     that the earth nurtures,
  And the sea's arms brim
  With hostile beasts;
  And lights blossom, suspended high up
  Between earth and sky;   590
  And winged things and ones that tread the ground
     could also tell of
  The whirlwinds' tempestuous rage.

  But man's over-daring
     thought—who could tell of this,   595
  And of the all-daring lusts of women
  Audacious in their hearts,
  Dwelling together with disasters for mortals?
  Female-ruling implacable passion conquers the   600
     marriages
  Of beasts and of mortals.

Human Time (T10–T13)

T10 (≠ DK) Sophocles, *Oedipus at Colonus*

[OEDIPUS:]   [. . .] it is only for the gods
  That there is no old age nor ever death.

τὰ δ' ἄλλα συγχεῖ πάνθ' ὁ παγκρατὴς χρόνος.
610   φθίνει μὲν ἰσχὺς γῆς, φθίνει δὲ σώματος,
θνῄσκει δὲ πίστις, βλαστάνει δ' ἀπιστία,
καὶ πνεῦμα ταὐτὸν οὔποτ' οὔτ' ἐν ἀνδράσιν
φίλοις βέβηκεν οὔτε πρὸς πόλιν πόλει.
[. . .] μυρίας ὁ μυρίος
χρόνος τεκνοῦται νύκτας ἡμέρας τ' ἰών [. . .].

T11 (≠ DK) Soph. *Aj.* 646–49

[AI.]   ἅπανθ' ὁ μακρὸς κἀναρίθμητος χρόνος
φύει τ' ἄδηλα καὶ φανέντα κρύπτεται·
κοὐκ ἔστ' ἄελπτον οὐδέν, ἀλλ' ἁλίσκεται
χὠ δεινὸς ὅρκος χαὶ περισκελεῖς φρένες.

T12 (≠ DK) Soph. Frag. 918 R

πάντ' ἐκκαλύπτων ὁ χρόνος εἰς τὸ φῶς ἄγει

T13 (≠ DK) Soph. *Hipponous* Frag. 301 R

[. . .] ὡς ὁ πάνθ' ὁρῶν
καὶ πάντ' ἀκούων πάντ' ἀναπτύσσει χρόνος

All others things all-mastering Time overwhelms.
The earth's strength withers, the body's withers,   610
Trust dies, distrust blossoms,
And the spirit never continues the same, neither
   among men
Who are friends nor for one city to another one.
                    [. . .] countless time
Fathers countless nights and days as it proceeds
   [. . .].

T11 (≠ DK) Sophocles, *Ajax*

[AJAX:] Lengthy and unnumbered time makes
   All unseen things grow and conceals them once re-
      vealed;
   And there is nothing so unexpected but they are
      caught fast,
   Fearsome oath and rigid resolutions.

T12 (≠ DK) Sophocles, Fragment from an unidentified
play

   Time, uncovering all things, brings them to light.

T13 (≠ DK) Sophocles, Fragment from *Hipponous*

        [. . .] for time, which sees all
and hears all, unfolds all things.

Kinds of Human Excellence and
Fallibility (T14–T39)
The Varieties of Human Excellence (T14–T16)

T14 (≠ DK) Hom. *Il.* 11.784

αἰὲν ἀριστεύειν καὶ ὑπείροχον ἔμμεναι ἄλλων
[. . .].

T15 (≠ DK) Hom. *Od.*

a 8.167–71, 174–75

οὕτως οὐ πάντεσσι θεοὶ χαρίεντα διδοῦσιν
ἀνδράσιν, οὔτε φυὴν οὔτ᾽ ἂρ φρένας οὔτ᾽
ἀγορητύν.
ἄλλος μὲν γάρ τ᾽ εἶδος ἀκιδνότερος πέλει ἀνήρ,
170   ἀλλὰ θεὸς μορφὴν ἔπεσι στέφει· οἱ δέ τ᾽ ἐς αὐτὸν
τερπόμενοι λεύσσουσιν [. . .].
ἄλλος δ᾽ αὖ εἶδος μὲν ἀλίγκιος ἀθανάτοισιν,
175   ἀλλ᾽ οὔ οἱ χάρις ἀμφὶ περιστέφεται ἐπέεσσιν
[. . .].

b 9.5–11

5   οὐ γὰρ ἐγώ γέ τί φημι τέλος χαριέστερον εἶναι
ἢ ὅτ᾽ ἐυφροσύνη μὲν ἔχῃ κάτα δῆμον ἅπαντα,
δαιτυμόνες δ᾽ ἀνὰ δώματ᾽ ἀκουάζωνται ἀοιδοῦ
ἥμενοι ἑξείης, παρὰ δὲ πλήθωσι τράπεζαι

REFLECTIONS ON GODS AND MEN

Kinds of Human Excellence and
Fallibility (T14–T39)
The Varieties of Human Excellence (T14–T16)

T14 (≠ DK) Homer, *Iliad* [Peleus to his son Achilles:]

Always to be the best and to be superior to the others
[. . .].

T15 (≠ DK) Homer, *Odyssey*

a [Odysseus to Euryalus:]

The gods do not give delightful things to all men in
the same way,
Neither bodily shape nor intelligence nor eloquence.
For one man is weak in his appearance,
But the god garlands his words with beauty, and upon   170
him
Men look with delight [. . .]
And then another is similar to the gods in his
appearance,
But no delight is set as a garland upon his words   175
[. . .].

b [Odysseus to Alcinous:]

I think that no fulfillment (*telos*) is more delightful   5
Than when festivity holds sway over all the people,
And banqueters throughout the rooms listen to a
bard
While they sit next to one another, and beside them
the tables are full

103

σίτου καὶ κρειῶν, μέθυ δ᾽ ἐκ κρητῆρος ἀφύσσων
10   οἰνοχόος φορέῃσι καὶ ἐγχείῃ δεπάεσσι·
τοῦτό τί μοι κάλλιστον ἐνὶ φρεσὶν εἴδεται εἶναι.

c 11.489–91

βουλοίμην κ᾽ ἐπάρουρος ἐὼν θητευέμεν ἄλλῳ,
ἀνδρὶ παρ᾽ ἀκλήρῳ, ᾧ μὴ βίοτος πολὺς εἴη,
ἢ πᾶσι νεκύεσσι καταφθιμένοισιν ἀνάσσειν.

T16 (≠ DK) Sapph. Frag. 16.1–4

ο]ἰ μὲν ἱππήων στρότον, οἰ δὲ πέσδων,
οἰ δὲ νάων φαῖσ᾽ ἐπ[ὶ] γᾶν μέλαι[ν]αν
ἔ]μμεναι κάλλιστον, ἔγω δὲ κῆν᾽ ὅτ-
τω τις ἔραται.

Uses and Abuses of Human Language (T17–T21)
Poetry and Truth (T17–T19)

T17 (> ad 3 B1) Hes. *Th.* 26–28

ποιμένες ἄγραυλοι, κάκ᾽ ἐλέγχεα, γαστέρες οἶον,
ἴδμεν ψεύδεα πολλὰ λέγειν ἐτύμοισιν ὁμοῖα,
ἴδμεν δ᾽ εὖτ᾽ ἐθέλωμεν ἀληθέα γηρύσασθαι.

Of bread and meats, and drawing wine from the
    mixing bowl
The cup-bearer carries it about and pours it into their   10
    cups.
This seems in my mind to be the loveliest thing.

c [The shade of dead Achilles to Odysseus:]

I would prefer to work the earth laboring for another
    man,
Some man without his own land, who did not have a
    lot to live on,
Then to lord it over all the perished dead.

T16 (≠ DK) Sappho, Fragment

Some say that a host of horsemen, others one of
    footsoldiers,
Others one of ships, is the most beautiful thing
On the black earth: but I say it is that thing, whatever
    it is,
        That one loves.

Uses and Abuses of Human Language (T17–T21)
        Poetry and Truth (T17–T19)

T17 (> ad 3 B1) Hesiod, *Theogony* [The Muses to the
shepherd Hesiod:]

Field-dwelling shepherds, ignoble disgraces, mere
    bellies:
We know how to say many false things (*pseudea*)
    similar to genuine ones (*etuma*),
But we know, when we wish, how to proclaim true
    things (*alêthea*).

T18 (≠ DK) Solon Frag. 29

πολλὰ ψεύδονται ἀοιδοί

T19 (≠ DK) Pind. *Nem.* 7.20–24

ἐγὼ δ πλέον᾿ ἔλπομαι
λόγον Ὀδυσσέος ἢ πάθαν
  διὰ τὸν ἁδυεπῆ γενέσθ᾿ Ὅμηρον·
ἐπεὶ ψεύδεσ οἱ ποτανᾷ τε μαχανᾷ
σεμνὸν ἔπεστί τι· σοφία
  δὲ κλέπ ει παράγοισα μύθοις. τυφλὸν δ᾿ ἔχει
ἦτορ ὅμιλς ἀνδρῶν ὁ πλεῖστος.

The Power of Persuasion (T20–T21)

T20 (≠ DK) Aesch. *Ag.* 385–86

[χο.] βιᾶτει δ᾿ ἁ τάλαινα Πειθώ,
  προβ́ύλου παῖς ἄφερτος Ἄτας.

T21 (≠ DK Soph. Frag. 865 R

δεινὸν τὸ τᾶς Πειθοῦς πρόσωπον

T18 (≠ DK) Solon, Fragment from a poem probably in elegiac couplets

Poets tell many lies.

T19 (≠ DK) Pindar, *Nemeans*

I myself believe
That Odysseus' story is greater than his suffering
    Because of sweet-songed Homer,
For on his lies (*pseudesi*) and winged craft (*mâkhanâ*)
There resides a sort of majesty; and skill (*sophia*)
    Deceives, misleading with stories. And the great
        swarm
Of men possess a blind heart [. . .].

The Power of Persuasion (T20–T21)

T20 (≠ DK) Aeschylus, *Agamemnon*

[CHORUS:] Wretched Persuasion commits violence,
    The unendurable child of counseling Madness.

T21 (≠ DK) Sophocles, Fragment from an unidentified play

Awe-inspiring is Persuasion's face.

Nature and Consequences of Justice
and Injustice (T22–T34)
Justice and Injustice in This World (T22–T31)

T22 (≠ DK) Hom. *Il.* 18.497–508

λαοὶ δ᾽ εἰν ἀγορῇ ἔσαν ἀθρόοι· ἔνθα δὲ νεῖκος
ὠρώρει, δύο δ᾽ ἄνδρες ἐνείκεον εἵνεκα ποινῆς
ἀνδρὸς ἀποφθιμένου. ὃ μὲν ηὔχετο πάντ᾽
   ἀποδοῦναι
500 δήμῳ πιφαύσκων, ὃ δ᾽ ἀναίνετο μηδὲν ἑλέσθαι·
ἄμφω δ᾽ ἔσθην ἐπὶ ἴστορι πεῖραρ ἑλέσθαι.
λαοὶ δ᾽ ἀμφοτέροισιν ἐπήπυον ἀμφὶς ἀρωγοί·
κήρυκες δ᾽ ἄρα λαὸν ἐρήτυον. οἱ δὲ γέροντες
εἵατ᾽ ἐπὶ ξεστοῖσι λίθοις ἱερῷ ἐνὶ κύκλῳ,
505 σκῆπτρα δὲ κηρύκων ἐν χέρσ᾽ ἔχον ἠεροφώνων·
τοῖσιν ἔπειτ᾽ ἤισσον, ἀμοιβηδὶς δ᾽ ἐδίκαζον.
κεῖτο δ᾽ ἄρ᾽ ἐν μέσσοισι δύω χρυσοῖο τάλαντα,
τῷ δόμεν, ὃς μετὰ τοῖσι δίκην ἰθύντατα εἴποι.

Nature and Consequences of Justice
and Injustice (T22–T34)
Justice and Injustice in This World (T22–T31)

T22 (≠ DK) Homer, *Iliad* [Description of a scene on the shield Hephaestus makes for Achilles:]

> The people were gathered in the marketplace; there
>   a quarrel
> Had arisen, and two men were quarreling over the
>   blood price
> For a man who had been killed. The one man swore
>   he had paid back everything,
> Speaking to the people, but the other refused to   500
>   accept [or: denied that he had received] anything
>   at all;
> And both were going for an arbitrator, to win the
>   decision.
> People were cheering both men, to help each of
>   them.
> But heralds held the people back, and the elders
> Were sitting on polished stones in a sacred circle,
> Holding in their hands the staves of the loud-voiced   505
>   heralds.
> They sprang up with these, and gave judgment in
>   turns.
> And amidst them there lay on the ground two talents
>   of gold,
> To be given to the one among them who spoke the
>   straightest judgment.

T23 (≠ DK) Hes. *Th.*

a 881–85

αὐτὰρ ἐπεί ῥα πόνον μάκαρες θεοὶ ἐξετέλεσσαν,
Τιτήνεσσι δὲ τιμάων κρίναντο βίηφι,
δή ῥα τότ᾽ ὤτρυνον βασιλευέμεν ἠδὲ ἀνάσσειν
Γαίης φραδμοσύνῃσιν Ὀλύμπιον εὐρύοπα Ζῆν
ἀθανάτων· ὁ δὲ τοῖσιν ἐὺ διεδάσσατο τιμάς.

b 901–3

δεύτερον ἠγάγετο λιπαρὴν Θέμιν, ἣ τέκεν Ὥρας,
Εὐνομίην τε Δίκην τε καὶ Εἰρήνην τεθαλυῖαν,
αἵ τ᾽ ἔργ᾽ ὠρεύουσι καταθνητοῖσι βροτοῖσι [. . .].

T24 (≠ DK) Hes. *Op.* 225–31, 238–55

225 οἳ δὲ δίκας ξείνοισι καὶ ἐνδήμοισι διδοῦσιν
ἰθείας καὶ μή τι παρεκβαίνουσι δικαίου,
τοῖσι τέθηλε πόλις, λαοὶ δ᾽ ἀνθέουσιν ἐν αὐτῇ·
Εἰρήνη δ᾽ ἀνὰ γῆν κουροτρόφος, οὐδέ ποτ᾽ αὐτοῖς
ἀργαλέον πόλεμον τεκμαίρεται εὐρύοπα Ζεύς·
230 οὐδέ ποτ᾽ ἰθυδίκῃσι μετ᾽ ἀνδράσι λιμὸς ὀπηδεῖ
οὐδ᾽ ἄτη, θαλίης δὲ μεμηλότα ἔργα νέμονται.
[. . .]

110

T23 (≠ DK) Hesiod, *Theogony*

a

> But when the blessed gods had completed their toil,
> And by force had reached a settlement with the
>   Titans regarding honors,
> Then by the counsels of Earth they urged Olympian
>   far-seeing Zeus
> To become king and to rule over the immortals;
> And he divided their honors well for them.

b

> Second [scil. after Intelligence (*Mêtis*)], he [i.e. Zeus]
>   married bright Ordinance (*Themis*), who gave
>   birth to the Seasons (*Hôrai*),
> Lawfulness (*Eunomia*) and Justice (*Dikê*) and
>   blooming Peace (*Eirênê*),
> Who care for the works of mortal human beings [. . .].

T24 (≠ DK) Hesiod, *Works and Days*

> But those who give straight judgments to foreigners   225
>   and fellow citizens
> And do not turn aside from justice at all,
> Their city blooms and the people in it flower.
> For them, Peace, the nurse of the young, is on the
>   earth,
> And far-seeing Zeus never marks out painful war;
> Nor does famine attend straight-judging men,   230
> Nor calamity, but they share out in festivities the
>   fruits of the labors they care for.
> [. . .]

οἷς δ᾽ ὕβρις τε μέμηλε κακὴ καὶ σχέτλια ἔργα,
τοῖς δὲ δίκη· Κρονίδης τεκμαίρεται εὐρύοπα
Ζεύς.

240 πολλάκι καὶ ξύμπασα πόλις κακοῦ ἀνδρὸς
       ἀπηύρα,
ὅστις ἀλιτραίνει καὶ ἀτάσθαλα μηχανάαται.
τοῖσιν δ᾽ οὐρανόθεν μέγ᾽ ἐπήγαγε πῆμα Κρονίων,
λιμὸν ὁμοῦ καὶ λοιμόν· ἀποφθινύθουσι δὲ λαοί·
οὐδὲ γυναῖκες τίκτουσιν, μινύθουσι δὲ οἶκοι

245 Ζηνὸς φραδμοσύνῃσιν Ὀλυμπίου· ἄλλοτε δ᾽ αὖτε
ἢ τῶν γε στρατὸν εὐρὺν ἀπώλεσεν ἢ ὅ γε τεῖχος
ἢ νέας ἐν πόντῳ Κρονίδης ἀποτείνυται αὐτῶν.

ὦ βασιλῆς, ὑμεῖς δὲ καταφράζεσθε καὶ αὐτοί
τήνδε δίκην· ἐγγὺς γὰρ ἐν ἀνθρώποισιν ἐόντες

250 ἀθάνατοι φράζονται, ὅσοι σκολιῇσι δίκῃσιν
ἀλλήλους τρίβουσι θεῶν ὄπιν οὐκ ἀλέγοντες.
τρὶς γὰρ μύριοί εἰσιν ἐπὶ χθονὶ πουλυβοτείρῃ
ἀθάνατοι Ζηνὸς φύλακες θνητῶν ἀνθρώπων,
οἵ ῥα φυλάσσουσίν τε δίκας καὶ σχέτλια ἔργα,

255 ἠέρα ἑσσάμενοι, πάντῃ φοιτῶντες ἐπ᾽ αἶαν.

T25 (≠ DK) Solon

a Frag. 4–8, 30–39

ἡμετέρη δὲ πόλις κατὰ μὲν Διὸς οὔποτ᾽ ὀλεῖται

But to those who care only for evil outrageousness
    and cruel deeds,
Far-seeing Zeus, Cronus' son, marks out justice.
Often even a whole city suffers because of an evil   240
    man
Who sins and devises wicked deeds.
Upon them, Cronus' son brings forth woe from the
    sky,
Famine together with pestilence, and the people die
    away;
The women do not give birth, and the household are
    diminished
By the cunning of Olympian Zeus. And at another   245
    time
Cronus' son destroys their broad army or their wall,
Or he takes vengeance upon their ships on the sea.

As for you kings, too, ponder this justice yourselves.
For among human beings there are immortals nearby,
Who take notice of all those who with crooked   250
    judgments
Grind one another down and have no care for the
    gods' retribution.
Thrice ten thousand are Zeus' immortal guardians
Of mortal human beings upon the bounteous earth,
And they watch over judgments and cruel deeds,
Clad in invisibility, walking everywhere upon the   255
    earth.

T25 (≠ DK) Solon, Elegiac poems

a

Our city will never be destroyed through the fate of
    Zeus

αἶσαν καὶ μακάρων θεῶν φρένας ἀθανάτων·
τοίη γὰρ μεγάθυμος ἐπίσκοπος ὀβριμοπάτρη
Παλλὰς Ἀθηναίη χεῖρας ὕπερθεν ἔχει·
5   αὐτοὶ δὲ φθείρειν μεγάλην πόλιν ἀφραδίῃσιν
ἀστοὶ βούλονται χρήμασι πειθόμενοι,
δήμου θ᾽ ἡγεμόνων ἄδικος νόος, οἷσιν ἑτοῖμον
ὕβριος ἐκ μεγάλης ἄλγεα πολλὰ παθεῖν·
[. . .]
30   ταῦτα διδάξαι θυμὸς Ἀθηναίους με κελεύει,
ὡς κακὰ πλεῖστα πόλει Δυσνομίη παρέχει·
Εὐνομίη δ᾽ εὔκοσμα καὶ ἄρτια πάντ᾽ ἀποφαίνει,
καὶ θαμὰ τοῖς ἀδίκοις ἀμφιτίθησι πέδας·
τραχέα λειαίνει, παύει κόρον, ὕβριν ἀμαυροῖ,
35   αὐαίνει δ᾽ ἄτης ἄνθεα φυόμενα,
εὐθύνει δὲ δίκας σκολιάς, ὑπερήφανά τ᾽ ἔργα
πραΰνει· παύει δ᾽ ἔργα διχοστασίης,
παύει δ᾽ ἀργαλέης ἔριδος χόλον, ἔστι δ᾽ ὑπ᾽
αὐτῆς
πάντα κατ᾽ ἀνθρώπους ἄρτια καὶ πινυτά.

b Frag. 13.15–17, 25–32

οὐ γὰρ δὴν θνητοῖς ὕβριος ἔργα πέλει,
ἀλλὰ Ζεὺς πάντων ἐφορᾷ τέλος [. . .].

114

Or the intentions of the blessed immortal gods;
For such a great-hearted guardian, Pallas Athena,
  Born of a mighty father, holds her hands over it.
But the citizens themselves are willing, by their   5
    follies
  And obedience to money, to destroy this great city,
And unjust is the mind of the people's leaders, for
    whom it is made ready
  That they will suffer many pains because of their
    great arrogance (*hybris*).
[. . .]
This my heart bids me teach the Athenians: 30
  That Lawlessness (*Dysnomia*) gives the city
    countless evils,
But Lawfulness (*Eunomia*) makes all things ordered
    and well-fitting,
  And often puts fetters on the unjust.
She smoothes the rough, stops excess, weakens
    arrogance,
  Withers the blooming flowers of disaster,   35
Straightens crooked judgments, softens arrogant
    deeds,
  And stops acts of civil strife,
And stops the anger of evil contention. Under her
  All things among men are well-fitting and wise.

b

  For the works of arrogance do not last long for
    mortals.
No, Zeus looks upon the outcome of all things [. . .].

25 τοιαύτη Ζηνὸς πέλεται τίσις· οὐδ᾽ ἐφ᾽ ἑκάστῳ
    ὥσπερ θνητὸς ἀνὴρ γίγνεται ὀξύχολος,
    αἰεὶ δ᾽ οὔ ἑ λέληθε διαμπερές, ὅστις ἀλιτρὸν
    θυμὸν ἔχῃ, πάντως δ᾽ ἐς τέλος ἐξεφάνη·
    ἀλλ᾽ ὁ μὲν αὐτίκ᾽ ἔτεισεν, ὁ δ᾽ ὕστερον· οἱ δὲ
        φύγωσιν
30 αὐτοί, μηδὲ θεῶν μοῖρ᾽ ἐπιοῦσα κίχῃ,
    ἤλυθε πάντως αὖτις· ἀναίτιοι ἔργα τίνουσιν
    ἢ παῖδες τούτων ἢ γένος ἐξοπίσω.

c Frag. 9.1–4

ἐκ νεφέλης πέλεται χιόνος μένος ἠδὲ χαλάζης,
    βροντὴ δ᾽ ἐκ λαμπρῆς γίγνεται ἀστεροπῆς·
ἀνδρῶν δ᾽ ἐκ μεγάλων πόλις ὄλλυται, ἐς δὲ
        μονάρχου
    δῆμος ἀϊδρίῃ δουλοσύνην ἔπεσεν.

d Frag. 12

ἐξ ἀνέμων δὲ θάλασσα ταράσσεται· ἢν δέ τις
        αὐτὴν
    μὴ κινῇ, πάντων ἐστὶ δικαιοτάτη.

T26 (≠ DK) Theogn.

a 197–208

χρῆμα δ᾽ ὃ μὲν Διόθεν καὶ σὺν δίκῃ ἀνδρὶ
        γένηται

116

Such is the vengeance of Zeus: he is not quick to   25
      anger,
   Like a mortal man, at everything,
But whoever has a wicked heart does not ever escape
      his notice
   And in the end certainly he is exposed.
But one man pays immediately, another later, and
      those who themselves escape
   And the gods' pursuing destiny does not catch   30
      them,
It certainly comes at some other time; the innocent
      pay for their deeds,
   Either their children or their descendants later.

c

From a cloud comes the force of the snow and hail,
   And thunder is born from brilliant lightning;
From great men comes a city's destruction, and in its
      foolishness
   The people fall under the slavery of a monarch.

d

From winds comes the sea's agitation; but if
   It is not stirred up, it is the most just of all things.

T26 (≠ DK) Theognis, Elegiac poems

a

A possession that comes to a man from Zeus, and
      with justice

117

καὶ καθαρῶς, αἰεὶ παρμόνιμον τελέθει·
εἰ δ' ἀδίκως παρὰ καιρὸν ἀνὴρ φιλοκερδέι θυμῷ
200   κτήσεται, εἴθ' ὅρκῳ πὰρ τὸ δίκαιον ἑλών,
αὐτίκα μέν τι φέρειν κέρδος δοκεῖ, ἐς δὲ τελευτήν
αὖθις ἔγεντο κακόν, θεῶν δ' ὑπερέσχε νόος.
ἀλλὰ τάδ' ἀνθρώπων ἀπατᾷ νόον· οὐ γὰρ ἐπ' αὐτοῦ
τίνονται μάκαρες πρήγματος ἀμπλακίας,
205   ἀλλ' ὁ μὲν αὐτὸς ἔτεισε κακὸν χρέος, οὐδὲ
φίλοισιν
ἄτην ἐξοπίσω παισὶν ἐπεκρέμασεν·
ἄλλον δ' οὐ κατέμαρψε δίκη· θάνατος γὰρ
ἀναιδής
πρόσθεν ἐπὶ βλεφάροις ἕζετο κῆρα φέρων.

b 731–36, 741–52

Ζεῦ πάτερ εἴθε γένοιτο θεοῖς φίλα τοῖς μὲν
ἀλιτροῖς
ὕβριν ἀδεῖν, καί σφιν τοῦτο γένοιτο φίλον
θυμῷ, σχέτλια ἔργα· μετὰ φρεσὶ δ' ὅστις
†ἀθήνης
ἐργάζαιτο, θεῶν μηδὲν ὀπιζόμενος,
735   αὐτὸν ἔπειτα πάλιν τεῖσαι κακά, μηδ' ἔτ' ὀπίσσω
πατρὸς ἀτασθαλίαι παισὶ γένοιντο κακόν·
[. . .]
741   ταῦτ' εἴη μακάρεσσι θεοῖς φίλα· νῦν δ' ὁ μὲν ἔρδων
ἐκφεύγει, τὸ κακὸν δ' ἄλλος ἔπειτα φέρει.

118

And purely, lasts forever;
But if a man acquires it unjustly, unduly, with a
    greedy spirit,
  Or seizes it by an oath against what is just,   200
At first he thinks he is getting a profit, but in the end
  It turns out badly, and the mind (*noos*) of the gods
    overcomes him.
But these things deceive the minds of men, for it is
    not at the very moment
  That the blessed gods punish an act of sinfulness,
But one man pays his evil debt himself, and does not   205
    hang destruction
  Over his own children later;
While another one is not overtaken by justice, since
    ruthless death
  Settles first on his eyelids, bringing him doom.

b

Father Zeus, if only it pleased the gods that
    outrageous arrogance (*hybris*)
  Delighted sinners and that this pleased them
In their hearts: wicked deeds; but that whoever acted
    in their minds †. . .†,
  Without any regard for the gods,
Would then pay an evil penalty himself, and that evil   735
    later
  Would not come about for children by their
    father's sins. [. . .]
If only this pleased the blessed gods! But as it is, the   741
    perpetrator
  Gets away, and then another man gets misery.

καὶ τοῦτ᾽, ἀθανάτων βασιλεῦ, πῶς ἐστι δίκαιον,
ἔργων ὅστις ἀνὴρ ἐκτὸς ἐὼν ἀδίκων,
745 μῆτιν᾽ ὑπερβασίην κατέχων μήθ᾽ ὅρκον ἀλιτρόν,
ἀλλὰ δίκαιος ἐών, μὴ τὰ δίκαια πάθῃ;
τίς δή κεν βροτὸς ἄλλος ὁρῶν πρὸς τοῦτον
    ἔπειτα
ἄζοιτ᾽ ἀθανάτους, καὶ τίνα θυμὸν ἔχων,
ὁππότ᾽ ἀνὴρ ἄδικος καὶ ἀτάσθαλος, οὔτε τευ
    ἀνδρὸς
750 οὔτε τευ ἀθανάτων μῆνιν ἀλευόμενος,
ὑβρίζῃ πλούτῳ κεκορημένος, οἱ δὲ δίκαιοι
τρύχονται χαλεπῇ τειρόμενοι πενίῃ;

T27 (≠ DK) Pind.

a Frag. 169a 1–5

νόμος ὁ πάντων βασιλεύς
θνατῶν τε καὶ ἀθανάτων
ἄγει δικαιῶν τὸ βιαιότατον
ὑπερτάτᾳ χειρί. τεκμαίρομαι
ἔργοισιν Ἡρακλέος [. . .].

b Frag. 213

πότερον δίκᾳ τεῖχος ὕψιον
ἢ σκολιαῖς ἀπάταις ἀναβαίνει
ἐπιχθόνιον γένος ἀνδρῶν,
δίχα μοι νόος ἀτρέκειαν εἰπεῖν.

120

And this, king of the immortals: how is it just
    That a man who keeps away from unjust deeds
And does not commit any transgression or a wicked   745
    oath,
    But is just, suffers unjustly?
What other mortal, looking upon him, would then
    Revere the immortals? What spirit would he have,
Whenever an unjust and wicked man, who does not
    avoid the wrath
    Of any man or of any of the deathless gods,   750
Commits an outrage, sated in wealth, while the just
    Are worn out and wasted away by harsh poverty?

T27 (≠ DK) Pindar, Fragments

a

    Law (*nomos*), king of all,
    Of mortals and of immortals,
    Leads them, rendering the greatest violence just
    By his supreme hand. I cite as witness
    Heracles' deeds [. . .].

b

    Whether the race of men on the earth
    Ascends the loftier wall by means of justice
    or by crooked deceits—
    my mind is divided in saying this precisely.

T28 (≠ DK) Aesch. *Ag.* 250

[χο.]   Δίκα δὲ τοῖς μὲν παθοῦσιν μαθεῖν ἐπιρρέπει
[. . .].

T29 (≠ DK) Aesch. *Eum.*

a 517–37

[χο.]   ἔσθ᾿ ὅπου τὸ δεινὸν εὖ,
         καὶ φρενῶν ἐπίσκοπον
         δεῖμ᾿ ἄνω καθήμενον·
520   ξυμφέρει
         σωφρονεῖν ὑπὸ στένει.
         τίς δὲ μηδὲν ἐν †φάει†
         καρδίας δέος τρέφων—
         ἢ πόλις, βροτός θ᾿ ὁμοί-
525   ως—ἔτ᾿ ἂν σέβοι Δίκαν;

         μήτ᾿ ἄναρκτον βίον
         μήτε δεσποτούμενον
         αἰνέσῃς.
530   παντὶ μέσῳ τὸ κράτος θεὸς ὤπασεν,
         ἄλλ᾿ ἄλλᾳ δ᾿ ἐφορεύει.
         ξύμμετρον δ᾿ ἔπος λέγω·
         δυσσεβίας μὲν ὕβρις τέκος ὡς ἐτύμως,
535   ἐκ δ᾿ ὑγιείας
         φρενῶν ὁ πᾶσιν φίλος
         καὶ πολύευκτος ὄλβος.

T28 Aeschylus, *Agamemnon*

[CHORUS:]   Justice weighs out learning to those
          who suffer [. . .].

T29 (≠ DK) Aeschylus, *Eumenides*

a

[CHORUS:] Sometimes terror is good,
          And, a sentinel for minds,
          Dread, seated on high (?):
          There is a benefit   520
          In wisdom coming with duress.
          For he who does not at all nourish
          His heart's dread in †light†—
          Either a city, or a mortal in the same
          Way—would still revere justice?   525

          Neither the life without a ruler
          Nor the one under a despot
          Should you praise.
          To all in the middle a god   530
          Has granted strength, though he oversees
          Differently in different places.
          I speak an appropriate word:
          In truth, arrogant violence
          Is impiety's child;
          But from health   535
          Of the mind comes all-loving
          And all-invoked prosperity.

b 696–702

[ΑΘ.]   τὸ μήτ᾿ ἄναρχον μήτε δεσποτούμενον
       ἀστοῖς περιστέλλουσι βουλεύω σέβειν,
       καὶ μὴ τὸ δεινὸν πᾶν πόλεως ἔξω βαλεῖν·
       τίς γὰρ δεδοικὼς μηδὲν ἔνδικος βροτῶν;
       τοιόνδε τοι ταρβοῦντες ἐνδίκως σέβας
       ἔρυμα τε χώρας καὶ πόλεως σωτήριον
       ἔχοιτ᾿ ἄν, οἷον οὔτις ἀνθρώπων ἔχει [. . .].

T30 (31 B135) Soph. *Ant.* 450–60

[ΑΝ.]   οὐ γάρ τί μοι Ζεὺς ἦν ὁ κηρύξας τάδε,
       οὐδ᾿ ἡ ξύνοικος τῶν κάτω θεῶν Δίκη
       τοιούσδ᾿ ἐν ἀνθρώποισιν ὥρισεν νόμους,
       οὐδὲ σθένειν τοσοῦτον ᾠόμην τὰ σὰ
       κηρύγμαθ᾿ ὥστ᾿ ἄγραπτα κἀσφαλῆ θεῶν
455   νόμιμα δύνασθαι θνητά γ᾿ ὄνθ᾿ ὑπερδραμεῖν.
       οὐ γάρ τι νῦν γε κἀχθές, ἀλλ᾿ ἀεί ποτε
       ζῇ ταῦτα, κοὐδεὶς οἶδεν ἐξ ὅτου ᾿φάνη.
       τούτων ἐγὼ οὐκ ἔμελλον, ἀνδρὸς οὐδενὸς
       φρόνημα δείσασ᾿, ἐν θεοῖσι τὴν δίκην
       δώσειν.

b

[ATHENA:] Neither absence of a ruling power nor submission to an absolute master—
This is what I advise the citizens to defend and to revere,
And not to cast fear altogether from the city.
For what mortal who fears nothing is just?
If you fear justly the object of such a veneration
You will have protection for your country and salvation for your city
Such as no one among men possesses [. . .].

T30 (31 B135) Sophocles, *Antigone*

[ANTIGONE:] For me, it was not Zeus who made that [i.e. Creon's] proclamation,
Nor did Justice, who dwells with the gods below,
Stipulate such laws to be valid among humans;
Nor did I suppose that your proclamations were so strong
That they, being mortal, could outrun
The unwritten and immovable ordinances of the gods.   455
For they are not of now and of yesterday, but for all eternity
Do they live, and no one knows when they appeared.
So I was not, out of fear of any man's spirit,
Going to make myself liable to the gods because of them.

T31 (≠ DK) Soph. *OT* 863–96

[xo.] εἴ μοι ξυνείη φέροντι μοῖρα τὰν
        εὔσεπτον ἁγνείαν λόγων
865   ἔργων τε πάντων, ὧν νόμοι πρόκεινται
        ὑψίποδες, οὐρανίᾳ 'ν
        αἰθέρι τ κνωθέντες, ὧν Ὄλυμπος
        πατὴρ μόνος, οὐδέ νιν
        θνατὰ φύσις ἀνέρων
870   ἔτικτεν, οὐδὲ μήποτε λά-
        θα κατακοιμάσῃ·
        μέγας ἐν τούτοις θεός, οὐδὲ γηράσκει.

        ὕβρις φυτεύει τύραννον· ὕβρις, εἰ
        πολλῶν ὑπερπλησθῇ μάταν
875   ἃ μὴ 'πίκαιρα μηδὲ συμφέροντα,
        ἀκρότατα γεῖσ' ἀναβᾶσ'
        ἀπότομον ὤρουσεν εἰς ἀνάγκαν,
        ἔνθ' οὐ ποδὶ χρησίμῳ
        χρῆται. τὸ καλῶς δ' ἔχον
880   πόλει πάλαισμα μήποτε λῦ-
        σαι θεὸν αἰτοῦμαι·
        θεὸν οὐ λήξω ποτὲ προστάταν ἴσχων.

        εἰ δέ τις ὑπέροπτα χερσὶν
        ἢ λόγῳ πορεύεται,
885   Δίκας ἀφόβητος, οὐδὲ
        δαιμόνων ἕδη σέβων,
        κακά νιν ἕλοιτο μοῖρα,

126

T31 (≠ DK) Sophocles, *Oedipus the Tyrant*

[CHORUS:] May my destiny help me
To practice reverent purity in words
And in all deeds for which the laws are fixed   865
Standing on high, sired in
The heavenly aether, those of which Olympus
Alone is father, nor did
Men's mortal nature
Father them, nor will oblivion ever put them to   870
    sleep:
For in them god is great and never does he grow
    old.

Arrogance (*hubris*) makes a tyrant grow—
Arrogance, if it is overfull of many things in vain,
Inopportune, unprofitable,   875
Climbing up to the roof-top it plunges into sheer
    necessity,
Where it finds no useful footing. But the contention
That is good for the city—I pray that god never   880
    destroy that.
For never will I cease to hold a god as our protector.
If someone proceeds overweening in hands or
    word,
Unintimidated by Justice nor revering the deities'   885
    shrines—
May an evil destiny catch him
Because of his ill-fortuned luxury,

δυσπότμ~υ χάριν χλιδᾶς,
εἰ μὴ τὸ κέρδος κερδανεῖ δικαίως
890   καὶ τῶν ἰσέπτων ἔρξεται,
ἢ τῶν ἀίκτων θίξεται ματάζων.
τίς ἔτι ποτ᾽ ἐν τοῖσδ᾽ ἀνὴρ θυμοῦ βέλη
εὔξεται ψυχᾶς ἀμύνειν;
895   εἰ γὰρ αἱ τοιαίδε πράξεις τίμιαι,
τί δεῖ μ~ χορεύειν;

894 εὔξεται Musgrave: ἔρξεται mss.: τεύξεται Hölscher

The Afterlife (T32–T34)

T32 Pind.

a (> ad 31 B145) *Ol.* 2.53–54, 56–77

ὁ μὰν πλοῦτος ἀρεταῖς δεδαιδαλμένος
    φέρει τῶν τε καὶ τῶν
καιρὸν βαθεῖαν ὑπέχων μέριμναν ἀγροτέραν
    [. . .]
    εἰ δέ νιν ἔχων τις οἶδεν τὸ μέλλον,
ὅτι θανόντων μὲν ἐν-
    θάδ᾽ αὐτίκ᾽ ἀπάλαμνοι φρένες
ποινὰς ἔτεισαν—τὰ δ᾽ ἐν τᾷδε Διὸς ἀρχᾷ
ἀλιτρὰ κατὰ γᾶς δικάζει τις ἐχθρᾷ
60   λόγον φράσαις ἀνάγκᾳ·

ἴσαις δὲ νύκτεσσιν αἰεί,
ἴσαις δ᾽ ἁμέραις ἅλιον ἔχοντες, ἀπονέστερον

128

If he does not acquire profit justly
Nor refrains from irreverence   890
Or in his folly lays hand on things untouchable.
Among such people, what man will boast
That he wards off the gods' shafts from his breast?
For if these are the kinds of practices that are held   895
   in honor,
Why need I dance [scil. at the festivals of the gods]?

The Afterlife (T32–T34)

T32 Pindar

a (> ad 31 B146) *Olympians*

Wealth ornamented by virtues
   brings the occasion for some things and for others,
Repressing down deep fierce anxiety [. . .].
   If someone who possesses it knows what is to
     come,
That of those who have died here
   the helpless spirits (*phrenes*) immediately
Pay the penalty—and for the sins in this realm of
     Zeus
Someone passes judgment below the earth,
Speaking with hateful necessity;   60

But always possessing the sunlight in equal nights
And in equal days, good men receive

ἐσλοὶ δέκονται βίοτον, οὐ χθόνα τα-
 ράσσοντες ἐν χερὸς ἀκμᾷ
οὐδὲ πόντιον ὕδωρ
65 κεινὰν παρὰ δίαιταν, ἀλλὰ παρὰ μὲν τιμίοις
θεῶν οἵτινες ἔχαιρον εὐορκίαις
 ἄδακρυν νέμονται
αἰῶνα, τοὶ δ᾽ ἀπροσόρατον ὀκχέοντι πόνον.

ὅσοι δ᾽ ἐτόλμασαν ἐστρὶς
ἑκατέρωθι μείναντες ἀπὸ πάμπαν ἀδίκων ἔχειν
70 ψυχάν, ἔτειλαν Διὸς ὁδὸν παρὰ Κρό-
 νου τύρσιν· ἔνθα μακάρων
νᾶσον ὠκεανίδες
αὖραι περιπνέοισιν· ἄνθεμα δὲ χρυσοῦ φλέγει,
τὰ μὲν χερσόθεν ἀπ᾽ ἀγλαῶν δενδρέων,
 ὕδωρ δ᾽ ἄλλα φέρβει,
ὅρμοισι τῶν χέρας ἀναπλέκοντι καὶ στεφάνους

75 βουλαῖς ἐν ὀρθαῖσι Ῥαδαμάνθυος,
ὃν πατὴρ ἔχει μέγας ἑτοῖμον αὐτῷ πάρεδρον,
πόσις ὁ πάντων Ῥέας
 ὑπέρτατον ἐχοίσας θρόνον.

b (≠ DK) Frag. 131a

ὄλβιοι δ᾽ ἅπαντες αἴσᾳ λυσιπόνων τελετᾶν.

130

A life free of toil, not worrying
    the earth nor the sea's water with the might of
      their hands
For a meager living; but instead, beside those   65
    honored
By the gods, those who rejoiced in good oaths
    pass a tearless
Existence, while the others endure pain impossible to
    look upon.

But all those who have managed, staying three times
In both places, to keep their soul away from all
    injustices,
They travel the road of Zeus to Cronus
    tower; there around the Island   70
Of the Blessed blow the ocean winds, and flowers of
    gold blaze,
Some on the ground from gleaming trees,
    while water nourishes others,
They weave garlands for their hands and crowns

In the straight decrees of Rhadamanthys,   75
Whom the great father keeps seated ready beside
    him,
The husband of Rhea, who possesses the loftiest
    throne of all.

b (≠ DK) Fragment

Blessed [scil. are] all those who have a share in the rites
that release from toil.

c (≠ DK) Frag. 131b

σῶμα μὲν πςντων ἕπεται θανάτῳ περισθενεῖ,
ζωὸν δ᾽ ἔτι λείπεται αἰῶνος εἴδω-
λον· τὸ γὰρ ἐστι μόνον
ἐκ θεῶν· εὕδ‿ δὲ πρασσόντων μελέων, ἀτὰρ εὐ-
δόντεσσιν ἐν πολλοῖς ὀνείροις
δείκνυσι τερπνῶν ἐφέρποισαν χαλεπῶν τε κρίσιν.

d (ad 31 B146) Frag. 133

οἷσι δὲ Φερςεφόνα ποινὰν παλαιοῦ πένθεος
δέξεται, ἐς τὸν ὕπερθεν ἅλιον κείνων ἐνάτῳ ἔτει
ἀνδιδοῖ ψυχὰς πάλιν, ἐκ τᾶν βασιλῆες ἀγαυοί
καὶ σθένει ϸραιπνοὶ σοφίᾳ τε μέγιστοι
ἄνδρες αὔξεντ᾽· ἐς δὲ τὸν λοιπὸν χρόνον ἥροες ἁ-
γνοὶ πρὸς ἀνθρώπων καλέονται.

e (≠ DK) Frag. 137

ὄλβιος ὅστις ἰδὼν κεῖν᾽ εἶσ᾽ ὑπὸ χθόν·
οἶδε μὲν βίου τελευτάν,
οἶδεν δὲ διίσδοτον ἀρχάν.

c (≠ DK) Fragment

The body of all men obeys overwhelming death,
But a living image of the vital force (*aiōn*) still
    remains:
    for that alone
Comes from the gods. It sleeps while the limbs are
    acting,
    but to men as they sleep, in many dreams
It reveals the approaching choice of delights or of
    pains.

d (> 31 B146) Fragment

For those from whom Persephone accepts requital
For her ancient grief [scil. the murder of her son
    Dionysus by the Titans], in the ninth year she
    sends
Their souls back up to the upper sun; from them rise
    up noble kings
And men quick in strength and those who are
    greatest in wisdom,
And for the rest of time they are called
    Sacred heroes by men.

e (≠ DK) Fragment

Blessed is he who sees them [i.e. the Eleusinian
    mysteries] and then goes beneath the earth;
    he knows the end of life
And knows too its god-given beginning.

133

T33 (≠ DK) Lamellae osseae saec. V a. Chr. Olbiae repertae

a Frag. 463 T Bernabé

> βίος, θάνατος, βίος
> ἀλήθεια
> Διό(νυσος) Ὀρφικοί

b Frag. 464 T Bernabé

> εἰρήνη πόλεμος
> ἀλήθεια ψεῦδος
> Διόν(υσος)

c Frag. 465 T Bernabé

> Διόν(υσος)
> ⟨ψεῦδος⟩ ἀλήθεια
> σῶμα ψυχή

> ⟨ψεῦδος⟩ Vinogradov

T34 (cf. 1 B17–20) Lamella aurea ca. 400 a. C. n. Hipponii reperta (Frag. 474 F Bernabé)

> Μναμοσύνας τόδε ἔργον. ἐπεὶ ἂν μέλλησι
>   θανεῖσθαι
> εἰς Ἀίδαο δόμους εὐήρεας, ἔστ᾽ ἐπὶ δεξιὰ κρήνα,
> πὰρ δ᾽ αὐτὰν ἑστακῦα λευκὰ κυπάρισσος·

T33 (≠ DK) Bone tablets from Olbia, 5th century BC

a

>   life death life
>   truth
>   Dion(ysus) Orphic men

b

>   peace war
>   truth falsehood [or: lie]
>   Dion(ysus)

c

>   Dion(ysus)
>   ‹falsehood [or: lie]› truth
>   body soul

T34 (cf. 1 B17–20) Orphic gold leaf from Hipponion, ca. 400 BC

>   This is the work of Mnemosyne [i.e. the goddess of
>   memory]: when you [i.e. the initiate] are about to
>   die
>   Into the well-constructed houses of Hades, there is
>   on the right a spring,
>   And beside it standing a white cypress;

ἔνθα κατερχόμεναι ψυχαὶ νεκύων ψύχονται.

5 ταύτας τᾶς κράνας μηδὲ σχεδὸν ἐγγύθεν ἔλθῃς.
πρόσθεν δὲ εὑρήσεις τᾶς Μναμοσύνας ἀπὸ
λίμνας
ψυχρὸν ὕδωρ προρέον· φύλακες δὲ ἐπύπερθεν
ἔασι.
οἳ δέ σε εἰρήσονται ἐνὶ φρασὶ πευκαλίμαισι
ὅττι δὴ ἐξερέεις Ἄιδος σκότος ὀρφνήεντος.
10 εἰπόν· "Γῆς παῖς εἰμι καὶ Οὐρανοῦ ἀστερόεντος·
δίψαι δ' εἰμ' αὖος καὶ ἀπόλλυμαι· ἀλλὰ δότ' ὦκα
ψυχρὸν ὕδωρ πιέναι τῆς Μνημοσύνης ἀπὸ
λίμνης."
καὶ δή τοι ἐρέουσιν ὑποχθονίῳ βασιλείᾳ·
καὶ δώσουσι πιεῖν τᾶς Μναμοσύνας ἀπὸ λίμνας
15 καὶ δὴ καὶ σὺ πιὼν ὁδὸν ἔρχεαι ἄν τε καὶ ἄλλοι
μύσται καὶ βάκχοι ἱερὰν στείχουσι κλεεινοί.

Varieties of Human Wisdom (T35–T39)
The Wisdom of the Seven Sages (T35–T38)

T35 (10.3) Demetr. Phal. in Stob. 3.1.172 (= Frag. 114 Wehrli)

[1] Κλεόβουλος Εὐαγόρου Λίνδιος ἔφη·

1. μέτρον ἄριστον. 2. πατέρα δεῖ αἰδεῖσθαι. 3. εὖ
τὸ σῶμα ἔχειν καὶ τὴν ψυχήν. 4. φιλήκοον εἶναι

Going down there, the souls (*psukhai*) of the dead
    cool off (*psukhontai*).
Do not go anywhere even near these springs.   5
Further on you will find cold water that flows forth
From the pool of Mnemosyne. There are guards set
    over it.
They will ask you, in their wise minds,
Why you are exploring the shadow of gloomy Hades.
Say: "I am a son of Earth and of starry Sky.   10
I am parched with thirst and am being destroyed.
    Come, give quickly
Cold water to drink from the pool of Mnemosyne."
And they will announce you to the queen under the
    earth,
And they will give you to drink from the pool of
    Mnemosyne;
And then you too, after you have drunk, will go on   15
    the holy road where the others,
Initiates and Bacchants, walk in glory.

Varieties of Human Wisdom (T35–T39)
The Wisdom of the Seven Sages (T35–T38)

T35 (10.3) Demetrius of Phalerum, *Apophthegms of the
Seven Sages,* in Stobaeus

[1] Cleobulus of Lindus, son of Euagoras, said:

1. Measure is best. 2. Revere your father. 3. Be well
in body and in soul. 4. Enjoy listening and don't talk

καὶ μὴ πολύλαλον. 5. πολυμαθῆ[1] ἢ ἀμαθῆ. 6.
γλῶσσαν εὔφημον κεκτῆσθαι. 7. ἀρετῆς οἰκεῖον,[2]
κακίας ἀλλότριον. 8. ἀδικίαν μισεῖν. 9. εὐσέβειαν φυλάσσειν. 10. πολίταις τὰ βέλτιστα
συμβουλεύειν 11. ἡδονῆς κρατεῖν. 12. βίᾳ μηδὲν
πράττειν. 13. τέκνα παιδεύειν. 14. τύχῃ εὔχεσθαι.
15. ἔχθρας διαλύειν. 16. τὸν τοῦ δήμου ἐχθρὸν
πολέμιον νομίζειν. 17. γυναικὶ μὴ μάχεσθαι
μηδὲ ἄγαν φρονεῖν ἀλλοτρίων παρόντων· τὸ
μὲν γὰρ ἄνοιαν, τὸ δὲ μανίαν δύναται παρέχειν.
18. οἰκέτας μεθύοντας μὴ κολάζειν· εἰ δὲ μή,
δόξεις παροινεῖν. 19. γαμεῖν ἐκ τῶν ὁμοίων. ἐὰν
γὰρ ἐκ τῶν κρειττόνων, δεσπότας, οὐ συγγενεῖς
κτήσῃ. 20. μὴ ἐπιγέλα τῷ σκώπτοντι· ἀπεχθὴς
γὰρ ἔσῃ τοῖς σκωπτομένοις. 21. εὐποροῦντα μὴ
ὑπερήφανον εἶναι, ἀποροῦντα μὴ ταπεινοῦσθαι.

---

[1] πολυμαθῆ μᾶλλον Diog. Laert. 1.92   [2] οἰκεῖον ‹εἶναι› Hense

[2] Σόλων Ἐξηκεστίδου Ἀθηναῖος ἔφη·

1. μηδὲν ἄγαν. 2. κριτὴς μὴ κάθησο· εἰ δὲ μή,
τῷ ληφθέντι ἐχθρὸς ἔσῃ. 3. ἡδονὴν φεῦγε, ἥτις
λύπην τίκτει. 4. φύλασσε τρόπου καλοκαγαθίαν
ὅρκου πιστοτέραν. 5. σφραγίζου τοὺς μὲν λόγους σιγῇ, τὴν δὲ σιγὴν καιρῷ. 6. μὴ ψεύδου,
ἀλλ' ἀλήθευε. 7. τὰ σπουδαῖα μελέτα. 8. τῶν γονέων μὴ λέγε δικαιότερα. 9. φίλους μὴ ταχὺ

too much. 5. [Scil. It is better] to know a lot than to know nothing. 6. Possess a tongue that speaks auspiciously. 7. A kinsman of virtue, a stranger to evil. 8. Hate injustice. 9 Preserve piety. 10. Counsel your fellow-citizens what is best. 11. Dominate over pleasure. 12. Do nothing with violence 13. Educate your children. 14. Pray to fortune. 15. Settle enmities. 16. Consider the people's adversary to be your enemy. 17. Do not fight with your wife, or be arrogant when others are present: the one can make you seem foolish, the other insane. 18. Do not punish your slaves when they are inebriated: otherwise it is you who will seem to be drunken. 19. Marry from your own social class; for if you marry superiors, you will acquire masters, not relatives. 20. Do not laugh with a mocker; for you will be hated by those he mocks. 21. If you are affluent do not be arrogant, if you are poor do not abase yourself.

[2] Solon of Athens, son of Execestides, said:

1. Nothing in excess. 2. Do not sit as a judge: otherwise you will be hated by the accused. 3. Flee pleasure that begets pain. 4. Preserve nobility of character, more credible than an oath. 5. Seal your discourses with silence, and silence with the right moment. 6. Do not lie, but tell the truth. 7. Devote yourself to serious matters. 8. Do not speak more justly than your parents. 9. Do not acquire friends

κτῶ, οὓς δ᾿ ἂν κτήσῃ, μὴ ταχὺ ἀποδοκίμαζε. 10. ἄρχεσθαι μαθών, ἄρχειν ἐπιστήσῃ. 11. εὐθύνας ἑτέρους ἀξιῶν διδόναι, καὶ αὐτὸς ὕπεχε. 12. συμβούλευε μὴ τὰ ἥδιστα, ἀλλὰ τὰ βέλτιστα. 13. τοῖς πολίταις μὴ θρασύνου. 14. μὴ κακοῖς ὁμίλει. 15. χρῶ τοῖς θεοῖς. 16. φίλους εὐσέβει. 17. ὃ ἂν¹ ἴδῃς μὴ λέγε. 18. εἰδὼς σίγα. 19. τοῖς ἑαυτοῦ πρᾷος ἴσθι. 20. τὰ ἀφανῆ τοῖς φανεροῖς τεκμαίρου.

¹ ὃ ἂν ‹μὴ› Wdz

[3] Χείλων Δαμαγήτου Λακεδαιμόνιος ἔφη·

1. γνῶθι σαυτόν. 2. πίνων, μὴ πολλὰ λάλει· ἁμαρτήσῃ γάρ. 3. μὴ ἀπείλει τοῖς ἐλευθέροις· οὐ γὰρ δίκαιον. 4. μὴ κακολόγει τοὺς πλησίον· εἰ δὲ μὴ, ἀκούσῃ ἐφ᾿ οἷς λυπηθήσῃ. 5. ἐπὶ τὰ δεῖπνα τῶν φίλων βραδέως πορεύου, ἐπὶ δὲ τὰς ἀτυχίας ταχέως. 6. γάμους εὐτελεῖς ποιοῦ. 7. τὸν τετελευτηκότα μακάριζε. 8. πρεσβύτερον σέβου. 9. τὸν τὰ ἀλλότρια περιεργαζόμενον μίσει. 10. ζημίαν αἱροῦ μᾶλλον ἢ κέρδος αἰσχρόν· τὸ μὲν γὰρ ἅπαξ λυπήσει, τὸ δὲ ἀεί. 11. τῷ δυστυχοῦντι μὴ ἐπιγέλα. 12. τραχὺς ὤν, ἥσυχον σεαυτόν πάρεχε, ὅπως σε αἰσχύνωνται μᾶλλον, ἢ φοβῶνται. 13. τῆς ἰδίας οἰκίας προστάτει. 14. ἡ γλῶσσά σου μὴ προτρεχέτω τοῦ νοῦ. 15. θυμοῦ

quickly, but those that you do acquire do not reject quickly. 10. If you have learned how to be ruled you will know how to rule. 11. If you demand that others be examined, then submit to examination yourself too. 12. Do not counsel what is most pleasant, but what is best. 13. Do not be arrogant with regard to your fellow-citizens. 14. Do not associate with wicked people. 15. Consult the oracles of the gods. 16. Respect your friends. 17. Do not say what you see. 18. If you know, remain silent. 19. Be gentle to your own people. 20. Estimate what is invisible by what is visible.

[3] Chilon of Lacedaemon, son of Damagetus, said:

1. Know yourself. 2. When you drink do not speak too much: for you will commit a wrong. 3. Do not threaten free men; for that is not just 4. Do not speak ill of those nearby; otherwise you will hear things that will cause you pain. 5. Go slowly to your friends' dinners, but quickly to their misfortunes. 6. Arrange inexpensive weddings. 7. Bless the deceased. 8. Respect an older man. 9. Hate the man who meddles in other people's affairs. 10. Prefer loss rather than shameful gain: for the one will cause you pain one time, the other forever. 11. Do not laugh at the unfortunate. 12. If you are harsh, show yourself to be gentle, so that people will feel respect for you rather than fear. 13. Lord it over your own household. 14. Your tongue should not run faster than your mind. 15. Dominate over anger.

κράτει. 16. μὴ ἐπιθύμει ἀδύνατα. 17a. ἐν ὁδῷ μὴ σπεῦδε προάγειν, 17b. μηδὲ τὴν χεῖρα κινεῖν· μανικὸν γάρ. 18. νόμοις πείθου. 19. ἀδικούμενος διαλλάσσου· ὑβριζόμενος τιμωροῦ.

[4] Θαλῆς Ἐξαμίου Μιλήσιος ἔφη·

1. ἐγγύα, πάρα δ᾽ ἄτα. 2. φίλων παρόντων καὶ ἀπόντων μέμνησο. 3. μὴ τὴν ὄψιν καλλωπίζου, ἀλλ᾽ ἐν τοῖς ἐπιτηδεύμασιν ἴσθι καλός. 4. μὴ πλούτει κακῶς. 5. μή σε διαβαλλέτω λόγος πρὸς τοὺς πίστεως κεκοινωνηκότας. 6. κολακεύειν γονεῖς μὴ ὄκνει. 7. μὴ προσδέχου τὸ φαῦλον. 8. οἵους ἂν ἐράνους ἐνέγκῃς τοῖς γονεῦσι, τούτους αὐτοὺς ἐν τῷ γήρᾳ παρὰ τῶν τέκνων προσδέχου. 9. χαλεπὸν τὸ εὖ γνῶναι. 10. ἥδιστον τὸ ἐπιθυμίας τυχεῖν. 11. ἀνιαρὸν ἀργία. 12. βλαβερὸν ἀκρασία. 13. βαρὺ ἀπαιδευσία. 14. δίδασκε καὶ μάνθανε τὸ ἄμεινον. 15. ἀργὸς μὴ ἴσθι, μηδ᾽ ἂν πλουτῇς. 16. κακὰ ἐν οἴκῳ κρύπτε. 17. φθόνου χάριν μὴ οἰκτείρου. 18. μέτρῳ χρῶ. 19. μὴ πᾶσι πίστευε. 20. ἄρχων κόσμει σεαυτόν.

[5] Πιττακὸς Ὑρραδίου Λέσβιος ἔφη·

1. καιρὸν γνῶθι. 2. ὃ μέλλεις ποιεῖν μὴ λέγε·

16. Do not desire what is impossible. 17a. On the road do not hasten to be first, 17b. and do not gesture with your hand, for that is typical of the insane. 18. Obey the laws. 19. If you suffer injustice, be reconciled; if you suffer outrageous mistreatment, avenge yourself.

[4] Thales of Miletus [cf. **THAL. P16–P17**], son of Examyes, said:

1. Give a pledge, and disaster is near. 2. Be mindful of your friends when they are present and also when they are absent. 3. Do not beautify your appearance, but be beautiful in your way of life. 4. Do not become rich by wickedness. 5. Let no word bring discredit for you upon those who share your trust. 6. Do not hesitate to flatter your parents. 7. Do not accept what is substandard. 8. The kinds of benefits you give to your parents, accept these yourself in old age from your children. 9. It is difficult to know the good. 10. The most pleasant thing is to obtain what one desires. 11. Laziness is vexatious. 12. Lack of self-control (*akrasia*) is harmful. 13. Lack of education is burdensome. 14. Teach and learn what is better. 15. Do not be inactive, even if you are wealthy. 16. Conceal evils within the house. 17. Because of envy, do not show pity. 18. Use measure. 19. Do not trust all. 20. If you are performing a magistracy, keep yourself orderly in appearance.

[5] Pittacus of Lesbos, son of Hyrras, said:

1. Know the right moment. 2. Do not say what you

143

ἀποτυχὼν γὰ⸱ καταγελασθήσῃ. 3. τοῖς ἐπιτη-
δείοις χρῶ. 4. ὅσα νεμεσᾷς τῷ πλησίον, αὐτὸς
μὴ ποίει. 5. ⸱πραγοῦντα μὴ ὀνείδιζε· ἐπὶ γὰρ
τούτοις νέμε⸱ις θεῶν κάθηται. 6. παρακαταθή-
κας ἀπόδος. ⸱. ἀνέχου ὑπὸ τῶν πλησίον μικρὰ
ἐλαττούμενος 8. τὸν φίλον κακῶς μὴ λέγε, μηδ᾽
εὖ τὸν ἐχθρό⸱· ἀσυλλόγιστον γὰρ τὸ τοιοῦτον.
9. δεινὸν συ⸱ ἰδεῖν τὸ μέλλον, ἀσφαλὲς τὸ γενόμενον. 10. π⸱στὸν γῆ, ἄπιστον θάλασσα. 11.
ἄπληστον κ⸱ρδος. 12. κτῆσαι ἀίδια· θεραπείαν,
εὐσέβειαν, ⸱αιδείαν, σωφροσύνην, φρόνησιν,
ἀλήθειαν, π⸱⸱τιν, ἐμπειρίαν, ἐπιδεξιότητα, ἑται-
ρείαν, ἐπιμέ⸱ειαν, οἰκονομίαν, τέχνην.

[6] Βίας Τευτα⸱ίδου Πριηνεὺς ἔφη·

1. οἱ πλεῖσ⸱⸱ι ἄνθρωποι κακοί. 2. ἐς τὸ ἔσοπτρον
ἐμβλέψαντες δεῖ, εἰ μὲν καλὸς φαίνῃ, καλὰ ποιεῖν, εἰ δὲ αἰ⸱χρός, τὸ τῆς φύσεως ἐλλιπὲς διορ-
θοῦσθαι τῇ καλοκαγαθίᾳ. 3. βραδέως ἐγχείρει·
ὃ δ᾽ ἂν ἄρ⸱ῃ, διαβεβαιοῦ. 4. μίσει τὸ ταχὺ λα-
λεῖν, μὴ ἁ⸱άρτῃς· μετάνοια γὰρ ἀκολουθεῖ. 5.
μήτ᾽ εὐήθη⸱ ἴσθι, μήτε κακοήθης. 6. ἀφροσύνην
μὴ προσδέ⸱ου. 7. φρόνησιν ἀγάπα. 8. περὶ θεῶν
λέγε, ὡς ⸱σὶ θεοί. 9. νόει τὸ πραττόμενον. 10.
ἄκουε πο⸱λά. 11. λάλει καίρια. 12. πένης ὢν
πλουσίοις μὴ ἐπιτίμα, ἢν μὴ μέγα ὠφελῇς. 13.
ἀνάξιον ἄ⸱δρα μὴ ἐπαίνει διὰ πλοῦτον. 14. πεί-
σας λαβέ μὴ βιασάμενος. 15. ὅ τι ἂν ἀγαθὸν

are going to do; for if you do not succeed you will
be laughed at. 3. Use what is suitable. 4. Whatever
you rebuke your neighbor for, do not do it yourself.
5. Do not speak ill of the man who fares badly; for
the vengeance of the gods is set upon these things.
6. Repay sureties. 7. Accept to be a little bit less than
your neighbors. 8. Do not speak ill of a friend nor
well of an enemy, for such a thing is illogical. 9. It
is terrible to see the future, safe to see the past.
10. The earth is reliable, the sea is unreliable.
11. Gain is insatiable. 12. Acquire what is eternal:
service, piety, education, moderation prudence,
truth, credibility, experience, cleverness, comrade-
ship, diligence, housekeeping, skill.

[6] Bias of Priene, son of Teutamides, said:

1. Most humans are bad. 2. You should look into a
mirror: if you look fine, then do fine things; if you
look ugly, correct by nobility the defect of your nature. 3. Set to work slowly; but where you begin,
persist. 4. Hate fast talking, do not commit a wrong:
for regret follows after. 5. Be neither simple-minded
nor evil-minded. 6. Do not accept folly. 7. Cherish
prudence. 8. Say about the gods that they exist. 9.
Think about what you are doing. 10. Listen a lot. 11.
Speak opportunely. 12. If you are poor, do not rebuke the wealthy, unless you are benefiting them
greatly thereby. 13. Do not praise an unworthy man
because of his wealth. 14. Take by persuasion, not
by force. 15. Whatever good you do, ascribe to the

145

πράσσῃς, θεούς, μὴ σεαυτὸν αἰτιῶ. 16. κτῆσαι
ἐν μὲν νεότητι εὐπραξίαν, ἐν δὲ τῷ γήρᾳ σοφίαν. 17. ἕξεις ἔργῳ μνήμην, καιρῷ εὐλάβειαν,
τρόπῳ γενναιότητα, πόνῳ ἐγκράτειαν, φόβῳ
εὐσέβειαν, πλούτῳ φιλίαν, λόγῳ πειθώ, σιγῇ
κόσμον, γνώμῃ δικαιοσύνην, τόλμῃ ἀνδρείαν,
πράξει δυναστείαν, δόξῃ ἡγεμονίαν.

[7] Περίανδρος Κυψέλου Κορίνθιος ἔφη·

1. μελέτα τὸ πᾶν. 2a. καλὸν ἡσυχία· 2b. ἐπι-
σφαλὲς προπέτεια. 3. κέρδος αἰσχρὸν φύσεως
κατηγορία. 4. δημοκρατία κρεῖττον τυραννίδος.
5. αἱ μὲν ἡδοναὶ θνηταί, αἱ δ᾽ ἀρεταὶ ἀθάνατοι.
6. εὐτυχῶν μὲν μέτριος ἴσθι, ἀτυχῶν δὲ φρόνι-
μος. 7. φειδόμενον κρεῖττον ἀποθανεῖν ἢ ζῶντα
ἐνδεῖσθαι. 8. σεαυτὸν ἄξιον παρασκεύαζε τῶν
γονέων. 9. ζῶν μὲν ἐπαινοῦ, ἀποθανὼν δὲ μα-
καρίζου. 10. φίλοις εὐτυχοῦσι καὶ ἀτυχοῦσιν ὁ
αὐτὸς ἴσθι. 11. ὃν ἂν ἑκὼν ὁμολογήσῃς πονη-
ρόν, παράβαινε. 12. λόγων ἀπορρήτων ἐκφορὰν
μὴ ποιοῦ. 13. λοιδοροῦ ὡς ταχὺ φίλος ἐσόμενος.
14. τοῖς μὲν νόμοις παλαιοῖς χρῶ, τοῖς δ᾽ ὄψοις
προσφάτοις. 15. μὴ μόνον τοὺς ἁμαρτάνοντας
κόλαζε, ἀλλὰ καὶ τοὺς μέλλοντας κώλυε. 16.
δυστυχῶν κρύπτε, ἵνα μὴ τοὺς ἐχθροὺς εὐφρά-
νῃς.

gods, not yourself. 16. Acquire proper conduct in youth, wisdom in old age. 17. You will acquire reputation by your deed, discretion by [scil. choosing] the right moment, nobility by your character, self-control by your effort, piety by your fear, friendship by your wealth, obedience by your speech, orderliness by your silence, justice by your judgment, manliness by your courage, dominion by your action, supremacy by your fame.

[7] Periander of Corinth, son of Cypselus, said:

1. Practice is all. 2a. Calmness is fine; 2b. rashness is dangerous. 3. Shameful gain is an accusation against your nature. 4. Democracy is better than tyranny. 5. Pleasures are mortal, but virtues immortal. 6. If you are fortunate, be moderate if unfortunate, prudent. 7. It is better to die being frugal than to live not having enough. 8. Make yourself worthy of your parents. 9. Be praised while you are alive, be blessed when you have died. 10. Be the same to your friends both when they are fortunate and when they are unfortunate. 11. Avoid the man that you yourself recognize to be wicked. 12. Do not reveal secret words. 13. Blame like someone who wants to quickly become a friend. 14. Use laws that are ancient but food that is fresh. 15. You should not only punish those who commit wrong, but also prevent those who are intending to do so. 16. If you are unfortunate, conceal it, so that you will not make your enemies happy.

T36 (≠ DK) Pin. Frag. 35b

σοφοὶ δὲ καὶ τὸ μηδὲν ἄγαν ἔπος αἴνη-
σαν περισσῶς.

T37 (cf. 80 A25) Simon. Frag. 542

1 ἄνδρ’ ἀγαθὸν μὲν ἀλαθέως γενέσθαι
χαλεπὸν χερσίν τε καὶ ποσὶ καὶ νόῳ
τετράγωνον ἄνευ ψόγου τετυγμένον·
   . . .

11 οὐδέ μοι ἐμμελέως τὸ Πιττάκειον
νέμεται, καίτοι σοφοῦ παρὰ φωτὸς εἰ-
ρημένον· χαλεπὸν φάτ’ ἐσθλὸν ἔμμεναι.
θεὸς ἂν μόνος τοῦτ’ ἔχοι γέρας, ἄνδρα δ’ οὐκ
15 ἔστι μὴ οὐ κακὸν ἔμμεναι,
ὃν ἀμήχανος συμφορὰ καθέλῃ·
πράξας γὰρ εὖ πᾶς ἀνὴρ ἀγαθός,
κακὸς δ’ εἰ κακῶς [
[ἐπὶ πλεῖστον δὲ καὶ ἄριστοί εἰσιν
20 [οὓς ἂν οἱ θεοὶ φιλῶσιν.]
τοὔνεκεν οὔ ποτ’ ἐγὼ τὸ μὴ γενέσθαι
δυνατὸν διζήμενος κενεὰν ἐς ἄ-
πρακτον ἐλπίδα μοῖραν αἰῶνος βαλέω,
πανάμωμον ἄνθρωπον, εὐρυεδέος ὅσοι
25 καρπὸν αἰνύμεθα χθονός·
ἐπὶ δ’ ὑμῖν εὑρὼν ἀπαγγελέω.
πάντας δ’ ἐπαίνημι καὶ φιλέω,

19–20 paraphrasis Platonica sententiae Simonideae

T36 (≠ DK) Pindar, Fragment

> The wise have also praised surpassingly
> > The saying, "nothing in excess."

T37 (cf. 80 A25) Simonides, Fragments of an encomium for Scopas (cf. **PROT. D42**)

> For a man to be truly good (*agathos*)   1
> Is difficult, four-square in his hands, feet, and mind,
> Constructed without any blemish.
> . . .
> Nor does Pittacus' saying seem well-said to me,   11
> Although it was spoken by a wise man:
> > He said that it is difficult to be good (*esthlos*).
> Only a god could have that honor: a man
> > Cannot help being bad,   15
> When irresistible disaster seizes hold of him.
> When he is doing well, every man is good;
> But when badly, he is bad.
> [And for the most part those are the best ones
> Whom the gods love.][1]   20
> And for that reason I myself shall never
> Throw away my portion of life onto an empty, futile
> > hope
> > Looking for what cannot come about, the
> completely blameless man
> > Among all of us who enjoy the fruit of the broad   25
> earth.
> I shall tell you when I have found one.
> I praise and love all men,

[1] The words in brackets are a paraphrase by Plato of the contents of these lines of Simonides.

ἑκὼν ὅστις ἔρξῃ
μηδὲν αἰσχρόν· ἀνάγκα
30   δ᾿ οὐδὲ θεοὶ μάχονται.

T38 (< 58C.4) Iambl. *VP* 83

ἔστι δ᾿ αὕτη ἡ ἀρτὴ τῇ τῶν ἑπτὰ σοφιστῶν λεγομένη
σοφίᾳ. καὶ γὰρ ἐκεῖνοι ἐζήτουν οὐ τί ἐστι τἀγαθόν,
ἀλλὰ τί μάλιστα; οὐδὲ τί τὸ χαλεπόν, ἀλλὰ τί τὸ
χαλεπώτατον; ὅτι τὸ αὑτὸν γνῶναί ἐστιν· οὐδὲ τί τὸ
ῥᾴδιον, ἀλλὰ τί τὸ ῥᾷστον; ὅτι τὸ ἔθει χρῆσθαι. τῇ
τοιαύτῃ γὰρ σοφίᾳ μετηκολουθηκέναι ἔοικε τὰ τοι-
αῦτα ἀκούσματα· πρότεροι γὰρ οὗτοι Πυθαγόρου ἐγένοντο.

Human Wisdom and the Study of Nature (T39)

T39 (≠ DK) Pind.

a Frag. 61

τί ἔλπεαι σοφίαν ἔμμεν, ἂν ὀλίγον τοι
ἀνὴρ ὑπὲρ ἀνδρὸς ἴσχει;
οὐ γὰρ ἔσθ᾿ ὅπως τὰ θεῶν
βουλεύματ᾿ ἐρευνάσει βροτέᾳ φρενί·
θνατᾶς δ᾿ ἀπὸ ματρὸς ἔφυ.

b Frag. 209

τοὺς φυσιολογοῦντας ἔφη Πίνδαρος
ἀτελῆ σοφίας καρπὸν δρέπειν.

150

Whoever does nothing shameful willingly: but against
  necessity
Not even do the gods fight.   30

T38 (< 58C.4) Iamblichus, *Life of Pythagoras*

This [i.e. the wisdom of the Pythagorean *akousmata*, cf.
PYTH. c D15] is the same as the so-called wisdom of the
Seven Sages. For they too investigated not what the good
is, but what it is most of all; nor what is difficult, but what
is the most difficult (that is, to know oneself); nor what is
easy, but what is the easiest (that is, to follow habit). For
the *akousmata* of this sort seem to be later than this kind
of wisdom: for these [i.e. the Seven Sages] lived before
Pythagoras.

Human Wisdom and the Study of Nature (T39)

T39 (≠ DK) Pindar, Fragments

a

What do you expect wisdom to be, if it is only by a
  little
That one man possesses it more than another?
For it is impossible for him
To discover the gods' plans with a human mind
  (*phreni*):
He was born of a mortal mother.

b

Pindar said that the philosophers of nature
  "pluck the fruit of wisdom before it is ripe."

151

EARLY IONIAN THINKERS
PART 1

4. PHERECYDES [PHER.]

The ancient sources date Pherecydes' maturity toward the middle of the sixth century BC (544/40), making him younger than Anaximander. But the chronological data are not certain enough to allow us to say which man is the likelier candidate for the title of the most ancient author of philosophy in prose—if indeed the term "philosophy" is meaningful in the case of Pherecydes. But what is certain is that he represents an interesting transitional figure between two types of discourse, theogony and cosmogony, which were becoming differentiated from one another at that time. Already Aristotle described Pherecydes' thought as "mixed."

Scholastic reconstructions, distorting somewhat the chronology, attribute to Pherecydes the same kind of function within the Italic line of descent as Thales' within the Ionian one: he is said to have been Pythagoras' teacher, as Thales was Anaximander's. This line of descent gave rise to stories often repeated in antiquity [cf. **PYTH. a P12–P15**] but is most probably fictitious.

BIBLIOGRAPHY

Edition

H. S. Schibli. *Pherekydes of Syros* (Oxford, 1990).

Studies

H. Granger. "The Theologian Pherecydes of Syros and the Early Days of Natural Philosophy," *Harvard Studies in Classical Philology* 103 (2007): 135–63.

M. L. West. "Three Presocratic Cosmogonies," *Classical Quarterly* 13 (1963): 157–72.

———. *Early Greek Philosophy and the Orient* (Oxford, 1971), pp. 28–75.

OUTLINE OF THE CHAPTER

P

D

PHERECYDES [7 DK]

P

Chronology (P1–P4)

P1 (< A1) Diog. Laert. 1.121

γέγονε δὲ κατὰ τὴν πεντηκοστὴν καὶ ἐνάτην Ὀλυμπιάδα.

P2 (< A2) *Suda* Φ.214

Φερεκύδης, Βάβυος, Σύριος [. . .] · γέγονε δὲ κατὰ τὸν
Λυδῶν βασιλέα Ἀλυάττην, ὡς συγχρονεῖν τοῖς ζ' σοφοῖς καὶ τετέχθαι περὶ τὴν με'[1] Ὀλυμπιάδα [. . . = **P6**].

<blockquote>
[1] με'] νε' G: μθ' Rohde
</blockquote>

P3 (< A5) Cic. *Tusc.* 1.16.38

[. . . = **R14**] antiquus sane; fuit enim meo regnante gentili
[. . .].

PHERECYDES

P

Chronology (P1–P4)

P1 (< A1) Diogenes Laertius
He lived during the 59th Olympiad [= 544/40].

P2 (< A2) *Suda*

Pherecydes, son of Babys, of Syros [. . .]; he lived at the time of Alyattes, king of the Lydians [i.e. 605/560], so that he was contemporary with the Seven Sages and was born around the 45th Olympiad [= 600/596].[1]

[1] This is often corrected to the 49th Olympiad (584/80) on the supposition that the indication given in **P1** refers to Pherecydes' *floruit* (forty years old).

P3 (< A5) Cicero, *Tusculan Disputations*

[. . . scil. he was] quite ancient, for he lived during the reign of my ancestor and namesake [i.e. Servius Tullius, 578/35].

159

P4 (8 Schibli) Ps.-Luc. *Long.* 22

[. . .] Φερεκύδης ὁ Σύριος [. . .] ὀγδοήκοντα καὶ πέντε.

His Teachers (P5–P7)
Did He Have a Greek Teacher? (P5)

P5 (< A1) Diog. Laert. 1.116

Φερεκύδης Βάβυος Σύριος, καθά φησιν Ἀλέξανδρος
ἐν Διαδοχαῖς [FGrHist 273 F85], Πιττακοῦ διακήκοε.

Or Did He Learn from Oriental Sources? (P6–P8)

P6 (< A2) *Suda* Φ.214

[. . . = **P2**] αὐτὸν δὲ οὐκ ἐσχηκέναι καθηγητήν, ἀλλ’
ἑαυτὸν ἀσκῆσαι, κτησάμενον τὰ Φοινίκων ἀπόκρυφα
βιβλία [. . . = **R5a**].

P7 (< B4) Eus. *PE* 1.10.50 (= Ph. Bybl., *FHG* III Frag.
9)

παρὰ Φοινίκων δὲ καὶ Φερεκύδης λαβὼν τὰς ἀφορ-
μὰς ἐθεολόγησε περὶ τοῦ παρ’ αὐτῷ λεγομένου Ὀφί-
ονος θεοῦ καὶ τῶν Ὀφιονιδῶν [. . .].

P8 (38 Schibli) Flav. Jos. *Apion.* 1.14

ἀλλὰ μήν [. . . = **D4**] Φερεκύδην τε τὸν Σύριον καὶ

160

P4 (≠ DK) Ps.-Lucian, *Long-lived Men*

[. . .] Pherecydes of Syros [. . . scil. lived] eighty-five years.

His Teachers (P5–P7)
Did He Have a Greek Teacher? (P5)

P5 (< A1) Diogenes Laertius

Pherecydes, son of Babys, of Syros, studied with Pittacus,[1]
as Alexander says in his *Successions*.

[1] One of the Seven Sages, cf. **MOR. T35[5].**

Or Did He Learn from Oriental Sources? (P6–P8)

P6 (< A2) *Suda*

[. . .] he did not have a teacher himself, but he trained
himself after he had acquired the secret books of the
Phoenicians.

P7 (< B4) Philon of Byblos in Eusebius, *Evangelical Preparation*

Pherecydes, taking his starting point from the Phoenicians, expressed theological doctrines about the god that
he calls Ophion and the Ophionids [cf. **D11–D12**] [. . .].

P8 (≠ DK) Flavius Josephus, *Against Apion*

But as for [. . .] Pherecydes of Syros, Pythagoras, and

Πυθαγόραν καὶ Θαλητα πάντες συμφώνως ὁμολογοῦσιν Αἰγυπτίων καὶ Χαλδαίων γενομένους μαθητὰς
[. . . = **R7**].

His Student Pythagoras (P9)

P9 (< A2) Suda Φ.14

[. . . = **P2**] διδαχθῆναι δὲ ὑπ᾽ αὐτοῦ Πυθαγόραν λόγος
[. . . = **P6**].

Predictions (P10)

P10 (< A1) Diog. Laert. 1.116–17

πολλὰ δὲ καὶ θαυμάσια λέγεται περὶ αὐτοῦ· καὶ γὰρ
παρὰ τὸν αἰγιαλὸν τῆς Σάμου περιπατοῦντα καὶ ναῦν
οὐριοδρομοῦσαν ἰδόντα εἰπεῖν ὡς μετ᾽ οὐ πολὺ[1] κατα-
δύσεται· καὶ ἐν ὀφθαλμοῖς αὐτοῦ καταδῦναι. καὶ ἀνι-
μηθέντος ἐκ φρέατος ὕδατος πιόντα προειπεῖν ὡς εἰς
τρίτην ἡμέραν ἔσοιτο σεισμός, καὶ γενέσθαι. ἀνιόντα
τε εἰς Ὀλυμπίαν[2] ἐν Μεσσήνῃ[3] τῷ ξένῳ Περιλάῳ συμ-
βουλεῦσαι ἐξοικίσαι μετὰ τῶν οἰκείων· καὶ τὸν μὴ
πεισθῆναι, Μεσσήνην δὲ ἑαλωκέναι. [117] καὶ Λακε-
δαιμονίοις εἰπεῖν μήτε χρυσὸν τιμᾶν μήτε ἄργυρον,
ὥς φησι Θεόπομπος ἐν Θαυμασίοις [FGrHist 115 F71]·

[1] μετ᾽ οὐ πολὺ rec.: οὐ μετ᾽ οὐ πολὺ ΒΡΦ: οὐ μετὰ πολὺ
Diels   [2] εἰς Ὀλυμπίαν ΒΡΦ: ἀπ᾽ Ὀλυμπίας Casaubon

Thales, everyone agrees that they were students of the
Egyptians and Chaldaeans [. . .].

His Student Pythagoras (P9)

P9 (< A2) *Suda*

There is a report that Pythagoras was taught by him [cf.
PYTH. a P12–P15].

Predictions (P10)

P10 (< A1) Diogenes Laertius

Many marvels are reported about him. While he was walking on the beach of Samos, he saw a boat sailing with a fair
wind and said that soon it would sink—and it sank before
his eyes. When he drank water drawn from a well, he
predicted that there would be an earthquake two days
later—and it happened. When he traveled to Olympia, he
advised his host Perilaus in Messene to leave his home
together with his household—but he was not persuaded,
and Messene was captured. [117] He told the Lacedaemonians to hold neither gold nor silver in honor, as Theopompus says in his *Marvels;* he had received this order in a

---

3 ἐν Μεσσήνῃ von der Mühll: ἐς Μεσσήνην (Μεσή- PΦ)
BP¹Φ: ἐκ Μεσσήνης Richards

προστάξαι δὲ αὐτῷ ὄναρ τοῦτο τὸν Ἡρακλέα, ὃν καὶ τῆς αὐτῆς νυκτὸς τοῖς βασιλεῦσι κελεῦσαι Φερεκύδῃ πείθεσθαι. ἔνιοι δὲ Πυθαγόρᾳ περιάπτουσι ταῦτα [. . . = **P14**].

Pherecydes at Sparta (P11–P12)

P11 (23 Schibli) Plut. *Agis* 10. 6

ἐπεὶ Τέρπανδρόν γε[1] καὶ Θάλητα καὶ Φερεκύδην ξένους ὄντας, ὅτι τὰ αὐτὰ τῷ Λυκούργῳ διετέλουν ᾄδοντες καὶ φιλοσοφοῦντες, ἐν Σπάρτῃ τιμηθῆναι διαφερόντως.

[1] τε mss., corr. Reiske

P12 (25 Schibli) Plut. *Pelop.* 21.3

[. . .] Φερεκύδην τε τὸν σοφὸν ὑπὸ Λακεδαιμονίων ἀναιρεθέντα καὶ τὴν δορὰν αὐτοῦ κατά τι λόγιον ὑπὸ τῶν βασιλέων φρουρουμένην [. . .].

Death: The Role of Pythagoras (P13–P16)

P13 (32 Schibli) Arist. *HA* 5.30 556b30–557a3

ἐνίοις δὲ τοῦτο συμβαίνει τῶν ἀνθρώπων νόσημα, ὅταν ὑγρασία πολλὴ ἐν τῷ σώματι ᾖ· καὶ διεφθάρησάν τινες ἤδη τοῦτον τὸν τρόπον, ὥσπερ Ἀλκμᾶνά τέ φασι τὸν ποιητὴν καὶ Φερεκύδην τὸν Σύριον.

dream from Heracles, who that same night ordered the
kings to obey Pherecydes. But some people attach this
story to Pythagoras [cf. **R13**].

Pherecydes at Sparta (P11–P12)

P11 (≠ DK) Plutarch, *Agis*

Although Terpander, Thales, and Pherecydes were foreigners, they are particularly honored in Sparta because
they constantly sang and proclaimed philosophically the
same things as Lycurgus.

P12 (≠ DK) Plutarch, *Pelopidas*

[. . .] Pherecydes the sage was killed by the Lacedaemonians and, in conformity with an oracle, his skin was preserved by the kings [. . .].[1]

[1] Presumably this is the trace of a story of ritual sacrifice, of
which the details are obscure.

Death: the Role of Pythagoras (P13–P16)

P13 (≠ DK) Aristotle, *History of Animals*

This disease [i.e. phthiriasis] affects certain humans when
there is an abundance of moisture in the body; and some
people have already died in this way, like, they say, Alcman
the poet, and Pherecydes of Syros.

P14 (< A1) Diog. Laert. 1.117–18

[. . . = **P10**] φησὶ δ᾽ Ἕρμιππος [*FGrHist* 1026 F20]
πολέμου συνεστῶτος Ἐφεσίοις καὶ Μάγνησι βουλό-
μενον τοὺς Ἐφεσίους νικῆσαι πυθέσθαι τινὸς παριόν-
τος πόθεν εἴη· τοῦ δ᾽ εἰπόντος "ἐξ Ἐφέσου," "ἕλκυσόν
με τοίνυν," ἔφη, "τῶν σκελῶν καὶ θὲς εἰς τὴν τῶν
Μαγνήτων χώραν, καὶ ἀπάγγειλόν σου τοῖς πολίταις
μετὰ τὸ νικῆσαι αὐτόθι με θάψαι· ἐπεσκηφέναι τε
ταῦτα Φερεκύδην." [118] ὁ μὲν <οὖν>[1] ἀπήγγειλεν· οἱ
δὲ μετὰ μίαν ἐπελθόντες κρατοῦσι τῶν Μαγνήτων,
καὶ τὸν Φερεκύδην μεταλλάξαντα θάπτουσιν αὐτόθι
καὶ μεγαλοπρεπῶς τιμῶσιν. ἔνιοι δέ φασιν ἐλθόντα
εἰς Δελφοὺς ἀπὸ τοῦ Κωρυκίου ὄρους αὐτὸν δισκῆ-
σαι. Ἀριστόξενος δ᾽ ἐν τῷ Περὶ Πυθαγόρου καὶ τῶν
γνωρίμων αὐτοῦ φησι [Frag. 14 Wehrli] νοσήσαντα
αὐτὸν ὑπὸ Πυθαγόρου ταφῆναι ἐν Δήλῳ. οἱ δὲ φθει-
ριάσαντα τὸν βίον τελευτῆσαι· ὅτε καὶ Πυθαγόρου
παραγενομένου καὶ πυνθανομένου πῶς διακέοιτο, δια-
βαλόντα τῆς θύρας τὸν δάκτυλον εἰπεῖν, "χροῖ δῆλα."

[1] <οὖν > Cobet

P15 (< A4) Diod. Sic. 10.3.4

ὅτι Πυθαγόρας πυθόμενος Φερεκύδην τὸν ἐπιστάτην
αὐτοῦ γεγενημένον ἐν Δήλῳ νοσεῖν καὶ τελέως[1] ἐσχά-
τως ἔχειν, ἔπλευσεν ἐκ τῆς Ἰταλίας εἰς τὴν Δῆλον.

[1] τελέως del. Cobet

P14 (< A1) Diogenes Laertius

[...] Hermippus says that during a war between the Ephesians and the Magnesians, he [i.e. Pherecydes] wanted the Ephesians to win and so asked someone who was passing by where he was from. When that man answered, "From Ephesus," he said, "Then drag me by the legs and put me down in the territory of the Magnesians and proclaim to your fellow citizens that after their victory they must bury me right there; and that it is Pherecydes who has commanded these things." [118] So the man made this proclamation, and they attacked the next day and gained victory over the Magnesians; and they buried Pherecydes, who had died, right there and honored him magnificently. But some say that he went to Delphi and threw himself from Mount Corycius. Aristoxenus says in his book *On Pythagoras and His Disciples* that at the end of his illness he was buried by Pythagoras at Delos. Others say that he died of phthiriasis; and when Pythagoras who was there, asked how he was doing, he stuck his finger through the door and said, "It is clear from my skin."

P15 (< A4) Diodorus Siculus

When Pythagoras found out that Pherecydes, who had become his tutor, was sick in Delos and finally was near death, he sailed from Italy to Delos. There he took care of

ἐκεῖ δὲ χρόνον ἱκανὸν τὸν ἄνδρα γηροτροφήσας, πᾶσαν εἰσηνέγκατο σπουδὴν ὥστε τὸν πρεσβύτην ἐκ τῆς νόσου διασῶσαι. κατισχυθέντος² δὲ τοῦ Φερεκύδου διὰ τὸ γῆρας καὶ διὰ τὸ μέγεθος τῆς νόσου, περιέστειλεν αὐτὸν κηδεμονικῶς, καὶ τῶν νομιζομένων ἀξιώσας ὡσανεί τις υἱὸς πατέρα πάλιν ἐπανῆλθεν εἰς τὴν Ἰταλίαν.

² κατισχύσαντος mss., corr. Reiske

P16 (28 Schibli) Heracl. Lemb. in Diog. Laert. 8.40

Ἡρακλείδης δέ φησιν [*FHG* III Frag. 6] ἐν τῇ τῶν Σατύρου βίων ἐπιτομῇ μετὰ τὸ θάψαι Φερεκύδην ἐν Δήλῳ ἐπανελθεῖν εἰς Ἰταλίαν [. . .].

the old man for a considerable time and applied all his efforts to save him from his illness. But when Pherecydes has been defeated by old age and the seriousness of his illness, he wrapped up his body carefully and after he had honored him with the traditional rites, like a son for his father, he returned once again to Italy.

P16 (≠ DK) Heraclides Lembos in Diogenes Laertius

Heraclides says in his *Epitome of Satyrus' Lives* that he [i.e. Pythagoras] returned to Italy after he had buried Pherecydes in Delos.

See also **PYTH. a P12, P15**

PHERECYDES [7 DK]

D

Title and Contents of Pherecydes' Book (D1–D4)

D1 (< A2) *Suda* Φ 214

ἔστι δὲ ἅπαντα ἃ συνέγραψε, ταῦτα· Ἑπτάμυχος ἤτοι
Θεοκρασία ἢ Θεογονία. ἔστι δὲ θεολογία¹ ἔχουσα
θεῶν γένεσιν καὶ διαδοχάς.²

¹ ἐν βιβλίοις ιʹ post θεολογία habent mss, del. Jacoby ut ad
Pherecydum Atheniensem spectantia   ² διαδόχους mss.,
corr. Preller

D2 (< A1) Diog. Laert. 1.116

τοῦτόν φησι Θεόπομπος [*FGrHist* 115 F71] πρῶτον
περὶ φύσεως καὶ θεῶν ῞Ελλησι² γράψαι.

¹ καὶ <γενέσεως> Gomperz   ² ῞Ελλησι del. Diels: <ἐν
τοῖς> ῞Ελλησι Marcovich

D3 (A11) Max. Tyr. *Diss.* 4.4.5

ἀλλὰ καὶ τοῦ Συρίου τὴν ποίησιν σκόπει, τὸν Ζῆνα

170

PHERECYDES

D

Title and Contents of Pherecydes' Book (D1–D4)

D1 (< A2) *Suda*

These are all of his writings: *The Seven Nooks*[1] or *Mixture of the Gods* or *Theogony.* It is a theology comprising the birth and successions of the gods.

   [1] **D6** speaks of *Five Nooks*.

D2 (< A1) Diogenes Laertius

Theopompus says that he was the first to write for the Greeks about nature and the gods.

D3 (A11) Maximus of Tyre, *Philosophical Orations*

Consider also the poetry of the man from Syros: Zeus,

καὶ τὴν Χθονίην καὶ τὸν ἐν τούτοις Ἔρωτα καὶ τὴν
Ὀφιονέως γένεσιν καὶ τὴν θεῶν μάχην καὶ τὸ δένδρον
καὶ τὸν πέπλον.

D4 (38 Schibli) Flav. Jos. *Apion.* 1.14

ἀλλὰ μὴν καὶ τοὺς περὶ τῶν οὐρανίων τε καὶ θείων
πρώτους παρ' Ἕλλησι φιλοσοφήσαντας, οἷον Φερεκύδην τε τὸν Σύρον [. . . = **P8**].

The Principles (D5–D7)

D5 (< B1) Diog. Laert. 1.119

[. . .] τό τε βιβλίον [. . .] οὗ ἡ ἀρχή· Ζὰς μὲν καὶ
Χρόνος ἦσαν[1] **ἀεὶ καὶ Χθονίη ἦν**·[2] **Χθονίη δὲ ὄνομα
ἐγένετο Γῆ ἐπειδὴ αὐτῇ Ζὰς γῆν**[3] **γέρας διδοῖ.**

[1] ἦσαν Diels: ἧς B: εἰς P¹(Q): εἷς Pˣ   [2] χθόνην B, χθὼν
ἦν P: corr. Casaubon   [3] γην B: γῆ P¹(Q): eras. Pˣ

D6 (< A8) Dam. *Princ.* 124b (= Eudem. Frag. 117 Wehrli)

Φερεκύδης δὲ ὁ Σύριος [. . .] τὸν δὲ Χρόνον ποιῆσαι
ἐκ τοῦ γόνου ἑαυτοῦ πῦρ καὶ πνεῦμα καὶ ὕδωρ [. . .]
ἐξ ὧν ἐν πέντε μυχοῖς διῃρημένων πολλὴν ἄλλην γενεὰν συστῆναι θεῶν τὴν πεντέμυχον καλουμένην [. . .]
[cf. **R23**].

Chthoniê, Eros who is among them, the birth of Ophioneus,[1] the battle of the gods, the tree, and the robe [cf.
D5, D8, D9, D10–D12].

[1] A monster, whose name suggests a snake, cf. **R27**.

D4 (≠ DK) Flavius Josephus, *Against Apion*

But as for those who were the first among the Greeks to
philosophize about celestial phenomena and divine matters, like Pherecydes of Syros [. . .].

The Principles (D5–D7)

D5 (< B1) Diogenes Laertius

[. . .] the book [. . .] its beginning is: **Zas** [i.e. Zeus] **and
Chronos were always, and Chthonie was. But the
name of Chthonie became Earth when Zas gave her
the earth as a present** [cf. **R4**].

D6 (< A8) Eudemus in Damascius, *On the Principles*

Pherecydes of Syros [scil. says] [. . .] that Chronos made
out of his own seed fire, breath, and water [. . .] out of
which, when they had been distributed in five nooks, was
created another numerous generation of gods, called **"the
five-nook"** one [. . .].

D7 (< B1a) Ach. Tat. *Introd. Arat.* 3

Θαλῆς δὲ ὁ Μιλήσιος καὶ Φερεκύδης ὁ Σύριος ἀρχὴν
τῶν ὅλων τὸ ὕδωρ ὑφίστανται, ὃ δὴ καὶ χάος καλεῖ ὁ
Φερεκύδης [. . . = **R22**].

Zas' Cosmogonic Marriage (D8–D10)

D8 (< B3) Procl. *In Tim.* 3 *ad* 32c (vol. 2, p. 54.28–30
Diehl)

[. . .] ὁ Φερεκύδης ἔλεγεν εἰς Ἔρωτα μεταβεβλῆσθαι
τὸν Δία μέλλοντα δημιουργεῖν [. . . cf. **R24**].

D9 (B2) P. Grenf. 2.11 ed. Schibli (et al.)

[Col. 1] [αὐ]τῶι ποιοῦσιν τὰ ο[ἰ]κία | πολλά τε καὶ
μεγάλα· | ἐπεὶ δὲ ταῦτα ἐξετέ[5]λεσαν πάντα καὶ
χρή|ματα καὶ θεράποντας | καὶ θεραπαίνας καὶ |
τἆλλα ὅσα δεῖ πάντα, | ἐπεὶ δὴ πάντα ἑτοῖ[10]μα
γίγνεται, τὸν γάμον ποιεῦσιν. κἀπει(δὴ τρίτη ἡμέρη
γί|γνεται τῶι γάμωι, τό | τε ⌊Ζὰς ποιεῖ φᾶρος μέ[15]
γα τε καὶ καλόν· καὶ | ἐν αὐτῶ[ι] ποικ[ίλλει Γῆν | καὶ
Ὠγη[νὸν καὶ τὰ Ὠ|γηνοῦ [δώματα] . . .

[Col. 2] [βουλόμενος] | γάρ σεο τοὺς γάμου[ς | εἶναι,
τούτωι σε τιμ[έω. | σὺ δέ μοι χαῖρε καὶ σύ[ν| [5]ι

Col. 1 1 αὐ]τῶι suppl. Diels, 16–18 Γῆν . . . δώματα suppl.
edd. ex Clem. Alex *Strom.* 6.9.4, cett. suppl. Grenfell-Hunt
Col. 2 1 βουλό*μενος* suppl. Weil, 4–5 σύ[νι]σθι Blass

D7 (< B1a) Achilles Tatius, *Introduction to Aratus' Phae-nomena*

Thales of Miletus and Pherecydes of Syros posit as the principle of all things water, which Pherecydes also calls **Chaos** [. . .].

Zas' Cosmogonic Marriage (D8–D10)

D8 (< B3) Proclus, *Commentary on Plato's* Timaeus

[. . .] Pherecydes of Syros said that when Zeus was about to begin his work of creation, he transformed himself into **Eros** [. . .].

D9 (B2) Grenfell Papyrus

[Col. 1] . . . **for him** [i.e. Zas] **they make buildings, many and great; and when they had finished them all, the objects, male servants, female servants, and everything else that is necessary, when then everything is ready, they perform the wedding. And when the third day of the wedding comes, then Zas makes a robe, great and beautiful, and on it he embroiders Earth, Ogenos** [i.e. Ocean], **and the houses of Ogenos** . . .

[Col. 2] [Zeus speaks to Chthoniê:] . . . **"since I want this marriage to be yours, it is you that I honor with this. But you, receive my greeting and be my wife." They**

σθι. ταῦτά φασεν ἀν[α]καλυπτήρια πρῶτον | γενέ-
σθαι, ἐκ τούτου δ[ὲ | ὁ νόμος ἐγένε[το] καὶ | θεοῖσι
καὶ ἀνθρ[ώπ]οι|[10]σιν. ἡ δέ μι[ν ἀμείβε|ται δεξα-
μ[ένη εὖ τὸ | φᾶ ρος . . .

10–12 suppl. Diels, cett. Grenfell-Hunt   3 ς (600) in marg.

D10 (< B2) Clem. Alex. *Strom.* 6.53.5

[. . .] ἡ ὑπόπτερος δρῦς καὶ τὸ ἐπ᾽ αὐτῇ πεποικιλμένον
φᾶρος [. . .] [cf. R28].

War Against Ophioneus (D11–D12)

D11 (< B4) Orig. *Cels.* 6.42

Φερεκύδην δὲ πολλῷ ἀρχαιότερον γενόμενον Ἡρακλείτου μυθοποιεῖν[1] στρατείαν στρατείᾳ παρατατто-
μένην, καὶ τῆς μὲν ἡγεμόνα Κρόνον διδόναι τῆς ἑτέ-
ρας δὲ Ὀφιονέα, προκλήσεις τε καὶ ἁμίλλας αὐτῶν
ἱστορεῖν,[2] συνθήκας τε αὐτοῖς γίνεσθαι, ἵν᾽ ὁπότεροι
αὐτῶν εἰς τὸν Ωγηνὸν ἐμπέσωσι, τούτους μὲν εἶναι
νενικημένους, τοὺς δ᾽ ἐξώσαντας καὶ νικήσαντας τούτους ἔχειν τὸν οὐρανόν.

[1] μυθοποιίαν ms., corr. Bouhéreau   [2] ἱστορεῖ ms., corr.
Bouhéreau

D12 (< B4) Tert. *Cor.* 7.4

Saturnum Pherecydes ante omnes refert coronatum [. . .].

176

say that these were the first *anakalypteria*[1] that were
performed, and from this time this custom has existed, for both gods and men. And she answers him,
receiving the robe from him . . .

[1] A nuptial ceremony in ancient Greece during which the
groom unveiled the bride and gave her gifts.

D10 (< B2) Isidore in Clement of Alexandria, *Stromata*

[. . .] the **winged oak** and the **embroidered robe** on it
[. . .].

War Against Ophioneus (D11–D12)

D11 (< B4) Celsus in Origen, *Against Celsus*

Pherecydes, who is much more ancient than Heraclitus,
invented the myth of one army set in order against another
army, gave the command of the one to Cronus and of the
other to Ophioneus, and recounted their challenges and
combats, and that they made an accord according to which
whichever ones of them fell into Ogenos would be defeated, while those who expelled them and defeated them
would possess the heavens.

D12 (< B4) Tertullian, *On the Soldier's Garland*

Pherecydes reports that Saturn [i.e. Cronus, Khronos] was
crowned before everyone [. . .].[1]

[1] This doubtless refers to the victory of Cronus over Ophioneus.

Cosmology (D13–D15)

D13 (< B5) Orig. *Cels.* 6.42

κείνης δὲ τῆς μοίρας ἔνερθέν ἐστιν ἡ ταρταρίη
μοῖρα· φυλάσσουσι δ' αὐτὴν θυγατέρες Βορέου Ἅρ-
πυιαί τε καὶ Θύελλα, ἔνθα Ζεὺς ἐκβάλλει θεῶν ὅταν
τις ἐξυβρίσῃ.

D14 (< B6) Porph. *Antr.* 31

[. . .] καὶ τοῦ Συρίου Φερεκύδου μυχοὺς καὶ βόθρους
καὶ ἄντρα καὶ θύρας καὶ πύλας λέγοντος [. . .] [cf.
R26].

D15 (< B7) Porph. *Gaur.* 2.2

[. . .] παρὰ δὲ τῷ Φερεκύδῃ τὴν ἐκροὴν [. . .] [cf. **R18**].

Other References to the Gods (D16–D18)

D16 Hdn. *Mon. Lex.*

a (< B9) 7.5 (911.23–34 Lentz)

[. . .] καὶ ἡ Ῥέα Ῥῆ κέκληται ὑπὸ τοῦ Συρίου [. . .].

b (< B1) 6.14–16 (911.7–9 Lentz)

καὶ γὰρ Δὶς καὶ Ζῆν καὶ Δῆν καὶ Ζὰς καὶ Ζῆς παρὰ
Φερεκύδει κατὰ κίνησιν ἰδίαν.

PHERECYDES

Cosmology (D13–D15)

D13 (< B5) Celsus in Origen, *Against Celsus*

Below that portion is the portion of Tartarus. The daughters of Boreas, the Harpies and Thyella [i.e. Storm], **guard it. It is to there that Zeus banishes any of the gods when he commits an outrage.**

D14 (< B6) Porphyry, *The Cave of the Nymphs*

[. . .] and Pherecydes of Syros, who speaks of **nooks,** of **hollows,** of **caves,** of **doors,** of **gates** [. . .].

D15 (< B7) Porphyry, *To Gaurus on the Animation of the Embryo*

[. . .] the **outflow** in Pherecydes [. . .].

Other References to the Gods (D16–D18)

D16 Herodian, *On Particular Usages*

a (< B9)

[. . .] Rhea is called **Rê** by the man from Syros [. . .].

b (< B1)

For one finds **Dis, Zên, Dên, Zas,** and **Zês** in Pherecydes, according to the appropriate declension.

179

D17 (B12) Diog. Laert. 1.119

ἔλεγέ τε ὅτι οἱ θεοὶ τὴν τράπεζαν θυωρὸν καλοῦσιν.

D18 (< B13a) Plut. *Fac. orb. lun.* 938B

εἰ μὴ νὴ Δία φήσομεν [. . .] τὴν σελήνην [. . .], τρέφειν τοὺς ἄνδρας ἀμβροσίαν ἀνιεῖσαν[1] αὐτοῖς ἐφημέριον, ὡς Φερεκύδης ὁ παλαιὸς οἴεται σιτεῖσθαι τοὺς[2] θεούς.

---

[1] ἀνεῖσαν mss., corr. Emperius   [2] αὐτοὺς mss., corr. Wyttenbach

A Reference to the Hyades (D19)

D19 (B13) Schol. in Arat. *Phaen.* 172, p. 369.27

Ἱππίας [cf. **D36**] δὲ καὶ Φερεκύδης ἑπτά.

D17 (B12) Diogenes Laertius

And he also said that the gods call the [scil. banquet] table a **table for offerings.**

D18 (< B13a) Plutarch, *On the Face in the Moon*

Unless we say [. . .] that the moon [. . .] nourishes the men [scil. who live on it] by sending up ambrosia to them every day, as the ancient Pherecydes thinks that the gods themselves are fed.

A Reference to the Hyades (D19)

D19 (B13) Scholia on Aratus' *Phaenomena*

Hippias [cf. **D35**] and Pherecydes say [scil. that the Hyades] are seven in number.

PHERECYDES [7 DK]

R

The Earliest References and Allusions (R1–R3)

R1 (< 36 B4) Ion Chius in Diog. Laert. 1.120

Ἴων δ᾽ ὁ Χῖος φησιν περὶ αὐτοῦ·

ὣς ὁ μὲν ἠνορέῃ τε κεκασμένος ἠδὲ καὶ αἰδοῖ
καὶ φθίμενος ψυχῇ τερπνὸν ἔχει βίοτον,
εἴπερ Πυθαγόρης ἐτύμως ὁ σοφὸς περὶ πάντων
ἀνθρώπων γνώμας εἶδε καὶ ἐξέμαθεν.

R2 (p. 88 Schibli) Plat. *Soph.* 242c–d

ὁ μὲν ὡς τρία τὰ ὄντα, πολεμεῖ δὲ ἀλλήλοις ἐνίοτε
αὐτῶν ἄττα πῃ, τοτὲ δὲ καὶ φίλα γιγνόμενα γάμους
τε καὶ τόκους καὶ τροφὰς τῶν ἐκγόνων παρέχεται.

---

[1] It is possible but not certain, that Plato is implicitly alluding to Pherecydes.

PHERECYDES

The Earliest References and Allusions (R1–R3)

R1 (< 36 B4) Ion of Chios in Diogenes Laertius

Ion of Chios says about him [i.e. Pherecydes[1]]:

> Thus adorned with prowess and reverence,
> > He has a pleasant life for his soul even though he
> > is dead,
> If indeed Pythagoras, truly wise beyond all [or: about
> all things],
> > Made acquaintance with men's thoughts and knew
> > them thoroughly.

[cf. **PYTH. a P29**].

[1] The pronoun could also refer to Pythagoras, whose name appears in an epigram that Diogenes Laertius has just cited.

R2 (≠ DK) Plato, *Sophist*

[. . .] the one[1] says that there are three beings, that at one time some of them wage war against each other, and that at another they become friends, get married, have children, and raise their offspring [cf. **D5, D8–D12**].

R3 (< A7) Arist. *Metaph.* N4 1091b8–10

[. . .] ἐπεὶ οἵ γε μεμιγμένοι αὐτῶν καὶ τῷ μὴ μυθικῶς πάντα λέγειν, οἷον Φερεκύδης καὶ ἕτεροί τινες, τὸ γεννῆσαν πρῶτον ἄριστον τιθέασι [. . .].

Pherecydes' Book (R4–R9)
The First Prose Author (R4–R7)

R4 (9 Schibli) Plin. *Nat. hist.* 7.205

[. . .] prosam orationem condere Pherecydes Syrius instituit Cyri regis aetate, historiam Cadmus Milesius [. . .].

R5 (< A2) *Suda*

a Φ.214

[. . . = **P6**] πρῶτον δὲ συγγραφὴν ἐξενεγκεῖν πεζῷ λόγῳ τινὲς ἱστοροῦσιν, ἑτέρων τοῦτο εἰς Κάδμον τὸν Μιλήσιον φερόντων [. . . = **R15**].

b Φ.216

Πορφύριος [. .] ἐκεῖνον μόνον ἡγεῖται ἀρχηγὸν συγγραφῆς.

R6 (13 Schibli) Strab. 1.2.6

εἶτα ἐκείνην [sc. τὴν ποιητικὴν κατασκεύην] μιμούμενοι λύσαντες τὸ μέτρον, τἆλλα δὲ φυλάξαντες τὰ ποιητικὰ συνέγραψαν οἱ περὶ Κάδμον καὶ Φερεκύδη καὶ Ἑκαταῖον.

R3 (A7) Aristotle, *Metaphysics*

[. . .] those among them [i.e. the ancient poets] whose position is mixed, also because they do not say everything in a mythic way posit as the best that which engendered first, like Pherecydes and certain others [. . .].

Pherecydes' Book (R4–R9)
The First Prose Author (R4–R7)

R4 (≠ DK) Pliny, *Natural History*

[. . .] Pherecydes of Syros founded the composition of discourse in prose under the reign of Cyrus [= 559/29], Cadmus of Miletus did the same for history [. . .].

R5 (< A2) *Suda*

a

Some people report that he was the first to publish a treatise in prose, while others attribute this to Cadmos of Miletus [. . .].

b

Porphyrius [. . .] thinks that he alone [i.e. and not Pherecydes of Athens] was the originator of the [scil. prose] treatise.

R6 (≠ DK) Strabo, *Geography*

Then Cadmus, Pherecydes, and Hecataeus wrote treatises that imitated this [i.e. poetic presentation]: they abandoned meter but preserved all the other poetic features.

185

R7 (< 38 Schibli) Flav. Jos. *Apion.* 1.14

[. . . = **P8**] ὀλίγα συγγράψαι.

In Ionic Dialect (R8)

R8 Apoll. Dysc. *Pronom.*

a (B13) p. 65.15 Schneider

καὶ Φερεκύδης ἐν τῇ θεολογίᾳ καὶ ἔτι [. . . cf. **ATOM. R3a**] χρῶνται τῇ ἐμεῦ καὶ ἔτι τῇ ἐμέο.

b (B11) p. 92.20–93.2 Schneider

αἱ πληθυντικαὶ κοινολεκτοῦνται κατ᾿ εὐθεῖαν πρός τε Ἰώνων καὶ Ἀττικῶν, ἡμεῖς, ὑμεῖς, σφεῖς, ἔστι ⟨δὲ⟩[1] πιστώσασθαι καὶ τὸ ἀδιαίρετον τῆς εὐθείας παρ᾿ Ἰωσιν ἐκ τῶν περὶ Δημόκριτον [**ATOM. R3b**], Φερεκύδην [. . .].

[1] ⟨δὲ⟩ Wilamowitz

The Survival of His Book (R9)

R9 (< A1) Diog. Laert. 1.119

σῴζεται δὲ τοῦ Συρίου τό τε βιβλίον ὃ συνέγραψεν, οὗ ἡ ἀρχή· [. . . = **D5**].

R7 (≠ DK) Flavius Josephus, *Against Apion*

[. . .] they [i.e. Pherecydes, Pythagoras, and Thales] wrote only very little.

In Ionic Dialect (R8)

R8 Apollonius Dyscolus, *On Pronouns*

a (B13)

Pherecydes in his *Theology,* as well as [i e. Democritus] [. . .] often use ***"emeu"*** and also ***"emeo"*** [i.e. both the contracted and the uncontracted form of "my"].

b (B11)

In the nominative, the plural forms *hêmeis, humeis, spheis* ("we," "you," "they") are used by both Ionian and Attic writers, but the uncontracted forms of the nominative are also attested in Ionic writers in the writings of Democritus [cf. **ATOM. R3b**], Pherecydes, [. . .].

The Survival of His Book (R9)

R9 (< A1) Diogenes Laertius

Of the one from Syros [scil. not Pherecydes of Athens] the book he wrote is extant;[1] its beginning is [. . .].

---

[1] This might refer to the time of Diogenes Laertius, or to that of his (unknown) source.

One of the Seven Sages (R10)

R10 (cf. A2a) Diog. Laert. 1.42

Ἕρμιππος δ' ἐν τῷ Περὶ τῶν σοφῶν ἑπτακαίδεκά φησιν [Frag. 6 Wehrli], ὧν τοὺς ἑπτὰ ἄλλους ἄλλως αἱρεῖσθαι· εἶναι δὲ [. . .] Φερεκύδην [. . .].

Pherecydes as a Pythagorean (R11–R18)
The Initiator of the Pythagorean Line of Descent
of Greek Philosophy (R11–R12)

R11 (58 Schibli) Arist. in Diog. Laert. 2.46 (= Frag. 65 Rose)

[. . .] ἐφιλονείκεε [. . .] Θάλητι δὲ Φερεκύδης [. . .].

R12 (46b Schibli) Clem. Alex. *Strom.* 1.62.4

διδάσκαλος δὲ αὐτοῦ οὐδεὶς ἀναγράφεται, ὥσπερ οὐδὲ Φερεκύδου τοῦ Συρίου, ᾧ Πυθαγόρας ἐμαθήτευσεν.

A Substitution (R13)

R13 (< A6) Porph. apud Eus. *PE* 10.3.7–9 (< Frag. 408 Smith, p. 480.30–46)

[7] ταῦτ' οὖν τοῦ Ἄνδρωνος περὶ Πυθαγόρου ἱστορηκότος πάντα ὑφείλετο Θεόπομπος· [. . .] νῦν δὲ τὴν κλοπὴν δήλην πεποίηκεν ἡ τοῦ ὀνόματος μετάθεσις·

One of the Seven Sages (R10)

R10 (cf. A2a) Diogenes Laertius

Hermippus in his book *On the Sages* says [scil. that the Sages were] seventeen, out of whom different people made different selections of seven; and that they were [. . .] Pherecydes [. . .].

Pherecydes as a Pythagorean (R11–R18)
The Initiator of the Pythagorean Line of Descent
of Greek Philosophy (R11–R12)

R11 (≠ DK) Aristotle, *On the Poets,* in Diogenes Laertius

[. . .] Pherecydes was the rival of Thales [. . .].

R12 (≠ DK) Clement of Alexandria, *Stromata*

No teacher is recorded for him [i.e. Thales], just as there is none for Pherecydes of Syros either, with whom Pythagoras studied [cf. **P9**].

A Substitution (R13)

R13 (< A6) Porphyry in Eusebius, *Evangelical Preparation*

[7] All these stories that Andron has told about Pythagoras, Theopompus has purloined [. . .]. But as it is, the change of name renders the theft obvious. For he uses the

τοῖς μὲν γὰρ πράγμασι κέχρηται τοῖς αὐτοῖς, ἕτερον
δ᾽ ὄνομα μετενήνοχε· Φερεκύδην γὰρ τὸν Σύριον πε-
ποίηκε ταῦτα προλέγοντα. [8] οὐ μόνον δὲ τούτῳ τῷ
ὀνόματι ἀποκρύπτει τὴν κλοπήν, ἀλλὰ καὶ τόπων
μεταθέσει. τό τε γὰρ περὶ τῆς προρρήσεως τοῦ σει-
σμοῦ ἐν Μεταπονίῳ ὑπ᾽ Ἄνδρωνος ῥηθὲν ἐν Σύρῳ[1]
εἰρῆσθαί φησιν ὁ Θεόπομπος τό τε περὶ τὸ πλοῖον
οὐκ ἀπὸ Μεγάρων τῆς Σικελίας, ἀπὸ δὲ Σάμου φησὶ
θεωρηθῆναι· καὶ τὴν Συβάρεως ἅλωσιν ἐπὶ τὴν Μεσσήνης μετέθηκεν. [9] ἵνα δέ τι δοκῇ λέγειν περιττόν,
καὶ τοῦ ξένου προστέθεικε τοὔνομα, Περίλαον αὐτὸν
καλεῖσθαι λέγων.

[1] Συρίῳ mss., corr. Müller

Doctrina Rapprochements (R14–R18)
Metempsychosis (R14–R16)

R14 (< A5) Cic. *Tusc.* 1.16.38

[. . .] sed quod literis exstet, Pherecydes Syrius primus[1]
dixit animos esse nominum sempiternos [. . . = **P3**]. hanc
opinionem discipulus eius Pythagoras maxime confirmavit
[. . .].

[1] primum mss., corr. Bentley

R15 (< A2) Suda Φ.214

[. . . = **R5**] καὶ πρῶτον τὸν περὶ τῆς μετεμψυχώσεως
λόγον εἰσηγήσασθαι.

same events but substituted one name for the other. For he has made Pherecydes of Syros the one who made this prediction [cf. **P10**]. [8] And it is not only by this name that he conceals his theft, but also by a change of location. For while Andron located the story about the prediction of an earthquake at Metapontum, Theopompus says that it was made in Syros; and also the incident concerning the ship was seen not from Megara in Sicily but from Samos; and he has substituted the capture of Messene for that of Sybaris. [9] And finally, in order to create the impression that he was saying something extraordinary, he has also added the name of the host, saying that he was called Perilaus.

Doctrinal Rapprochements (R14–R18)
Metempsychosis (R14–R15)

R14 (< A5) Cicero, *Tusculan Disputations*

[. . .] to judge from written records, Pherecydes of Syros was the first to say that the souls of humans are eternal [. . .]. His disciple Pythagoras strongly supported this view [cf. **PYTH. c D4–D5**].

R15 (< A2) *Suda*

[. . .] [Scil. Some report that] he was the first to introduce the idea of metempsychosis.

R16 (< A5) Appon 5.23 (ad *Cn.* 3:5)

[. . . = **THAL. R4**] Ferecides autem vocabulo animam
hominis prior omnibus immortalem auditoribus suis tra-
didisse docetur, et eam esse vitam corporis, et unum nobis
de caelo spiratum, alterum credidit terrenis seminibus
comparatum.

  [1] spiritum RMpc

The One (R17)

R17 (< A7a) Plot. 5.1.9.28–30

[. . .] ὥστε τῶν ἀρχαίων οἱ μάλιστα συντασσόμενοι
τοῖς[1] Πυθαγόρου καὶ τῶν μετ᾽ αὐτὸν καὶ Φερεκύδου δὲ
περὶ ταύτην μὲν ἔσχον τὴν φύσιν.

  [1] αὐτοῖς mss., corr. Creuzer

Seed (R18)

R18 (B7) Porph. *Gaur.* 2 (p. 34.26–35.3 Kalbfleisch)

[. . .] πολὺς ὁ Νουμήνιος καὶ οἱ τὰς Πυθαγόρου ὑπο-
νοίας ἐξηγούμενοι, καὶ τὸν παρὰ μὲν τῷ Πλάτωνι ποταμὸν Ἀμέλητα *Rep.* 621a], παρὰ δὲ τῷ Ἡσιόδῳ [cf.
COSM. T7] καὶ τοῖς Ὀρφικοῖς [Frag. 344 F Bernabé]
τὴν Στύγα, παρὰ δὲ τῷ Φερεκύδῃ τὴν ἐκροὴν ἐπὶ τοῦ
σπέρματος ἐκδεχόμενοι [. . .].

R16 (< A5) Apponius, *Commentary on the Song of Songs*

[. . .] They say that a certain Pherecydes, before all others, taught his students the doctrine that the soul of man is immortal and that it is the life of the body, and he believed on the one hand that it is breathed into us from heaven and on the other that it is supplied by earthly seeds [cf. **PHER. R29; THAL. R43**].

The One (R17)

R17 (< A7a) Plotinus, *Enneads*

[. . .] so that among the ancients, those who most align themselves with the doctrines of Pythagoras and his successors as well as with those of Pherecydes were concerned with this nature [i.e. the One] [. . .].

Seed (R18)

R18 (B7) Porphyry, *To Gaurus on the Animation of the Embryo*

[. . .] the great Numenius and the interpreters of Pythagoras' hidden thought [cf. **PYTHS. R69**] understand as seed the river Ameles in Plato, the Styx in Hesiod and the Orphics, and the **outflow** in Pherecydes [. . .] [cf. **D15**].

Other Allegories and Interpretations (R19–R26)
The Form of the Narrative (R19)

R19 (A12) Procl. *In Tim.* 1 ad 22b–c (vol. 1, p. 129.15–16 Diehl)

[. . .] ἡ Πλάτωνος παράδοσις οὐκ ἔστι τοιαύτη αἰνιγματώδης, οἵα ἡ Φερεκύδου [. . .].

The Principles and Elements (R20–R26)

R20 (cf. A9) Herm. *Irris.* 12

[. . . = **R30**] Ζῆνα μὲν τὸν αἰθέρα, Χθονίην δὲ τὴν γῆν, Κρόνον δὲ τὸν χρόνον· ὁ μὲν αἰθὴρ τὸ ποιοῦν, ἡ δὲ γῆ τὸ πάσχον, ὁ δὲ χρόνος ἐν ᾧ τὰ γινόμενα.

R21 (A10) Sext. Emp. *Pyr. Hyp.* 3.30

Φερεκύδης μὲν γὰρ ὁ Σύριος γῆν εἶπε τὴν πάντων εἶναι ἀρχήν [. . .]

R22 (> B1a) Ach. Tat. *Introd. Arat.* 3

[. . . = **D7**] τὸ ὕδωρ [. . .], ὃ δὴ καὶ χάος καλεῖ ὁ Φερεκύδης, ὡς εἰκός, τοῦτο ἐκλεξάμενος παρὰ τοῦ Ἡσιόδου οὕτω λέγοντος·

ἤτοι μὲν πρώτιστα χάος γένετο.

παρὰ γὰρ τὸ χεῖσθαι ὑπολαμβάνει τὸ ὕδωρ χάος ὠνόμασθαι.

Other Allegories and Interpretations (R19–R26)
The Form of the Narrative (R19)

R19 (A12) Proclus, *Commentary on Plato's* Timaeus

[. . .] Plato's teaching [scil. on the war of ancient Athens against Atlantis] is not enigmatic in the same way as Pherecydes' is [. . .].

The Principles and Elements (R20–R26)

R20 (cf. A9) Hermias, *Satire on the Pagan Philosophers*

[. . .] Zeus the aether, Chthoniê the earth, and Cronus time (*khronos*): the aether is the agent, the earth the patient, the time that in which the things that come about exist.

R21 (A10) Sextus Empiricus, *Outlines of Pyrrhonism*

Pherecydes of Syros said that the principle of all things is the earth [. . .].

R22 (> B1a) Achilles Tatius, *Introduction to Aratus'* Phaenomena

[. . .] water, which Pherecydes also calls **"Chaos,"** having probably derived this name from Hesiod, who says, "In truth, first of all Chaos came to be" [**COSM. T11**]. For he thinks that water was called "Chaos" from the fact that it pours out (*kheisthai*).

R23 (> A8) Dam. *Princ.* 124b (= Eudem. Frag. 117 Wehrli)

Φερεκύδης δὲ ὁ Σύριος Ζᾶντα μὲν εἶναι[1] ἀεὶ καὶ Χρόνον καὶ Χθονίαν τὰς τρεῖς πρώτας ἀρχάς, τὴν μίαν φημὶ πρὸ τῶν δυεῖν καὶ τὰς δύο μετὰ τὴν μίαν, τὸν δὲ Χρόνον ποιῆσαι ἐκ τοῦ γόνου ἑαυτοῦ πῦρ καὶ πνεῦμα καὶ ὕδωρ, τὴν τριπλῆν, οἶμαι, φύσιν τοῦ νοητοῦ, ἐξ ὧν ἐν πέντε μυχοῖς διῃρημένων πολλὴν ἄλλην γενεὰν συστῆναι θεῶν τὴν **πεντέμυχον** καλουμένην, ταὐτὸν δὲ ἴσως εἰπεῖν, πεντέκοσμον.

[1] μένεναι mss., corr. Kopp

R24 (> B3) Procl. *In Tim.* 3 ad 32c (vol. 2, p. 54.28–55.2 Diehl)

καὶ ἴσως πρὸς τοῦτο ἀποβλέπων καὶ ὁ Φερεκύδης ἔλεγεν εἰς Ἔρωτα μεταβεβλῆσθαι τὸν Δία μέλλοντα δημιουργεῖν, ὅτι δὴ τὸν κόσμον ἐκ τῶν ἐναντίων συνιστὰς εἰς ὁμολογίαν καὶ φιλίαν ἤγαγε καὶ ταυτότητα πᾶσιν ἐνέσπειρε καὶ ἕνωσιν τὴν δι᾽ ὅλων διήκουσαν.

R25 (A9) Lyd. *Mens.* 4.3

ἥλιος αὐτὸς κατὰ Φερεκύδην.

R26 (B6) Porph. *Antr.* 31

[. . .] καὶ τοῦ Συρίου Φερεκύδου **μυχοὺς** καὶ **βόθρους**

R23 (> A8) Eudemus in Damascius, *On the Principles*

Pherecydes of Syros [scil. says] on the one hand that Zas always exists as well as Chronos and Chthonie, the three first principles—the first of these, I mean, before the other two, and these two after the first one—and on the other hand that Chronos made out of his seed fire, breath, and water—the triple nature, I suppose, of the intelligible—out of which, when they had been distributed in five nooks, arose another numerous generation of gods, called **"the five-nook"** one [cf. **D6**]—what is surely the same thing as "the five-cosmos" one.

R24 (> B3) Proclus, *Commentary on Plato's* Timaeus

And it is perhaps with a view toward this [scil. that love is the cause of the harmony in these products] that Pherecydes of Syros said that when Zeus was about to begin his work of creation, he transformed himself into **Eros,** because, since he was putting the world together out of the contraries, he led them to agreement and friendship and sowed in all things identity and the unity that pervades the universe [cf. **D8**].

R25 (A9) John Lydus, *On the Months*

He [i.e. Zeus] is the sun according to Pherecydes.

R26 (B6) Porphyry, *On the Cave of the Nymphs*

[. . .] and Pherecydes of Syros, who speaks of **nooks,** of

καὶ ἄντρα καὶ θύρας καὶ πύλας λέγοντος καὶ διὰ τούτων αἰνιττομένου τὰς τῶν ψυχῶν γενέσεις καὶ ἀπογενέσεις.[1]

[1] *καὶ ἀπογενέσεις* V: om. M

Pherecydes Among the Christians (R27–R30)
Does Pherecydes Derive His Inspiration from
Homer or the Bible? (R27)

R27 Orig. *Cels.*

a (< B5) 6.42

ταῦτα δὲ τὰ Ὁμήρου ἔπη οὕτω νοήσαντα[1] *τὸν Φερεκύδην φησὶν εἰρηκέναι τό· "κείνης δὲ τῆς μοίρας [. . .] ἐξυβρίσῃ"* [**D**13].

[1] *νοηθέντα* m., corr. Guiet

b (79 Schibli) 6.43

[. . .] μὴ κατανοήσας ὅτι τὰ πολλῷ οὐ μόνον Ἡρακλείτου καὶ Φερεκύδου ἀρχαιότερα ἀλλὰ καὶ Ὁμήρου Μωϋσέως γράμματα εἰσήγαγε τὸν περὶ τοῦ πονηροῦ τούτου καὶ ἐκπεσόντος τῶν οὐρανίων λόγον. ὁ γὰρ ὄφις, παρ' ὃν ὁ παρὰ τῷ Φερεκύδῃ γέγονεν Ὀφιονεὺς [. . .] τοιαῦτά τινα αἰνίσσεται [. . .].

hollows, of **caves,** of **doors,** of **gates,** and means by these terms allegorically the births and departures of the souls [cf. **D14**].

Pherecydes Among the Christians (R27–R30)
Does Pherecydes Derive His Inspiration from
Homer or the Bible? (R27)

R27 Origen, *Against Celsus*

a (< B5)

He [i.e. Celsus] says that it is because he understood these verses of Homer [*Iliad* 1.590–91 and 15.18–24][1] in this way that he [i.e. Pherecydes] said, **"Below that portion [. . .] he commits an outrage"** [= **D13**].

[1] The gods, including Hephaestus, who have come to the help of Hera (whom Zeus had suspended in the air), are expelled from Olympus.

b (≠ DK)

[. . .] he [i.e. Celsus] does not understand that Moses' writings, which are far more ancient not only than Heraclitus' and Pherecydes' but also than Homer's, introduced the story about this evil being [i.e. Satan], that he fell from the heavens. For the snake (*ophis*), from which Ophioneus is derived in Pherecydes, [. . .] allegorically signifies things of this sort [. . .] [cf. **D11**].

*Other Testimonia on Pherecydes' Dependence
upon the Scriptures (R28–R29)*

R28 (< B2) Clem. Alex. *Strom.* 6.53.5

[. . .] καὶ γάρ μοι δοκεῖ[1] τοὺς προσποιουμένους φιλο-
σοφεῖν ἵνα μάθωσι τί ἐστιν ἡ ὑπόπτερος δρῦς καὶ τὸ
ἐπ᾽ αὐτῇ πεποικιλμένον φᾶρος, πάντα ὅσα Φερεκύδης
ἀλληγορήσας ἐθεολόγησεν, λαβὼν[2] ἀπὸ τῆς τοῦ Χὰμ
προφητείας τὴν ὑπόθεσιν.

[1] δοκεῖ <διδάσκειν> vel <ἐλέγχειν> Früchtel   [2] λαβεῖν
Heyse

R29 (< A5) Appon. 5.22 (ad *Cn.* 3:5)

in priore enim 'filiarum adiuratione,' in 'caprearum et
cervorum' personas thalesianae et ferecidensis philosophiae intellegi diximus [. . .].

Hermias' Fatigue (R30)

R30 (cf. A9) Herm. *Irris.* 12

νευροκοποῦσι[1] γάρ μου τὴν ψυχὴν ἀρχαιότεροι τούτων γέροντες, Φερεκύδης μὲν ἀρχὰς εἶναι λέγων Ζῆνα
καὶ Χθονίην καὶ Κρόνον [. . . = **R20**].

[1] νευροκοπο οὖσι mss., corr. Hanson: νευροσπαστοῦσι
Usener

Other Testimonia on Pherecydes' Dependence upon the Scriptures (R28–R29)

R28 (< B2) Isidore in Clement of Alexandria, *Stromata*

[. . .] it seems to me that the pretenders are philosophizing in order to learn what are the **winged oak** and the **embroidered robe** on it [= **D10**], everything that Pherecydes has said allegorically in a theological form, taking his starting point from the prophecy of Cham [cf. Genesis 9:20–27].

R29 (< A5) Apponius, *Commentary on the Song of Songs*

For we said about the earlier 'adjuration of the daughters' that 'the roes and stags' are to be understood as the representatives of the philosophy of Thales and Pherecydes[1] [cf. **PHER. R16; THAL. R43**].

[1] The reference seems to be to his commentary (4:1) on *Cn.* 2.7 (where in fact he does not name Thales or Pherecydes, but the Platonists and the Stoics).

Hermias' Fatigue (R30)

R30 (cf. A9) Hermias, *Satire on the Pagan Philosophers*

Ancient philosophers earlier than those [scil. probably: Plato and Aristotle] exhaust my spirit—Pherecydes, when he says that the principles are Zeus, Chthoniê, and Cronus [. . .].

*An Apocryphal Correspondence between
Pherecydes and Thales (R31)*

R31 Diog. Laert.

a (Hercher 740) .43–44

Θαλῆς Φερεκύδει—πυνθάνομαί σε πρῶτον Ἰώνων
μέλλειν λόγους ἀμφὶ τῶν θείων χρημάτων ἐς τοὺς
Ἕλληνας φαίνειν. καὶ τάχα μὲν ἡ γνώμη τοι δικαίη
ἐς τὸ ξυνὸν καταθέσθαι γραφήν, μᾶλλον ἢ ἐφ᾽ ὁποιοι-
σοῦν ἐπιτρέπειν χρῆμα ἐς οὐδὲν ὄφελος. εἰ δή τοι
ἥδιον, ἐθέλω γενέσθαι λεσχηνώτης περὶ ὁτέων γρά-
φεις· καὶ ἢν κελεύῃς, παρὰ σὲ ἀφίξομαι ἐς Σῦρον.
[. . .] ἥξει γὰρ καὶ ὁ Σόλων, ἢν ἐπιτρέπῃς. [44] σὺ
μέντοι χωροφιλέων ὀλίγα φοιτέεις ἐς Ἰωνίην, οὐδέ σε
ποθὴ ἴσχει ἀνδρῶν ξείνων· ἀλλά, ὡς ἔλπομαι, ἑνὶ
μούνῳ χρῆμα πρόσκεαι τῇ γραφῇ. ἡμέες δὲ οἱ μηδὲν γράφοντες περιχωρέομεν τήν τε Ἑλλάδα καὶ
Ἀσίην.

b (test. 238 Wehrle) 1.122

Φερεκύδης Θαλῆ—εὖ θνήσκοις ὅταν τοι τὸ χρεὼν
ἥκῃ. νοῦσός με καταλελάβηκε δεδεγμένον τὰ παρὰ
σέο γράμματα. φθειρῶν ἔβρυον[1] πᾶς καί με εἶχεν
ἠπίαλος. ἐπέσκηψα δ᾽ ὦν τοῖσιν οἰκιήτῃσιν, ἐπήν με
καταθάψωσιν ἐς σὲ τὴν γραφὴν ἐνέγκαι. σὺ δὲ ἢν

---

[1] ἔβρυον Frobenius: ἔθυον mss.

PHERECYDES

An Apocryphal Correspondence between
Pherecydes and Thales (R31)

R31 (≠ DK) Diogenes Laertius

a

[Thales to Pherecydes:] I hear that you are going to be the first Ionian to set forth discourses on divine matters for the Greeks. And perhaps your decision is wise, to make your text public instead of entrusting it to any individuals, something that has no advantage. If you wish, I am willing to become your interlocutor for whatever you write; and if you ask me, I will come to you in Syros. [. . .] Solon will come too, if you permit. [44] You are attached to your country and so you come only rarely to Ionia, and the desire to meet foreigners does not possess you; but, as I suppose, you dedicate yourself to only one activity, writing—whereas we who write nothing travel throughout Greece and Asia.

b

[Pherecydes to Thales:] May you die well when your time comes. An illness has befallen me since I received your letter. I am completely full of lice and an ague has taken hold of me. So I have ordered my servants to carry my text to you after they have buried me. If you, together with the

203

δοκιμώσῃς σὺν τοῖς ἄλλοις σοφοῖς, οὕτω μιν φῆνον·
ἢν δὲ οὐ δοκιμώσητε, μὴ φήνῃς. ἐμοὶ μὲν γὰρ οὔκω
ἥνδανεν. ἔστι δὲ οὐκ ἀτρεκείη πρηγμάτων, οὐδ᾽ ὑπί-
σχνέομαί <κ>ου τὠληθὲς² εἰδέναι, ἄσσα δ᾽ ἂν ἐπι-
λέγω³ θεολογέων· τὰ ἄλλα χρὴ νοεῖν· ἅπαντα γὰρ
αἰνίσσομαι. [. . .]

---

² <κ>ου τὠληθὲς Diels post Reiske : οὕτω ληθὲς B: οὐ τω-
ληθὲς P¹ (ut vid.: οὕτω ἀληθὲς Q): οὐ τ᾽ ἀληθὲς P⁴   ³ ἐπι-
λέγω Menagius: ἐπιλέγῃ BP: ἐπιλέγῃ Dorandi

other sages, approve of it, publish it as it is; if you do not approve, do not publish it. As for myself, I am not yet satisfied with it. There is a lack of precision about the subject matter nor do I promise in any case that I know the truth, but only what I say when I speak about the gods. All other things one has to think about, for I hint at them all allegorically [. . .].

5. THALES [THAL.]

Thales' activity is situated at Miletus between the second half of the seventh century and the first decades of the sixth century BC. He is included in the canonical list of the seven "Sages," which goes back to an early date (**P1b,** cf. **R2–R4**). Histories of philosophy often present him as "the first philosopher," largely because of the way in which Aristotle introduces him in the *Metaphysics,* as the first to have practiced a philosophy of "nature" (**R9**). But the most ancient testimonia, notably those of Aristophanes and Herodotus rather suggest a multifaceted figure engaged above all in politics and (especially hydraulic) engineering. It is most likely that he left no writings behind, as is suggested by the fact that already Aristotle seems to have no direct knowledge of his ideas. A large number of mathematical and scientific discoveries are attributed to him by later authors, but it is usually difficult or impossible to say whether, and if so to what extent, they really do go back to him; in any case, we have put all these reports into the section on Thales' reception (**R13–R31**). In general, the distinction, maintained here as in the other chapters, between doctrine and reception is more hypothetical in the case of Thales than in most other ones.

BIBLIOGRAPHY

Edition

G. Wöhrle, ed. *The Milesians: Thales.* Co.l. Traditio Prae-
    socratica vol. 1 (Berlin, 2009), revised and enlarged
    English translation, 2014.

History of the Reception

H. Blumenberg. *The Laughter of the Thracian Woman: A
    Protohistory of Theory* (London, 2015).
A. Schwab. *Thales von Milet in der frühen christlichen
    Literatur* (Berlin-Boston, 2012).

OUTLINE OF THE CHAPTER

P

THALES [11 DK]

P

Chronology (P1)

P1 (< A1) Dio͡g Laert.

a 1.37–38

φησὶ δ᾽ Ἀπολ͜όδωρος ἐν τοῖς Χρονικοῖς [*FGrHist* 244
F28] γεγενῆσθαι αὐτὸν κατὰ τὸ πρῶτον ἔτος τῆς τρι-
ακοστῆς πέμ͜της[1] Ὀλυμπιάδος. ἐτελεύτησε δ᾽ ἐτῶν
ἑβδομήκοντα ὀκτώ, ἤ, ὡς Σωσικράτης φησίν [Frag. 1
Giannattasio ͜ ndria], ἐνενήκοντα· τελευτῆσαι γὰρ ἐπὶ
τῆς πεντηκοστῆς ὀγδόης Ὀλυμπιάδος, γεγονότα κατὰ
Κροῖσον [. .].

    [1] πέμπτης] ἐνάτης prop. Diels

b 1.22

καὶ πρῶτος ͜σοφὸς ὠνομάσθη ἄρχοντος Ἀθήνησι Δα-
μασίου, καθ᾽ ὃν καὶ οἱ ἑπτὰ σοφοὶ ἐκλήθησαν, ὥς
φησι Δημήτριος ὁ Φαληρεὺς ἐν τῇ τῶν Ἀρχόντων
ἀναγραφῇ ͜Frag. 149 Wehrli].

THALES

P

Chronology (P1)

P1 (< A1) Diogenes Laertius

a

Apollodorus in his *Chronicles* says that he was born in the first year of the 35th Olympiad [= 640/39].[1] He died at the age of seventy-eight; or, as Sosicrates says, at ninety; for he died during the 58th Olympiad [= 548/44], having lived at the time of Croesus [. . .].[2]

  [1] Diels suggested correcting "35th" to "39th" [= 624/23].
  [2] A competing ancient chronology (A2, A8 DK) dated Thales to the mid-eighth century BC.

b

And he was first called a "sage" when Damasius was archon in Athens [= 582/81]; it was during this time that the Seven Sages were named, as Demetrius of Phalerum says in his *Catalog of the Archons* [cf. **R2–R4**].

Origins and Family (P2)

P2 (< A1) Diog. Laert. 1.22

ἦν τοίνυν ὁ Θαλῆς, ὡς μὲν Ἡρόδοτος [cf. 1.170] καὶ Δοῦρις [FGrHist 76 F74] καὶ Δημόκριτός [cf. **ATOM. P23–P26**] φασι, πατρὸς μὲν Ἐξαμύου, μητρὸς δὲ Κλεοβουλίνης, ἐκ τῶν Θηλιδῶν,[1] οἵ εἰσι Φοίνικες, εὐγενέστατοι τῶν ἀπὸ Κάδμου καὶ Ἀγήνορος. [. . .] ἐπολιτογραφήθη δὲ ἐν Μιλήτῳ, ὅτε ἦλθε σὺν Νείλεω[2] ἐκπεσόντι Φοινίκης· ὡς δ' οἱ πλείους φασίν, ἰθαγενὴς Μιλήσιος ἦν καὶ γένους λαμπροῦ.

[1] Νηλειδῶν Bywater   [2] varia mss., corr. Diels

Alleged Education in Egypt (P3–P5)

P3 (< A1) Diog. Laert. 1.27

οὐδεὶς δὲ αὐτοῦ καθηγήσατο, πλὴν ὅτι εἰς Αἴγυπτον ἐλθὼν τοῖς ἱερεῦσι συνδιέτριψεν.

P4 (A11) Aët. 1.3.1 (Ps.-Plut.) [περὶ ἀρχῶν τί εἰσιν]

φιλοσοφήσας ἐν Αἰγύπτῳ ἦλθεν εἰς Μίλητον πρεσβύτερος.

P5 (A11) Iambl. VP 12

[. . .] προτρέψατο εἰς Αἴγυπτον διαπλεῦσαι καὶ τοῖς ἐν Μέμφιδι καὶ Διοσπόλει μάλιστα συμβαλεῖν ἱερεῦσι·

Origins and Family (P2)

P2 (< A1) Diogenes Laertius

Thales, as Herodotus, Duris, and Democritus [cf. **R1**] report, had as father Examuas and as mother Cleobuline, of the family of the Thelides, who are Phoenicians, the most noble of the descendants of Cadmus and Agenor. [. . .] He became a citizen of Miletus when he went there with Neileus, who had been exiled from Phoenicia. But according to what most authors report, he was of genuine Milesian lineage and belonged to an illustrious family.

Alleged Education in Egypt (P3–P5)

P3 (< A1) Diogenes Laertius

No one showed him the way, except that he went to Egypt and spent time with the priests.

P4 (A11) Aëtius

After he had practiced philosophy in Egypt, he came to Miletus as an old man.

P5 (A11) Iamblichus, *Life of Pythagoras*

[. . .] he exhorted him [i.e. Pythagoras] to sail to Egypt and to spend time above all with the priests of Memphis and

παρὰ γὰρ ἐκείνωι καὶ ἑαυτὸν ἐφωδιάσθαι ταῦτα, δι᾽
ἃ σοφὸς παρὰ τοῖς πολλοῖς νομίζεται.

Disciple of Pherecydes, Like Pythagoras?

See **PYTH. P13**

The Engineer (P6)

P6 (> A6) Hdt. 1.75

ὡς δὲ ἀπίκετο ἐπὶ τὸν Ἅλυν ποταμὸν ὁ Κροῖσος, τὸ
ἐνθεῦτεν, ὡς μὲν ἐγὼ λέγω, κατὰ τὰς ἐούσας γεφύρας
διεβίβασε τὸν στρατόν, ὡς δὲ ὁ πολλὸς λόγος Ἑλλήνων, Θαλῆς οἱ ὁ Μιλήσιος διεβίβασε. ἀπορέοντος
γὰρ Κροίσου ὅκως οἱ διαβήσεται τὸν ποταμὸν ὁ
στρατός (οὐ γὰρ δὴ εἶναι κω τοῦτον τὸν χρόνον τὰς
γεφύρας ταύτας), λέγεται παρεόντα τὸν Θαλῆν ἐν τῷ
στρατοπέδῳ ποιῆσαι αὐτῷ τὸν ποταμὸν ἐξ ἀριστερῆς
χειρὸς ῥέοντα τοῦ στρατοῦ καὶ ἐκ δεξιῆς ῥέειν, ποιῆσαι δὲ ὧδε. ἄνωθεν τοῦ στρατοπέδου ἀρξάμενον διώρυχα βαθέαν ὀρύσσειν ἄγοντα μηνοειδέα, ὅκως ἂν
τὸ στρατόπεδον ἱδρυμένον κατὰ νώτου λάβοι, ταύτῃ
κατὰ τὴν διώρυχα ἐκτραπόμενος ἐκ τῶν ἀρχαίων ῥε-
έθρων, καὶ αὖτις, παραμειβόμενος τὸ στρατόπεδον, ἐς
τὰ ἀρχαῖα ἐσβάλλοι, ὥστε, ἐπείτε καὶ ἐσχίσθη τάχιστα ὁ ποταμός, ἀμφοτέρῃ διαβατὸς ἐγένετο.

214

of Diospolis [i.e. Thebes]. For it was from them that he himself had obtained what made most people regard him as a sage.

See also **PHER. P7**

Disciple of Pherecydes, Like Pythagoras?

See **PYTH. P13**

The Engineer (P6)

P6 (> A6) Herodotus, *Histories*

When Croesus arrived at the river Halys, he got his army across it, as I say for my part, on bridges that existed at the time; but according to a report widespread among the Greeks, it was Thales of Miletus who got them across for him. For when Croesus could not figure out how to get his army across the river (for they say that these bridges did not yet exist at that time), they say that Thales, who was present in the camp, made the river, which was flowing on the left side of the army, flow on its right side too. And he did this in the following way: he dug a deep canal in the shape of a crescent beginning above the camp so that the water, diverted in this way along the canal from its original course, would flow around to the rear and then, once it had passed the camp, would flow into its original bed. So that as soon as the river had been split into two it became fordable on both sides.

The Political Advisor (P7–P8)

P7 (A4) Hdt. 1.170

χρηστὴ δὲ καὶ τρὶν ἢ διαφθαρῆναι Ἰωνίην Θαλέω
ἀνδρὸς Μιλησίω ἐγένετο, τὰ ἀνέκαθεν γένος ἐόντος
Φοίνικος, ὃς ἐκέλευε ἐν βουλευτήριον Ἴωνας ἐκτῆ-
σθαι, τὸ δὲ εἶαι ἐν Τέῳ (Τέων γὰρ μέσον εἶναι
Ἰωνίης), τὰς δὲ ἄλλας πόλιας οἰκεομένας μηδὲν ἧσ-
σον νομίζεσθαι κατά περ εἰ δῆμοι εἶεν.

P8 (< A1) Diog. Laert. 1.25

δοκεῖ δὲ καὶ ἐν τοῖς πολιτικοῖς ἄριστα βεβουλεῦσθαι.
Κροίσου γοῦν πέμψαντος πρὸς Μιλησίους ἐπὶ συμ-
μαχίᾳ ἐκώλυσεν· ὅπερ Κύρου κρατήσαντος ἔσωσε
τὴν πόλιν [. . . = **P11**].

Prediction of a Solar Eclipse (P9–P10)

P9 (A5) Hdt. 1.74

διαφέρουσι δέ σφι ἐπὶ ἴσης τὸν πόλεμον τῷ ἕκτῳ ἔτει
συμβολῆς γενομένης συνήνεικε ὥστε, τῆς μάχης
συνεστεώσης, τὴν ἡμέρην ἐξαπίνης νύκτα γενέσθαι.
τὴν δὲ μεταλλαγὴν ταύτην τῆς ἡμέρης Θαλῆς ὁ Μιλήσιος τοῖσι Ἴωσι προηγόρευσε ἔσεσθαι, οὖρον προ-
θέμενος ἐνιαυτὸν τοῦτον ἐν τῷ δὴ καὶ ἐγένετο ἡ μετα-
βολή.

---

[1] This solar eclipse occurred on May 28, 585 BC. It is uncertain whether Thales possessed the means to predict it.

THALES

The Political Advisor (P7–P8)

P7 (A4) Herodotus, *Histories*

Useful too [scil. like that of Bias of Priene], before the destruction of Ionia, was that [i.e. advice] of Thales of Miletus (who was Phoenician by descent). He urged that the Ionians establish a single council, which should be located in Teos (for Teos is in the middle of Ionia), and that the other inhabited cities should be considered as being nothing less than demes.

P8 (< A1) Diogenes Laertius

And he seems to have given excellent advice in political matters too. Indeed, when Croesus sent an embassy to the Milesians to propose an alliance, he prevented it; and this saved the city after Cyrus' victory.[1]

[1] Cyrus conquered Croesus and Lydia in the middle of the sixth century BC.

Prediction of a Solar Eclipse (P9–P10)

P9 (A5) Herodotus, *Histories*

After they [i.e. Alyattes and Cyaxares] had been waging war inconclusively, it came to pass at an encounter in the sixth year that just when they had engaged a battle, the day was suddenly transformed into night. Thales of Miletus had predicted to the Ionians that this transformation of the day would take place, and he had determined beforehand as the exact time the very year in which the change actually took place.[1]

217

P10 (A5) Clem. Alex. *Strom.* 1.65

Θαλῆν δὲ Εὔδημος ἐν ταῖς Ἀστρολογικαῖς ἱστορίαις
[Frag. 143 Wehrli] τὴν γενομένην ἔκλειψιν τοῦ ἡλίου
προειπεῖν φησι, καθ᾽ οὓς χρόνους συνῆψαν μάχην
πρὸς ἀλλήλους Μῆδοί τε καὶ Λυδοὶ βασιλεύοντος Κυ-
αξάρους μὲν τοῦ Ἀστυάγους πατρὸς Μήδων, Ἀλυάτ-
του δὲ τοῦ Κροίσου Λυδῶν [. . .] εἰσὶ δὲ οἱ χρόνοι ἀμφὶ
τὴν ν΄ Ὀλυμπιάδα.

Married? (P11)

P11 (< A1) Diog. Laert. 1.25–26

[. . . = **P8**] καὶ αὐτὸς[1] δέ φησιν, ὡς Ἡρακλείδης ἱστορεῖ [Frag. 45 Wehrli], μονήρη αὐτὸν γεγονέναι καὶ ἰδι-
αστήν. ἔνιοι δὲ καὶ γῆμαι αὐτὸν καὶ Κύβισθον υἱὸν
σχεῖν· οἱ δὲ ἄγαμον μεῖναι, τῆς δὲ ἀδελφῆς τὸν υἱὸν
θέσθαι [. . . = **P17a**].

   [1] καὶ αὐτὸς Κλύτος Menagius

Attitude to Life (P12–P15)
Indifference to Human Affairs (P12–P13)

P12 (A9) Plat. *Theaet.* 174a

[ΣΩ.] ὥσπερ καὶ Θαλῆν ἀστρονομοῦντα [. . .] καὶ ἄνω
βλέποντα, πεσόντα εἰς φρέαρ, Θρᾷττά τις ἐμμελὴς

218

P10 (A5) Clement of Alexandria, *Stromata*

Eudemus says in his *History of Astronomy* that Thales had predicted the solar eclipse which took place at the time when the Medes and the Lydians—Cyaxares, father of Astyages, was reigning over the Medes, and Alyattes, son of Croesus, over the Lydians—were joining battle with one another [. . .] This happened around the 50th Olympiad [= 580/76].

See also **R15–R18**

Married? (P11)

P11 (< A1) Diogenes Laertius

And yet he himself says, as Heraclides [scl. of Pontus] reports, that he lived in solitude and as a private person. Some say that he married and had a son named Cybisthus, others that he remained a bachelor but adopted his sister's son [. . .].

Attitude to Life (P12–P15)
Indifference to Human Affairs (P12–P13)

P12 (A9) Plato, *Theaetetus*

It is said [. . .] that Thales, while doing astronomy and looking upward, fell into a well, and that a witty and charming

καὶ χαρίεσσα θεραπαινὶς ἀποσκῶψαι λέγεται ὡς τὰ
μὲν ἐν οὐρανῷ προθυμοῖτο εἰδέναι, τὰ δ᾽ ἔμπροσθεν
αὐτοῦ καὶ παρὰ τόδας λανθάνοι αὐτόν.

P13 (59 A30) Arist. *EN* 6.7 1141b2–8

διὸ [. . . cf. **ANAXAG. P29**] καὶ Θαλῆν καὶ τοὺς τοιού-
τους σοφοὺς μὲν φρονίμους δ᾽ οὔ φασιν εἶναι, ὅταν
ἴδωσιν ἀγνοοῦντας τὰ συμφέροντα ἑαυτοῖς, καὶ
περιττὰ μὲν καὶ θαυμαστὰ καὶ χαλεπὰ καὶ δαιμόνια
εἰδέναι αὐτούς φασιν, ἄχρηστα δ᾽, ὅτι οὐ τὰ ἀνθρώ-
πινα ἀγαθὰ ζητοῦσιν.

Practicality (P14–P15)

P14 (Th 22 Wöhrle) Plat. *Rep.* 10 600a

[ΣΩ.] ἀλλ᾽ οἷα δὴ εἰς τὰ ἔργα σοφοῦ ἀνδρὸς πολλαὶ
ἐπίνοιαι καὶ εὐμήχανοι εἰς τέχνας ἤ τινας ἄλλας πράξεις λέγονται, ὥσπερ αὖ Θάλεώ τε πέρι τοῦ Μιλησίου
καὶ Ἀναχάρσιος τοῦ Σκύθου;

P15 (< A10) Arist. *Pol.* 1.11 1259a9–18

ὀνειδιζόντων γὰρ αὐτῷ διὰ τὴν πενίαν ὡς ἀνωφελοῦς
τῆς φιλοσοφίας οὔσης, κατανοήσαντά φασιν αὐτὸν

Thracian handmaiden made fun of him, saying that he was
eager to know what was in the sky but did not see what
was in front of him and at his feet.[1]

> [1] This anecdote, which may derive from Aesop (Fab. 40 Haus-
> rath, 65 Chambry) and was destined to enjoy an enormous
> success, is repeated and varied in a large number of texts (includ-
> ing e.g. **ANAXIMEN. R11a;** Diogenes Laertius 1.34; (Ps.?)-
> Hippolytus, *Refutation of All Heresies* 1.1; etc.

P13 (59 A30) Aristotle, *Nicomachean Ethics*

That [scil. because wisdom is knowing what is most honorable by nature] is why people say that [. . .] Thales and
men like that are wise but not prudent, when they see
that they do not know what is advantageous for themselves; and they say that what they know is extraordinary
and marvelous and difficult and divine—but useless, since
they do not try to find what is good for humans.

Practicality (P14–P15)

P14 (≠ DK) Plato, *Republic*

[Socrates:] Or, as would be appropriate for the accom-
plishments of a wise man, are many ingenious inventions
for the arts or any other practical activities reported [scil.
for Homer] as they are for Thales of Miletus and Anachar-
sis the Scythian?

P15 (< A10) Aristotle, *Politics*

As people reproached him on account of his poverty, saying that philosophy is useless, he is reported to have ascer-

ἐλαιῶν φορὰν ἐσομένην ἐκ τῆς ἀστρολογίας, ἔτι χει-
μῶνος ὄντος εὐπορήσαντα χρημάτων ὀλίγων ἀρρα-
βῶνας διαδοῦναι τῶν ἐλαιουργίων τῶν τ᾽ ἐν Μιλήτῳ
καὶ Χίῳ πάντων, ὀλίγου μισθωσάμενον ἅτ᾽ οὐθενὸς
ἐπιβάλλοντος· ἐπειδὴ δ᾽ ὁ καιρὸς ἧκε, πολλῶν ζη-
τουμένων ἅμα καὶ ἐξαίφνης, ἐκμισθοῦντα ὃν τρόπον
ἠβούλετο, πολλὰ χρήματα συλλέξαντα ἐπιδεῖξαι ὅτι
ῥᾴδιόν ἐστι πλουτεῖν τοῖς φιλοσόφοις, ἂν βούλωνται,
ἀλλ᾽ οὐ τοῦτ᾽ ἐστὶ περὶ ὃ σπουδάζουσιν.

Apothegms and Other Sayings (P16–P18)

P16 (< A1) Diog. Laert. 1.35

τῶν τε ἀδομένων αὐτοῦ τάδε εἶναι·

οὔ τι τὰ πολλὰ ἔπη φρονίμην ἀπεφήνατο δόξαν·
ἕν τι μάτευε σοφόν,
ἕν τι κεδνὸν αἱροῦ·
λύσεις[1] γὰρ ἀνδρῶν κωτίλων
γλώσσας ἀπεραντολόγους. [SH 521]

[1] δήσεις Diels

P17 (< A1) Diog. Laert.

a 1.26

[. . . = **P11**] ὅτε καὶ ἐρωτηθέντα διὰ τί οὐ τεκνοποιεῖ,
διὰ φιλοτεκνίαν εἰπεῖν. καὶ λέγουσιν ὅτι τῆς μητρὸς

tained on the basis of astronomy, while the winter was still in its course, that there was going to be a large crop of olives; with the little money he possessed, he paid deposits on all the olive-presses in Miletus and Chios, renting them cheaply since no one was competing with him. When the moment came, as all at once many people needed them suddenly, he rented them out at as high a price as he pleased and made a lot of money—thereby demonstrating that it is easy for philosophers to become rich if they wish, but that this is not what they are eager to do.

Apothegms and Other Sayings (P16–P18)[1]

[1] Some of these sayings are also attributed to the Seven Sages (cf. **MOR. T35**).

P16 (< A1) Diogenes Laertius

Among his songs there are the following:

> Many words do not manifest a sensible opinion.
> Search for one thing: what is wise.
> Choose one thing: what is good.
> For you will undo the endlessly talking tongues
> Of chattering men.

P17 (< A1) Diogenes Laertius

a

[. . .] When he was asked why he did not have children, he replied, "because of my love for children." And they say

ἀναγκαζούσης αὐτὸν γῆμαι, ἔλεγεν, οὐδέπω καιρός. εἶτα, ἐπειδὴ παρήβησεν ἐγκειμένης, εἰπεῖν, οὐκέτι καιρός.

b 1.33

Ἕρμιππος δ᾽ ἐν τοῖς Βίοις [Frag. 11 Wehrli] εἰς τοῦτον ἀναφέρει τὸ λεγόμενον ὑπό τινων περὶ Σωκράτους. ἔφασκε γάρ, φασί, τριῶν τούτων ἕνεκα χάριν ἔχειν τῇ τύχῃ· πρῶτον μὲν ὅτι ἄνθρωπος ἐγενόμην καὶ οὐ θηρίον, εἶτα ὅτι ἀνὴρ καὶ οὐ γυνή, τρίτον ὅτι Ἕλλην καὶ οὐ βάρβαρος.

c 1.35–37

φέρεται δὲ καὶ ἀποφθέγματα αὐτοῦ τάδε· πρεσβύτατον τῶν ὄντων θεός· ἀγένητον γάρ. κάλλιστον κόσμος· ποίημα γὰρ θεοῦ. μέγιστον τόπος· ἅπαντα γὰρ χωρεῖ. τάχιστον νοῦς· διὰ παντὸς γὰρ τρέχει. ἰσχυρότατον ἀνάγκη· κρατεῖ γὰρ πάντων. σοφώτατον χρόνος· ἀνευρίσκει γὰρ πάντα.

οὐδὲν ἔφη τὸν θάνατον διαφέρειν τοῦ ζῆν. σὺ οὖν, ἔφη τις, διὰ τί οὐκ ἀποθνήσκεις; ὅτι, ἔφη, οὐδὲν διαφέρει.

[36] πρὸς τὸν πυθόμενον τί πρότερον γεγόνοι, νὺξ ἢ ἡμέρα, ἡ νύξ, ἔφη, μιᾷ ἡμέρᾳ πρότερον.

ἠρώτησέ τις αὐτὸν εἰ λήθοι θεοὺς ἄνθρωπος ἀδικῶν· ἀλλ᾽ οὐδὲ διανοούμενος, ἔφη. πρὸς τὸν μοιχὸν

that when his mother tried to compel him to marry he would say, "It is not yet the right time," and then, as she insisted when he was no longer young, "It is no longer the right time."

b

Hermippus in his *Lives* attributes to him what certain people say about Socrates. For they say that he used to say that he was grateful to fortune for three things: first, that he was born a human being and not an animal; second, that he was born a man and not a woman; and third, that he was born a Greek and not a barbarian.

c

The following sayings of his are also reported: "The oldest of beings is god; for he is unborn." "The most beautiful thing is the world; for it was made by god." "The biggest thing is place; for it contains everything." "The fastest thing is mind; for it races through everything." "The strongest thing is necessity; for it rules over everything." "The wisest thing is time; for it discovers everything."

He said that death is not at all different from life. Someone said, "Then why don't you die?" He answered, "Because there is no difference."

[36] To the man who wanted to know which came about earlier, night or day, he replied, "Night, earlier by a day."

Someone asked him whether a man escapes the notice of the gods if he commits injustice; he answered, "not even

ἐρόμενον εἰ ὁμόσῃ¹ μὴ μεμοιχευκέναι, οὐ χεῖρον, ἔφη, μοιχείας ἐπιορκίε;²

ἐρωτηθεὶς τί δύσκολον, ἔφη, τὸ ἑαυτὸν γνῶναι· τί δὲ εὔκολον, τὸ ἄλλῳ ὑποθέσθαι· τί ἥδιστον, τὸ ἐπιτυγχάνειν· τί τὸ θεῖον, τὸ μήτε ἀρχὴν ἔχον μήτε τελευτήν. τί δὲ καινὸν εἴη τεθεαμένος ἔφη· γέροντα τύραννον.

πῶς ἄν τις ἀτυχίαν ῥᾷστα φέροι, εἰ τοὺς ἐχθροὺς χεῖρον πράσσοντας βλέποι· πῶς ἂν ἄριστα καὶ δικαιότατα βιώσαιμεν, ἐὰν ἃ τοῖς ἄλλοις ἐπιτιμῶμεν, αὐτοὶ μὴ δρῶμεν· [37] τίς εὐδαίμων, ὁ τὸ μὲν σῶμα ὑγιής, τὴν δὲ ψυχὴν³ εὔπορος, τὴν δὲ φύσιν⁴ εὐπαίδευτος.

φίλων παρόντων καὶ ἀπόντων μεμνῆσθαί φησι· μὴ τὴν ὄψιν καλλωπίζεσθαι, ἀλλὰ τοῖς ἐπιτηδεύμασιν εἶναι καλόν.

μὴ πλούτει φησί, κακῶς, μηδὲ διαβαλλέτω σε λόγος πρὸς τοὺς πίστεως κεκοινωνηκότας.

οὓς ἂν ἐράνους εἰσενέγκῃς, φησί, τοῖς γονεῦσιν, τοὺς αὐτοὺς προσδέχου καὶ παρὰ τῶν τέκνων.

---

¹ ὁμόσῃει mss., corr. Roeper   ² ita interpunxit Sternbach
³ ψυχὴν BP¹ (C): τύχην FP³   ⁴ φύσιν BP¹ (Q): ψυχὴν FP³

d 1.40

τούτου ἐστὶν τὸ Γνῶθι σαυτόν, ὅπερ Ἀντισθένης ἐν ταῖς Διαδοχαῖς Φημονόης εἶναί φησιν [FGrHist 508 F3], ἐξιδιοποιήσασθαι δὲ αὐτὸ Χίλωνα.

if he intends to." And to the adulterer who asked whether he should swear that he had not committed adultery, he answered, "Is not perjury worse than adultery?"

Asked what is difficult, he answered, "to know oneself"; what is easy, "to give advice to someone else"; what is most pleasant, "to have success"; what is divine "that which has neither beginning nor end"; what was the most unheard of thing he had seen, he said, "an old tyrant."

How one could most easily endure misfortune? "If one sees one's enemies doing worse." How we could live best and most justly? "If we do not do ourselves what we blame others for doing." [37] Who is happy? "He who is healthy in body, resourceful in spirit, well trained in nature."

He says that we should remember our friends, be they present or absent; not to beautify our appearance, but to be beautiful in what we do.

He says, "Do not enrich yourself dishonestly, nor let any utterance set you against those who share your trust."

He says, "The very same favors that you did for your parents, expect them from your children too."

d

To him belongs the saying "Know yourself," which Antisthenes in his *Successions* attributes to Phemonoê, saying that Chilon appropriated it for himself.

P18 (< A19) Apul. *Flor.* 18

"[. . .] satis [. . .] mihi fuerit mercedis [. . .] si id quod a me didicisti cum proferre ad quosdam coeperis, sibi non adsciveris, sed eius inventi me potius quam alium repertorem praedicaris."

Death (P19)

P19 (< A1) Diog. Laert. 1.39

ὁ δ' οὖν σοφὸς ἐτελεύτησεν ἀγῶνα θεώμενος γυμνικὸν ὑπό τε καύματος καὶ δίψους καὶ ἀσθενείας, ἤδη γηραιός.

Statue (P20)

P20 (< A1) Diog. Laert. 1.34 (< Lobon Frag. 1 Garulli]

[. . . = **R8**] ἐπιγεγράφθαι δ' αὐτοῦ ἐπὶ τῆς εἰκόνος τόδε·

τόνδε Θαλῆν Μίλητος 'Ιὰς θρέψασ' ἀνέδειξεν
ἀστρολόγων πάντων πρεσβύτατον σοφίη.

P18 (< A19) Apuleius, *Florida*

[to Mandrolytus of Priene, who offered to pay him whatever he wished for teaching him the calculation of the sun's orbit, cf. **R13**:] "It would be an adequate recompense for me [. . .] if, when you begin to tell people what you have learned from me, you do not attribute it to yourself but declare that I am the author of this discovery rather than anyone else."

Death (P19)

P19 (< A1) Diogenes Laertius

This sage died while he was observing an athletic competition, because of the heat, thirst, and his weakness, when he was already old.

Statue (P20)

P20 (< A1) Diogenes Laertius

[. . .] [Scil. Lobon says that] his statue bears the following inscription:

> Ionian Miletus nursed this man, Thales, and revealed
> him
> As the most venerable of all astronomers in
> wisdom.

Iconography (P21)

P21 (≠ DK) Richter I, pp. 82–83 and Figures 321–25; Richter-Smith, pp. 209–10 and Figures 171–72; Koch, "Ikonographie," in Flashar, Bremer, Rechenauer (2013), I.1, pp. 217–19.

THALES [11 DK]

D

Tha es (Probably) Left Behind
No Writings (D1–D2)

D1 (< A1) Diog Laert. 1.23

καὶ κατά τινας μὲν σύγγραμμα κατέλιπεν οὐδέν [. . .
= **R6**].

D2 (< Th 184 Wöhrle) Gal. *In. Hipp. Nat. hom.* 1.27 (=
p. 37.9–11 Mewaldt)

[. . .] ὅτι Θαλῆς ἀπεφήνατο στοιχεῖον μόνον εἶναι τὸ
ὕδωρ, ἐκ συγγράμματος αὐτοῦ δεικνύναι οὐκ ἔχομεν,
ἀλλ᾽ ὅμως ἅπασι καὶ τοῦτο πεπίστευται.

Water as the Principle (D3–D4)

D3 (< A12) Arist. *Metaph.* A3 983b18–22

τὸ μέντοι πλῆθος καὶ τὸ εἶδος τῆς τοιαύτης ἀρχῆς οὐ

THALES

D

Thales (Probably) Left Behind
No Writings (D1–D2)

D1 (< A1) Diogenes Laertius

According to some, he did not leave behind a written treatise [. . .].

D2 (≠ DK) Galen, *Commentary on Hippocrates'* On the Nature of Man

[. . .] we are not able to demonstrate on the basis of a treatise by Thales that he declared that water was the only element, even if this is what everyone believes.

Water as the Principle (D3–D4)

D3 (< A12) Aristotle, *Metaphysics*

However, not all [scil. of those earliest philosophers who assert that things comes from a substrate] say the same

τὸ αὐτὸ πάντες λέγουσιν, ἀλλὰ Θαλῆς μὲν [. . . = **R9**]
ὕδωρ φησὶν εἶναι (διὸ καὶ τὴν γῆν ἐφ᾽ ὕδατος ἀπεφήνατο εἶναι) [. . . = **R32a**].

D4 (< Th 210 Wöhrle) (Ps.-?) Hippol. *Ref.* 1.1

[. . . = **R12**] οὗτος ἔφη ἀρχὴν τοῦ παντὸς εἶναι καὶ
τέλος τὸ ὕδωρ. ἐκ γὰρ αὐτοῦ τὰ πάντα συνίστασθαι
πηγνυμένου καὶ πάλιν διανιεμένου ἐπιφέρεσθαί τε
αὐτῷ τὰ πάντα ἀφ᾽ οὗ καὶ σεισμοὺς καὶ πνευμάτων
συστροφὰς καὶ ἄστρων κινήσεις γίνεσθαι [. . . = **R39**].

The World (D5)

D5 (A13b) Aët. 2.1.2 (Ps.-Plut.) [περὶ κόσμου]

Θαλῆς καὶ οἱ ἀπ᾽ αὐτοῦ ἕνα τὸν κόσμον.

The Heavenly Bodies (D6)

D6 (A17a) Aët.

a 2.13.1 (Ps.-Plut.) [τίς ἡ οὐσία τῶν ἄστρων πλανητῶν
καὶ ἀπλανῶν]

Θαλῆς γεώδη μὲν ἔμπυρα δὲ τὰ ἄστρα.

b 2.20.9 (Stob.) [περὶ οὐσίας ἡλίου]

Θαλῆς γεοειδῆ τὸν ἥλιον.

thing regarding the number and the kind of a principle of this sort. But Thales [. . .] says it is water (and it is for this reason that he declared that the earth rests upon water) [. . .].

D4 (≠ DK) (Ps.-?) Hippolytus, *Refutation of All Heresies*

[. . .] He said that the beginning of everything and its end is water. For it is out of this that all things are formed, when it solidifies and liquefies in turn,[1] and all things rest upon it, and it is also from this that earthquakes, concentrations of winds, and the motions of the stars come [. . .].

[1] This explanation seems more like reconstruction (of Aristotelian origin) than information.

The World (D5)

D5 (A13b) Aëtius

Thales and those who follow him: there is [scil. only] one world.

The Heavenly Bodies (D6)

D6 (A17a) Aëtius

a

Thales: the stars are made of earth, but they are on fire.

b

Thales: the sun is made of earth.

The Earth (D7–D8)

D7 (< A14) Arist. *Cael.* 2.13 294a28–32

οἱ δ᾽ ἐφ᾽ ὕδατος κεῖσθαι. τοῦτον γὰρ ἀρχαιότατον παρειλήφαμεν τὸν λόγον, ὅν φασιν εἰπεῖν Θαλῆν τὸν Μιλήσιον, ὡς διὰ τὸ πλωτὴν εἶναι μένουσαν ὥσπερ ξύλον ἤ τι τοιοῦτον ἕτερον (καὶ γὰρ τούτων ἐπ᾽ ἀέρος μὲν οὐθὲν πέφυκε μένειν, ἀλλ᾽ ἐφ᾽ ὕδατος) [. . . = **R33a**].

D8 (< A15) Sen. *Quaest. nat.* 3.14

ait enim terrarum orbem aqua sustineri et vehi more navigii mobilitateque eius fluctuare, tum quum dicitur tremere. non est ergo mirum si abundat humor ad flumina fundenda, quum mundus in humore sit totus.

The Flooding of the Nile (D9)

D9 (A16) Aët. 4 1.1 (Ps.-Plut.) [περὶ Νείλου ἀναβάσεως]

Θαλῆς τοὺς ἐτησίας ἀνέμους οἴεται πνέοντας τῇ Αἰγύπτῳ ἀντιπροσώπους ἐπαίρειν τοῦ Νείλου τὸν ὄγκον διὰ τὸ τὰς ἐκροὰς αὐτοῦ τῇ παροιδήσει τοῦ ἀντιπαρήκοντος πελάγους ἀνακόπτεσθαι.

The Earth (D7–D8)

D7 (< A14) Aristotle, *On the Heavens*

The others say that it [i.e. the earth] rests on water. For the most ancient explanation that has come down to us, which they say that Thales of Miletus stated, is that it stays put because it floats like wood or something else of this sort (for by nature none of these things stays put in the air, but rather on water) [. . .].

D8 (< A15) Seneca, *Natural Questions*

For he says that the terrestrial globe rests upon water and moves like a boat and fluctuates by reason of its mobility when there is what is called an earthquake. So it is not surprising if there is an abundant quantity of fluid that pours forth as streams, since the whole world is located in a fluid.

The Flooding of the Nile (D9)

D9 (A16) Aëtius

Thales thinks that the Etesian winds that blow upon Egypt in the opposite direction raise the Nile's bulk because its outflow is driven back by the swelling of the sea which comes to meet it.[1]

---

[1] Herodotus 2.20 mentions this theory without attributing it to anyone.

Soul and Divinities (D10–D11)

D10 (< A22) Arist. *An.* 1.5 411a7–8

[. . .] Θαλῆς ᾠήθη πάντα πλήρη θεῶν εἶναι.

D11

a (A22) Arist. *An.* 1.2 405a19–21

ἔοικε δὲ καὶ Θαλῆς ἐξ ὧν ἀπομνημονεύουσι κινητικόν τι τὴν ψυχὴν ὑπολαβεῖν, εἴπερ τὸν λίθον ψυχὴν ἔχειν ὅτι τὸν σίδηρον κινεῖ.

b (< A1) Diog. Laert. 1.24

[. . . = **R37**] Ἀριστοτέλης [**D11a**] δὲ καὶ Ἱππίας [**HIP-PIAS D23**] φασὶν αὐτὸν καὶ ἀψύχοις μεταδιδόναι ψυχῆς, τεκμαιρόμενον ἐκ τῆς λίθου τῆς μαγνήτιδος καὶ τοῦ ἠλέκτρου.

Souls and Divinities (D10–D11)

D10 (< A22) Aristotle, *On the Soul*

[. . .] Thales thought that all things are full of gods.[1]

> [1] Cf. Plato, *Laws* 899b.

See also **R34a**

D11

a (A22) Aristotle, *On the Soul*

Thales too seems, from what is reported, to have thought that the soul is something that moves, for he says that the stone [i.e. the magnet] has a soul, given that it moves iron.

b (< A1) Diogenes Laertius

[. . .] Aristotle and Hippias say that he attributed a soul to inanimate beings too, judging from the evidence of the magnet and of amber.

THALES

R

Earliest Testimonies to His Fame
Xenophanes, Heraclitus, Herodotus,
and Democritus (R1)

R1 (< A1) Diog. Laert. 1.23

[. . . = **R15**] ὅθεν αὐτὸν καὶ Ξενοφάνης καὶ Ἡρόδοτος θαυμάζει. μαρτυρεῖ δ᾽ αὐτῷ καὶ Ἡράκλειτος καὶ Δημόκριτος.

Hippias

See **THAL. D11b**

Aristophanes

See **DRAM. T13–T14**

THALES

R

Earliest Testimonies to His Fame
Xenophanes, Heraclitus, Herodotus,
and Democritus (R1)

R1 (< A1) Diogenes Laertius

[. . .] That is why Xenophanes and Herodotus [cf. **P2, P6, P7, P9**] admire him. Heraclitus [cf. **HER. D26**] and Democritus [cf. **THAL. P2**] also bear witness to him.

Hippias

See **THAL. D11b**

Aristophanes

See **DRAM. T13–T14**

From the Sage to the Theoretician (R2–R4)

R2 (< Th 20 Wöhrle) Plat. *Prot.* 343a

[ΠΡ.] τούτων ἦν καὶ Θαλῆς ὁ Μιλήσιος καὶ Πιττακὸς
ὁ Μυτιληναῖος καὶ Βίας ὁ Πριηνεὺς καὶ Σόλων ὁ ἡμέ-
τερος καὶ Κλεόβουλος ὁ Λίνδιος καὶ Μύσων ὁ Χη-
νεύς, καὶ ἕβδομος ἐν τούτοις ἐλέγετο Λακεδαιμόνιος
Χίλων.

R3 (Th 110 Wöhrle) Plut. *Sol.* 3.8.1–3 80B–C

καὶ ὅλως ἔοικεν ἡ Θάλεω μόνου σοφία τότε περαίτερω
τῆς χρείας ἐξικέσθαι τῇ θεωρίᾳ· τοῖς δ᾽ ἄλλοις ἀπὸ
τῆς πολιτικῆς ἀρετῆς τοὔνομα τῆς σοφίας ὑπῆρξε.

R4 (< A1) Diog. Laert. 1.34

οἶδε δ᾽ αὐτὸν ἀστρονομούμενον καὶ Τίμων, καὶ ἐν τοῖς
Σίλλοις ἐπαινεῖ αὐτὸν λέγων [Frag. 23 Di Marco]·

οἷόν θ᾽ ἑπτὰ Θάλητα σοφῶν σοφὸν
⟨ἀστρονομῆσαι⟩[1] [. . . = **R8**]

---

[1] ⟨ἀστρονομῆσαι⟩ Magnelli

Alleged Writings (R5–R8)

R5 (< A11) Flav. Jos. *Apion.* 1.2

ἀλλὰ μὴν καὶ τοὺς περὶ τῶν οὐρανίων τε καὶ θείων

THALES

From the Sage to the Theoretician (R2–R4)

R2 (≠ DK) Plato, *Protagoras*

[Protagoras:] To such men [scil. those capable of making laconic pronouncements] belonged Thales of Miletus, Pittacus of Mytilene, Bias of Priene, our own Solon, Cleobulus of Lindos, Myson of Chenae, and people say that the seventh among them was Chilon of Sparta [cf. **MOR. T35**].

R3 (≠ DK) Plutarch, *Solon*

And in general it seems that at that time only Thales' wisdom, by reason of its theoretical aspect, went beyond practical necessity: the others [scil. of the Seven Sages] possess the name of wisdom from their excellence in politics.

R4 (< A1) Diogenes Laertius

Timon too knows of him as an astronomer, and he praises him in his *Mockeries* (*Silloi*), saying,

As, among the Seven Sages, Thales the sage
⟨practiced astronomy⟩ [. . .].

See also **P1b**

Alleged Writings (R5–R8)

R5 (< A11) Flavius Josephus, *Against Apion*

Everyone agrees unanimously that the first Greeks who

πρώτους παρ' Ἕλλησι φιλοσοφήσαντας, οἷον [. . . = **PHER. P8**] Θάλετα, πάντες συμφώνως ὁμολογοῦσιν [. . .] ὀλίγα συγγράψαι· καὶ ταῦτα τοῖς Ἕλλησιν εἶναι δοκεῖ πάντων ἀρχαιότατα, καὶ μόλις αὐτὰ πιστεύουσιν ὑπ' ἐκείνων ἐγράφθαι.

R6 (< A1) Diog. Laert. 1.23

[. . . = **D1**] ἡ γὰρ εἰς αὐτὸν ἀναφερομένη Ναυτικὴ ἀστρολογία Φώκου λέγεται εἶναι τοῦ Σαμίου. [. . .] κατά τινας δὲ μόνα δύο συνέγραψε, Περὶ τροπῆς καὶ Ἰσημερίας, τὰ ἄλλ' ἀκατάληπτα εἶναι δοκιμάσας.

R7 (< B1) Plut. *Pyth. orac.* 18 403A

[. . .] εἴ γε Θαλῆς ἐποίησεν ὡς ἀληθῶς εἰπεῖν ⟨τὴν⟩ εἰς αὐτὸν[1] ἀναφερομένην Ἀστρολογίαν.

> [1] ⟨τὴν⟩ εἰς αὐτὴν Turnebus: εἰς αὐτὴν mss.

R8 (< A1) Diog. Laert. 1.34

[. . . = **R4**] ἀστρονομήματα[1] δὲ γεγραμμένα ὑπ' αὐτοῦ φησι Λόβων ὁ Ἀργεῖος [Frag. 1 Garulli] εἰς ἔπη τείνειν διακόσια [. . .].

> [1] ἀστρονομήμ̣ατα BP¹(Q) F²: ἀστρονόμημα. τὰ F¹P⁴

philosophized about celestial phenomena and divine matters, like [. . .] Thales, [. . .] wrote only very little; these writings seem to the Greeks to be the most ancient ones of all, and they can scarcely believe that they were written by them.

R6 (< A1) Diogenes Laertius

[. . .] for the *Nautical Astronomy* attributed to him is said to be by Phocus of Samos. [. . .] But according to other people he wrote only two works, *On the Solstice* and *On the Equinox,* for he was of the opinion that everything else was impossible to know.

R7 (< B1) Plutarch, *On the Pythian Oracles*

[. . .] if Thales really did write the *Astronomy* that is attributed to him.

R8 (< A1) Diogenes Laertius

[. . .] Lobon of Argos says that what was written by him about astronomy amounts to two hundred lines [. . .].

See also **R44**

The Science of Nature (R9–R12)

R9 (< A12) Arist. *Metaph.* A3 983b20–21

[. . . = **D3**] Θαλῆς μὲν ὁ τῆς τοιαύτης ἀρχηγὸς φιλοσοφίας [. . . = **R32a**].

R10 (< B1) Simp. *In Phys.*, p. 23.29–32

Θαλῆς δὲ πρῶτος παραδέδοται τὴν περὶ φύσεως ἱστορίαν τοῖς Ἕλλησιν ἐκφῆναι, πολλῶν μὲν καὶ ἄλλων
προγεγονότων, ὡς καὶ τῷ Θεοφράστῳ δοκεῖ [< Frag.
225 FHS&G], αὐτὸς δὲ πολὺ διενεγκὼν ἐκείνων, ὡς
ἀποκρύψαι πάντας τοὺς πρὸ αὐτοῦ.

R11 (< A1) Diog. Laert. 1.23, 24

μετὰ δὲ τὰ πολιτικὰ τῆς φυσικῆς ἐγένετο θεωρίας.
[. . .] πρῶτος δὲ καὶ περὶ φύσεως διελέχθη, ὥς τινες.

R12 (< Th 210 Wöhrle) (Ps.-?) Hippol. *Ref.* 1.1

λέγεται Θαλῆν τὸν Μιλήσιον ἕνα τῶν ἑπτὰ σοφῶν
πρῶτον ἐπικεχωρηκέναι φιλοσοφίαν φυσικήν. [. . . =
D4]

*The Initiator of the Ionian Line of
Descent of Greek Philosophy*

See **DOX. T20, T21**

The Science of Nature (R9–R12)

R9 (< A12) Aristotle, *Metaphysics*

[. . .] Thales, the founder of this sort of philosophy [i.e. the one that asserts that things derive from one or more principles that serve as their substrate] [. . .]

R10 (< B1) Simplicius, *Commentary on Aristotle's* Physics

Thales is reported to have been the first to reveal the study of nature to the Greeks; many others had preceded him, as is the view of Theophrastus too, but he was far superior to them so that he eclipsed all his predecessors.

R11 (< A1) Diogenes Laertius

After having engaged in politics, he devoted himself to the observation of nature. [. . .] And he was the first to speak about nature as well, according to some people.

R12 (≠ DK) (Ps.-?) Hippolytus, *Refutation of All Heresies*

They say that Thales of Miletus, one of the Seven Sages, was the first to make an attempt at natural philosophy.

The Initiator of the Ionian Line of Descent of Greek Philosophy

See **DOX. T20, T21**

Scientific Discoveries Attributed to
Thales (R13–R31)
A General Catalog (R13)

R13 (< A19) Apul. *Flor.* 18

Thales Milesius ex septem illis sapientiae memoratis viris facile praecipuus (enim geometricae penes Graios primus repertor et naturae certissimus explorator et astrorum peritissimus contemplator) maximas res parvis lineis repperit: temporum ambitus, ventorum flatus, stellarum meatus, tonitruum sonora miracula, siderum obliqua curricula, solis annua reverticula: itidem lunae vel nascentis incrementa, vel senescentis dispendia, vel delinquentis obstiticula. idem sane iam proclivi senectute divinam rationem de sole commentus est; quam equidem non didici modo, verum etiam experiundo comprobavi: quoties sol magnitudine sua circulum, quem permeat, metiatur.

Scientific Discoveries Attributed to
Thales (R13–R31)[1]
A General Catalog (R13)

[1] Among the many other discoveries attributed to Thales are the armillary sphere (Cicero, *On the Republic* 1.22), the solstices (Heron, *Definitions* 138.11 = Eudemus, Frag. 145 Wehrli), and the phases of the moon and the equinoxes (Eusebius, *Evangelical Preparation* 10.14.10).

R13 (< A19) Apuleius, *Florida*

Thales of Miletus, the most preeminent by far of those Seven famous for their wisdom—indeed he was the first among the Greeks to discover geometry and was an unerring investigator of nature and a most experienced observer of the stars—discovered the greatest things by means of small lines: the procession of the seasons, the blowing of the winds, the course of the stars, the prodigious sounds of thunderclaps, the slanting trajectory of the stars, the yearly reversion of the sun; and so too the increases of the moon when it waxes, its decreases when it wanes, the obstacles when it is eclipsed. The same man, though already in advanced old age, invented a divine calculation with regard to the sun, which I not only learned but have also confirmed by experiment: it measures the orbit that the sun follows as a multiple of the sun's magnitude.

Astronomical Discoveries (R14–R25)
Trajectory and Size of the Sun (R14)

R14 (< A1) Diog. Laert. 1.24

πρῶτος δὲ καὶ τὴν ἀπὸ τροπῆς ἐπὶ τροπὴν πάροδον
εὗρε, καὶ πρῶτος τὸ τοῦ ἡλίου μέγεθος ‹τοῦ ἡλιακοῦ
κύκλου ὥσπερ καὶ τὸ τῆς σελήνης μέγεθος›[1] τοῦ σε-
ληναίου ἑπτακοσιοστὸν καὶ εἰκοστὸν μέρος ἀπεφήνατο κατά τινας.

[1] suppl. Diels

The Solar Eclipse (R15–R18)

R15 (< A1) Diog. Laert. 1.23

δοκεῖ δὲ κατά τινας πρῶτος ἀστρολογῆσαι καὶ ἡλια-
κὰς ἐκλείψεις καὶ τροπὰς προειπεῖν, ὥς φησιν Εὔδημος ἐν τῇ περὶ τῶν Ἀστρολογουμένων ἱστορίᾳ [Frag.
144 Wehrli] [. . . = **R1**].

R16 (< A17) Theon Sm. *Exp.*, p. 198.14–18

Εὔδημος ἱστορεῖ ἐν ταῖς Ἀστρολογίαις [Frag. 145
Wehrli] [. . .] Θαλῆς δὲ ἡλίου ἔκλειψιν καὶ τὴν κατὰ
τὰς τροπὰς αὐτοῦ περίοδον, ὡς οὐκ ἴση ἀεὶ συμβαί-
νει·

Astronomical Discoveries (R14–R25)
Trajectory and Size of the Sun (R14)

R14 (< A1) Diogenes Laertius

He was the first to discover the trajectory from one tropic
to the other, and according to some people the first to
declare that the size of the sun ‹is the 720th part of the
solar circle, and the size of the moon› is the 720th part of
the lunar one.

The Solar Eclipse (R15–R18)

R15 (< A1) Diogenes Laertius

Some people are of the view that he was the first to do
astronomy and to predict solar eclipses and solstices, as
Eudemus says in his *History of Astronomy*.

R16 (< A17) Theon of Smyrna, *Mathematics Useful for
Understanding Plato* (extract from Dercyllides)

Eudemus reports in his *Astronomy* [. . .] that Thales [scil.
was the first to discover] the eclipse of the sun and the fact
that the periodicity of its revolutions is not always equal.

R17 (Th 91 Wöhrle) Aristarch. Samius in Comm. in *Od.*
20.156 (P.Oxy. 3710 Col. 2.36–43; vol. 53 [1986], 96–97,
ed. Haslam)

ὅτι ἐν νουμηνίαι αἱ ἐκλείψεις δηλο[ῖ] | Ἀρίσταρχος ὁ
Σάμ[ι]ος γράφων· ἔφη τε | ὁ μὲν Θαλῆς ὅτι ἐκλείπειν
τὸν ἥλ[ι]|ον σελήνης ἐπίπροσθεν αὐτῶι γεν|ομένης,
σημειουμέ[νης c. 6] . . . τῆς | ἡμέρας, ἐν ἧι ποιεῖται
τὴν ἔγλειψιν, | ἣ[ν] οἱ μὲν τριακάδα καλοῦσιν ο[ἱ] δὲ
νου|μηνίαν.

R18 (< A17a) Aët. 2.24.1 (Ps.-Plut.) [περὶ ἐκλείψεως
ἡλίου]

Θαλῆς πρῶτος ἔφη ἐκλείπειν τὸν ἥλιον τῆς σελήνης
αὐτὸν ὑπερχομένης κατὰ κάθετον, οὔσης φύσει γεώ-
δους· βλέπεσθαι δὲ τοῦτο κατοπτρικῶς[1] ὑποτιθεμένῳ
τῷ δίσκῳ.

[1] verbum obscurum et fortasse corruptum

The Light of the Moon (R19)

R19 (A17b) Aët. 2.28.5 (Stob.) [περὶ φωτισμῶν σε-
λήνης]

Θαλῆς πρῶτος ἔφη ὑπὸ τοῦ ἡλίου φωτίζεσθαι τὴν
σελήνην.

R17 (≠ DK) Aristarchus of Samos in an anonymous commentary on Homer's *Odyssey*

The fact that eclipses take place at the new moon is explained by Aristarchus of Samos, who writes, "Thales said that the sun is eclipsed when the moon comes to be located in front of it, the day on which it produces the eclipse (some people call this day 'the thirtieth' and others 'the new moon') being marked [. . .]."

R18 (< A17a) Aëtius

Thales was the first to say that an eclipse of the sun occurs when the moon, which by nature is made of earth, passes perpendicularly beneath it; this is seen in the manner of a mirror (?), when the disk comes to be placed under it.

The Light of the Moon (R19)

R19 (A17b) Aëtius

Thales was the first to say that the moon is illuminated by the sun.[1]

---

[1] This is a typical case of honorific attribution. In fact, the discovery belongs to Parmenides (**PARM. D28**).

Other Heavenly Bodies (R20–R22)

R20 (< A1) Diog. Laert. 1.23

Καλλίμαχος δ᾽ αὐτὸν οἶδεν εὑρετὴν τῆς ἄρκτου τῆς μικρᾶς λέγων ἐν τοῖς Ἰάμβοις οὕτως·

καὶ τῆς ἁμάξης ἐλέγετο σταθμήσασθαι
τοὺς ἀστερίσκους, ᾗ πλέουσι Φοίνικες
[Frag. 191.54–55 Pfeiffer]

R21 (A18) Plin. *Nat. hist.* 18

occasum matutinam Vergiliarum Hesiodus (nam huius quoque nomine exstat Astrologia) tradidit fieri, quum aequinoctium autumni conficeretur [Frag. 290 Merkelbach-West], Thales vigesimo quinto die ab aequinoctio [. . .].

R22 (B2) Schol. in Arat. 172, p. 369.24

Θαλῆς [. . .] δύο αὐτὰς εἶπεν εἶναι, τὴν μὲν βόρειον τὴν δὲ νότιον.

Zones of the Heavens (R23)

R23 (A13c) Aët 2.12.1 (Ps.-Plut.) [περὶ διαιρέσεως οὐρανοῦ]

Θαλῆς [. . .] μεμερίσθαι τὴν τοῦ παντὸς οὐρανοῦ σφαῖραν εἰς κύκλους πέντε, οὕστινας προσαγορεύουσι ζώνας [. . .].

Other Heavenly Bodies (R20–R22)

R20 (< A1) Callimachus in Diogenes Laertius

Callimachus knows of him as the discoverer of the Great
Bear, for he speaks in his *Iambs* as follows:

> And he was said to have numbered the little stars
> Of the Great Bear, by means of which the
>   Phoenicians navigate.

R21 (A18) Pliny, *Natural History*

Hesiod (for an *Astronomy* is also extant under his name)
reports that the morning setting of the Pleiades takes place
at the autumnal equinox, Thales twenty-five days after the
equinox [. . .].

R22 (B2) Scholia on Aratus' *Phaenomena*

Thales [. . .] said that there are two of them [i.e. the Hya-
des], the northern one and the southern one.

Zones of the Heavens (R23)

R23 (< A13c) Aëtius

Thales [. . .]: the sphere of the whole of heaven is divided
into five circles, which they [i.e. besides Thales, Pythagoras and his disciples] call zones.

Position of the Earth (R24)

R24 (A15) Aët. 3.11.1 (Ps.-Plut.) [περὶ θέσεως γῆς]

οἱ ἀπὸ Θάλεω τὴν γῆν μέσην [. . . = **XEN. D43**].

Division of the Year (R25)

R25 (< A1) Diog. Laert. 1.27

τάς τε ὥρας τοῦ ἐνιαυτοῦ φασιν αὐτὸν εὑρεῖν καὶ εἰς
τριακοσίας ἑξήκοντα πέντε ἡμέρας διελεῖν.

Geometrical Discoveries (R26–R31)
Theorems and Demonstrations (R26–R30)

R26 (A20) Procl. *In Eucl.* Prop. 15, theor. 8 (299.1–5
Friedlein)

τοῦτο τοίνυν τὸ θεώρημα δείκνυσιν, ὅτι δύο εὐθειῶν
ἀλλήλας τεμνουσῶν αἱ κατὰ κορυφὴν γωνίαι ἴσαι εἰσίν, εὑρημένον μέν, ὡς φησὶν Εὔδημος [Frag. 135
Wehrli], ὑπὸ Θαλοῦ πρώτου [. . .].

R27 (< A1) Diog. Laert. 1.24–25

παρά τε Αἰγυπτίων γεωμετρεῖν μαθόντα φησὶ Παμ-
φίλη [Frag. 1 Cagnazzi] πρῶτον καταγράψαι κύκλου τὸ
τρίγωνον ὀρθογώνιον, καὶ θῦσαι βοῦν. οἱ δὲ Πυθαγόραν φασίν, ὧν ἐστιν Ἀπολλόδωρος ὁ λογιστικός.

Position of the Earth (R24)

R24 (A15) Aëtius

The followers of Thales: the earth is in the center [. . .].

Division of the Year (R25)

R25 (< A1) Diogenes Laertius

They say that he was the one who discovered the seasons of the year and divided it into 365 days.

Geometrical Discoveries (R26–R31)
Theorems and Demonstrations (R26–R30)

R26 (A20) Proclus, *Commentary on the First Book of Euclid's* Elements

Thus this theorem demonstrates that when two straight lines intersect one another, the corresponding angles are equal, a discovery, as Eudemus says, first made by Thales [. . .].

R27 (< A1) Diogenes Laertius

Pamphilê says that after he learned geometry from the Egyptians, he was the first to inscribe a right triangle in a circle, and that he sacrificed a bull [scil. in celebration]. Others, including Apollodorus the arithmetician, say that it was Pythagoras [cf. **PYTH. c D7a**].

R28 (A20) Procl. *In Eucl.* Prop. 6, theor. 2 (250.20–251.2 Friedlein)

τῷ μὲν οὖν Θαλῇ τῷ παλαιῷ πολλῶν τε ἄλλων εὑρέσεως ἕνεκα καὶ τοῦδε τοῦ θεωρήματος χάρις. λέγεται γὰρ δὴ πρῶτος ἐκεῖνος ἐπιστῆσαι καὶ εἰπεῖν, ὡς ἄρα παντὸς ἰσοσκελοῦς αἱ πρὸς τῇ βάσει γωνίαι ἴσαι εἰσίν, ἀρχαικώτεροι δὲ τὰς ἴσας ὁμοίας προσειρηκέναι.

R29 (A20) Procl. *In Eucl.* Prop. 26, theor. 17 (352.14–18 Friedlein)

Εὔδημος δὲ ἐν ταῖς Γεωμετρικαῖς ἱστορίαις [Frag. 134 Wehrli] εἰς Θαλῆν τοῦτο ἀνάγει τὸ θεώρημα. τὴν γὰρ τῶν ἐν θαλάττῃ πλοίων ἀπόστασιν δι' οὗ τρόπου φασὶν αὐτὸν δεικνύναι τούτῳ προσχρῆσθαί φησιν ἀναγκαῖον.

R30 (A20) Procl. *In Eucl.* Def. 17 (157.10–11 Friedlein)

τὸ μὲν οὖν διχοτομεῖσθαι τὸν κύκλον ὑπὸ τῆς διαμέτρου πρῶτον Θαλῆν ἐκεῖνον ἀποδεῖξαί φασιν [. . .].

R28 (A20) Proclus, *Commentary on the First Book of Euclid's* Elements

We are indebted to ancient Thales for the discovery, among many other ones, in particular of the following theorem. For they say that he was the first to understand and to state that the angles at the base of every isosceles triangle are equal, even though he used the archaic expression "similar" for "equal."[1]

[1] Diels infers from this passage that Proclus or Eudemus was making use of a mathematical text that was attributed to Thales.

R29 (A20) Proclus, *Commentary on the First Book of Euclid's* Elements

Eudemus in his *History of Geometry* assigns this theorem [i.e. the equality of two triangles of which one side and the two neighboring angles are equal] to Thales. For he says that the method by which they say that he demonstrated the distance of ships on the sea requires that one make use of it.

R30 (A20) Proclus, *Commentary on the First Book of Euclid's* Elements

They say that the celebrated Thales was the first to demonstrate that a circle is divided into two by its diameter [. . .].

The Measurement of the Pyramids (R31)

R31

a (< A1) Diog. Laert. 1.27

ὁ δὲ Ἱερώνυμος [Frag. 40 Wehrli] καὶ ἐκμετρῆσαί φησιν αὐτὸν τὰς πυραμίδας ἐκ τῆς σκιᾶς, παρατηρή-
σαντα ὅτε ἡμῖν ἰσομεγέθης ἐστίν.

b (A21) Plin. *Nat. hist.* 36.82

mensuram altitudinis earum deprehendere invenit Thales
Milesius umbram metiendo qua hora par esse corpori
solet.

c (A21) Plut. *Sept. Sap. Conv.* 2 147A

τὴν βακτηρίαν στήσας ἐπὶ τῷ πέρατι τῆς σκιᾶς ἣν ἡ
πυραμὶς ἐποίει, γενομένων τῇ ἐπαφῇ τῆς ἀκτῖνος δυεῖν τριγώνων ἔδειξας, ὃν ἡ σκιὰ πρὸς τὴν σκιὰν λόγον εἶχε, τὴν πυραμίδα πρὸς τὴν βακτηρίαν ἔχουσαν.

*Aristotle's Reconstructions and Criticisms of
Thales' Arguments (R32–R34)*

R32

a (< A12) Arist. *Metaph.* A3 983b25–984a3

[. . . = **D3**] λαβὼν ἴσως τὴν ὑπόληψιν ταύτην ἐκ τοῦ

The Measurement of the Pyramids (R31)

R31

a (< A1) Hieronymus in Diogenes Laertius

Hieronymus says that he also measured [scil. the height of] the pyramids exactly on the basis of their shadow, by waiting for the moment when it [i.e. our shadow] has the same size as we do.

b (A21) Pliny, *Natural History*

Thales of Miletus discovered how to take their [i.e. the pyramids'] measure by measuring their shadow at the hour when it is equal to [scil. the height of] the body.

c (A21) Plutarch, *The Dinner of the Seven Wise Men*

You [i.e. Thales] placed a stick at the edge of the shadow which the pyramid made, and as two triangles were formed by contact with the sunbeam, you demonstrated that the pyramid is in the same ratio to the stick as the shadow of the one was to the shadow of the other.

Aristotle's Reconstructions and Criticisms of
Thales' Arguments (R32–R34)

R32

a (< A12) Aristotle, *Metaphysics*

[. . .] Perhaps he had derived this assumption [cf. **D3**]

πάντων ὁρᾶν τὴν τροφὴν ὑγρὰν οὖσαν καὶ αὐτὸ τὸ
θερμὸν ἐκ τούτου γιγνόμενον καὶ τούτῳ ζῶν (τὸ δ᾽ ἐξ
οὗ γίγνεται, τοῦτ᾽ ἐστὶν ἀρχὴ πάντων)—διά τε δὴ
τοῦτο τὴν ὑπόληψιν λαβὼν ταύτην καὶ διὰ τὸ πάντων
τὰ σπέρματα τὴν φύσιν ὑγρὰν ἔχειν· τὸ δ᾽ ὕδωρ ἀρχὴ
τῆς φύσεώς ἐστι τοῖς ὑγροῖς. εἰσὶ δέ τινες οἳ καὶ τοὺς
παμπαλαίους καὶ πολὺ πρὸ τῆς νῦν γενέσεως καὶ
πρώτους θεολογήσαντας οὕτως οἴονται περὶ τῆς φύσεως ὑπολαβεῖν. Ὠκεανόν τε γὰρ καὶ Τηθὺν ἐποίησαν τῆς γενέσεως πατέρας, καὶ τὸν ὅρκον τῶν θεῶν
ὕδωρ, τὴν καλουμένην ὑπ᾽ αὐτῶν Στύγα τῶν ποιη-
τῶν·[1] τιμιώτατον μὲν γὰρ τὸ πρεσβύτατον, ὅρκος δὲ
τὸ τιμιώτατόν ἐστιν. εἰ μὲν οὖν ἀρχαία τις αὕτη καὶ
παλαιὰ τετύχηκεν οὖσα περὶ τῆς φύσεως δόξα, τάχ᾽
ἂν ἄδηλον εἴη, Θαλῆς μέντοι λέγεται οὕτως ἀποφήνασθαι περὶ τῆς πρώτης αἰτίας.

[1] τῶν ποιητῶν secl. Christ

b (< Th 191 Wöhrle) Alex. *In Metaph.* A3, p. 26.16–18

εἰκότως τὸ "λέγεται οὕτως ἀποφήνασθαι"· οὐδὲν γὰρ
προφέρεται αὐτοῦ σύγγραμμα, ἐξ οὗ τις τὸ βέβαιον
ἕξει τοῦ ταῦτα λέγεσθαι τοῦτον τὸν τρόπον ὑπ᾽ αὐτοῦ.

from seeing that what nourishes all things is moist and that what is warm itself comes from this [i.e. water] and lives because of it (and what things come about from is the principle of all things)—it is for this reason then that he had this idea, and also from the fact that the seed of all things has a moist nature; and for things that are moist, water is the principle of their nature. But there are some people who think that those who spoke about the gods in ancient times, long before the present generation, and indeed were the first to do so, had formed the same conception about nature: for they made Ocean and Tethys the parents of becoming and the oath of the gods water, what they, being poets, called Styx [cf. **COSM. T6, T7**]; for what is most ancient is most honorable, and an oath is what is most honorable. Well, whether this really is a primeval and ancient view about nature, might well be unclear; however, at least as far as Thales is concerned, people say that he expressed himself in this way about the first cause.

b (≠ DK) Alexander of Aphrodisias, *Commentary on Aristotle's* Metaphysics

The phrase "people say that he expressed himself in this way" is appropriate; for no treatise by him is cited on the basis of which one could be certain that this was said by him in this way.

R33

a (< A14) Arist. *Cael.* 2.13 294a32–33

[. . . = **D7**] ὥσπερ οὐ τὸν αὐτὸν λόγον ὄντα περὶ τῆς γῆς καὶ τοῦ ὕδατος τοῦ ὀχοῦντος τὴν γῆν.

b (< A14) Simpl. *In Cael.* 522.16–18

[. . .] πρὸς ταύτην δὲ τὴν δόξαν ὁ Ἀριστοτέλης ἀντιλέγει μᾶλλον ἴσως ἐπικρατοῦσαν διὰ τὸ καὶ παρ' Αἰγυπτίοις οὕτως ἐν μύθου σχήματι λέγεσθαι καὶ τὸν Θαλῆν ἴσως ἐκεῖθεν τὸν λόγον κεκομικέναι.

R34

a (A22) Arist. *An.* 1.5 411a7–8

καὶ ἐν τῷ ὅλῳ δέ τινες αὐτὴν μεμεῖχθαί φασιν, ὅθεν ἴσως καὶ Θαλῆς ᾠήθη πάντα πλήρη θεῶν εἶναι [**D10**].

b (< A1) Diog. Laert. 1.27

[. . .] τὸν κόσμον ἔμψυχον καὶ δαιμόνων πλήρη.

Assimilations to Later Doctrines (R35–R39)

R35 (A23) Aët. 1.7.11 (Stob.) [περὶ θεοῦ]

Θαλῆς νοῦν τοῦ κόσμου τὸν θεόν, τὸ δὲ πᾶν ἔμψυχον

R33

a (< A14) Aristotle, *On the Heavens*

[. . .] as though the explanation given for the earth [cf. **D7**] did not apply as well to the water that bears the earth.

b (< A14) Simplicius, *Commentary on Aristotle's* On the Heavens

Aristotle contradicts this opinion, which perhaps is more prevalent because it is also stated among the Egyptians in the form of a myth and because Thales perhaps brought back this explanation from there.

R34

a (A22) Aristotle, *On the Soul*

Some people say that it [i.e. the soul] is mixed in with the whole, which is perhaps also the reason why Thales thought that all things are full of gods [cf **D10**].

b (< A1) Diogenes Laertius

[. . . he thought] that the universe is animate and full of divinities.

Assimilations to Later Doctrines (R35–R39)

R35 (A23) Aëtius

Thales: god is the intelligence of the world, the universe

ἅμα καὶ δαιμόνων πλῆρες· διήκειν δὲ καὶ διὰ τοῦ
στοιχειώδους ὑγροῦ δύναμιν θείαν κινητικὴν αὐτοῦ.

R36 (A22a) Aët. 4.2.1 (Ps.-Plut.) [περὶ ψυχῆς]

Θαλῆς ἀπεφήνατο πρῶτος τὴν ψυχὴν φύσιν ἀεικίνη-
τον ἢ αὐτοκίνητο.

R37 (< A1) Diog. Laert. 1.24

ἔνιοι δὲ καὶ αὐτὸν πρῶτον εἰπεῖν φασιν ἀθανάτους
τὰς ψυχάς· ὧν ἐστι Χοιρίλος ὁ ποιητής [*SH* 331] [. . .
= **D11b**].

R38 (A23) Cic. *Nat. deor.* 1.10.25

Thales enim Milesius, qui primus de talibus rebus quae-
sivit, aquam dixit esse initium rerum: deum autem, eam
mentem, quae ex aqua cuncta fingeret.

R39 (< Th 210 Wöhrle) (Ps.-?) Hippol. *Ref.* 1.1

[. . . = **D4**] καὶ τὰ πάντα φέρεσθαί τε καὶ ῥεῖν τῇ τοῦ
πρώτου ἀρχηγοῦ τῆς γενέσεως αὐτῶν φύσει συμ-
φερόμενα. θεὸν δὲ τοῦτ᾽ εἶναι, τὸ μήτε ἀρχὴν μήτε
τελευτὴν ἔχον.

is animated and at the same time full of divinities; and the divine power passes through the elementary moisture and moves it.

R36 (A22a) Aëtius

Thales was the first to state that the soul is a nature which is always in motion or which moves itself.[1]

¹ The disjunction is connected with a celebrated textual problem in Plato, *Phaedrus* 245c.

R37 (< A1) Diogenes Laertius

Some people also say that he was the first to say that souls are immortal; one of them is Choerilus the poet [. . .].

R38 (A23) Cicero, *On the Nature of the Gods*

For Thales of Miletus, who was the first to investigate these matters, said that water is the beginning of things, but that god is the intelligence capable of making all things out of water.

R39 (≠ DK) (Ps.-?) Hippolytus, *Refutation of All Heresies*

[. . .] And all things are borne along and flow, carried along by the nature of the first principle (*arkhêgos*) of their becoming. This, having neither beginning nor ending, is god.

Gnostic and Christian Interpretations (R40–R43)

R40 (< Th 145 Wöhrle) Iren. *Adv. haer.* 2.14.2

Thales quidem Milesius universorum generationem et initium aquam dixit esse: idem autem est dicere aquam et Bythum.

R41 (Th 213 Wöhrle) (Ps.-?) Hippol. *Ref.* 5.9.13

εἶναι δὲ τὸν ὄφιν λέγουσιν οὗτοι τὴν ὑγρὰν οὐσίαν, καθάπερ ὁ Μιλήσιος, καὶ μηδὲν δύνασθαι τῶν ὄντων ὅλως, ἀθανάτων ἢ θνητῶν, ἐμψύχων[1] ἢ ἀψύχων, συνεστηκέναι χωρὶς αὐτοῦ.

[1] τῶν ante ἐμψύχων del. Cruice

R42 (< Th 229 Wöhrle) Min. Fel. *Octav.* 19.4

sit Thales Milesius omnium primus, qui primus omnium de caelestibus disputavit. idem Milesius Thales rerum initium aquam dixit, deum autem eam mentem, quae ex aqua cuncta formaverit. esto[1] altior et sublimior aquae et spiritus ratio, quam ut ab homine potuerit inveniri, a Deo traditum; vides philosophi principalis nobiscum penitus opinionem consonare.

[1] eo *ms., corr. Vahlen*

R43 (< 7 A5) Appon. 5.22–23 (ad *Cn.* 3:5)

in priore enim 'filiarum adiuratione,' in 'caprearum et

Gnostic and Christian Interpretations (R40–R43)

R40 (≠ DK) Irenaeus, *Against Heresies*

Thales of Miletus said that water is the source and beginning of all things; but it is the same thing to say "water" and "Abyss" (*Buthos*)."[1]

> [1] According to some Gnostics, Bythos is the abyss out of which all things come.

R41 (≠ DK) (Ps.-?) Hippolytus, *Refutation of All Heresies*

These people [i.e. some Gnostics] say that the serpent is the moist substance, just like the Milesian [i.e. Thales], and that nothing at all of the things that are, immortal or mortal ones, animate or inanimate ones, is capable of being formed without it.

R42 (≠ DK) Minucius Felix, *Octavius*

Let Thales of Miletus be first of all, he who was the first of all to discuss celestial phenomena. This same Thales of Miletus said that water is the beginning of things, but that god is the mind (*mens*) that formed all things out of water. This theory of water and spirit (*spiritus*), too lofty and sublime to have been invented by a human being, may well have been transmitted by God. You see that the opinion of the founder of philosophy entirely agrees with ours.

R43 (< 7 A5) Apponius, *Commentary on the Song of Songs*

For we said about the earlier 'adjuration of the daughters'

cervorum' personas thalesianae et ferecidensis philosophiae intellegi diximus [= **PHER. R29**]. [. . .] [23] de quibus Thales nomine initium omnium rerum aquam in suo esse dogmate pronuntiavit, et inde omnia facta subsistere ab inviso et magno; causam vero motus aquae spiritum insidentem confirmat, simulque geometricam artem perspicaci sensu prior invenit, per quam suspicatus est unum rerum omnium creatorem [. . . = **PHER. R16**].

A Pseudepigraphic Text (R44)

R44 (B3) Ps.-Gal. *In Hipp. Hum.* 1.1

Θαλῆς μὲν εἴπερ καὶ ἐκ τοῦ ὕδατός φησι συνεστάναι πάντα, ἀλλ᾽ ὅμως καὶ τοῦτο βούλεται. ἄμεινον δὲ καὶ αὐτοῦ τὴν ῥῆσιν προσθεῖναι ἐκ τοῦ δευτέρου Περὶ τῶν ἀρχῶν ἔχουσαν ὧδέ πως· τὰ μὲν οὖν πολυθρύλητα τέτταρα, ὧν τὸ πρῶτον εἶναι ὕδωρ φαμὲν καὶ ὡσανεὶ μόνον στοιχεῖοι τίθεμεν, πρὸς σύγκρισίν τε καὶ πῆγνυσιν καὶ σύστασιν τῶν ἐγκοσμίων πρὸς ἄλληλα συγκεράννυται. πῶς δέ, ἤδη λέλεκται ἡμῖν ἐν τῷ πρώτῳ.

that 'the roes and stags' are to be understood as the representatives of the philosophy of Thales and Pherecydes.[1] [. . .] [23] Among these philosophers [i.e. the pure ones who can be compared to roes and stags], the one named Thales declared in his doctrine that water is the origin of all things, and that everything that has been made from this subsists because of a great invisible being, and he states that the cause of the movement of the water is the spirit that dwells within it. At the same time, it was he who by his intelligence was the first to discover the science of geometry, and this permitted him to surmise that there is only one creator of all things [cf. **PHER. R16, R29**].

[1] The reference seems to be to his commentary (4.1) on *Cn.* 2:7 (where in fact he does not name Thales or Pherecydes, but the Platonists and the Stoics).

A Pseudepigraphic Text (R44)

R44 (B3) Ps.-Galen, *Commentary on Hippocrates'* On Humors

Although Thales says that all things are constituted out of water, nonetheless he also wants this [i.e. that the elements are transformed into one another]. It is better to cite his own words from Book 2 of *On the Principles,* which are as follows: "Therefore the celebrated four, of which we say that the first is water and posit it as being as it were the only element, mix with one another for the combination, solidification, and composition of the things of this world. How this happens we have already said in Book 1."

269

6. ANAXIMANDER
[ANAXIMAND.]

The ancient sources situate the maturity of Anaximander of Miletus a little before the middle of the sixth century BC. Like Thales, of whom he is said to have been the disciple, he is credited by the biographical tradition with political activity, connected to the colonial expansion of Miletus. Again like Thales, various inventions are attributed to him, notably the *gnômôn*, the construction of a "sphere" (i.e. a tridimensional model of the universe), and a geographical map. His doctrine, unlike Thales', has outlines we can grasp. Only a single sentence of his has been transmitted in its original wording. But the fairly numerous testimonia indicate that Anaximander recounted the generation of the world and of its constitutive parts all the way to living beings, explained its present function, and envisaged its disappearance. Thus he stands at the origin of a new kind of investigation bearing upon the totality of the world. One tradition calls Anaximander the first Greek to have written a treatise on nature. Theophrastus called the style of the phrase he transmits "poetic"; nevertheless, this must have been a text in prose. The 'unlimited,' from which everything that exists derives and to which everything returns, and 'separation' are the two concepts that

have secured for Anaximander a place of honor in the
history of philosophy.

BIBLIOGRAPHY

Editions

G. Wöhrle et al., ed. *Die Milesier: Anaximander und
Anaximenes.* Coll. Traditio Praesocratica vol. 1 (Berlin,
2012).

Studies

C. H. Kahn. *Anaximander and the Origins of Greek Cosmology* (New York, 1960, 1994³).

OUTLINE OF THE CHAPTER

P

Chronology (P1–P3)
Origin and Intellectual Line of Descent (P4–P7)
Political Activity (P8)
Prediction (P9)
Character (P10)
Apothegm (P11)
Iconography (P12)

D

Anaximander's Book (D1–D3)
Terrestrial Map and Celestial Globe (D4–D5)
*Three Summaries Ultimately Deriving from Theophras-
tus (D6–D8)*

ANAXIMANDER [12 DK]

P

Chronology (P1–P3)

P1 (< A11) (Ps.?) Hippol. *Ref.* 1.6.7

οὗτος ἐγένετο κατὰ ἔτος τρίτον τῆς τεσσαρακοστῆς δευτέρας Ὀλυμπιάδος.

P2 (< A1) Diog. Laert. 2.2

[. . .] ὃς καί φησιν αὐτὸν ἐν τοῖς Χρονικοῖς [*FGrHist* 244 F29] τῷ δευτέρῳ ἔτει τῆς πεντηκοστῆς ὀγδόης Ὀλυμπιάδος ἐτῶν εἶναι ἑξήκοντα τεττάρων καὶ μετ᾽ ὀλίγον τελευτῆσαι ἀκμάσαντά πη μάλιστα κατὰ Πολυκράτη τὸν Σάμου τύραννον.[1]

[1] ἀκμάσαντά πη [. . .] τύραννον secl. Diels ut ab Anaximandro aliena

P3 (< A5) Plin. *Nat. hist.* 2.31

[. . .] Anaximander Milesius [. . .] Olympiade quinquagesima octava [. . . cf. **R15**].

ANAXIMANDER

P

Chronology (P1–P3)

P1 (< A11) (Ps.-?) Hippolytus, *Refutation of All Heresies*
He was born in the third year of the 42nd Olympiad [= 610/9 BC].

P2 (< A1) Diogenes Laertius
[. . .] He [i.e. Apollodorus of Athens] also says in his *Chronology* that he was sixty-four years old in the second year of the 58th Olympiad [= 547/6 BC] and that he died a little later, having reached his maturity approximately at the time of Polycrates, the tyrant of Samos.[1]

[1] This last indication causes some difficulty since Polycrates reigned from 538 to 522 BC, Anaximander cannot have reached his full maturity (forty years) at this time if he was sixty-four years old in 547/6.

P3 (< A5) Pliny, *Natural History*
[. . .] Anaximander of Miletus [. . .], at the time of the 58th Olympiad [= 548/44] [. . .].

Origin and Intellectual Line of Descent (P4–P7)

P4 (< A1) Diog. Laert. 2.1

Ἀναξίμανδρος Πραξιάδου Μιλήσιος [. . . = **D11**].

P5 (< A9) Simpl *In Phys.*, p. 24.13–14 (< Theoph. Frag. 226A FHS&G)

[. . . cf. **D6**] Ἀναξίμανδρος μὲν Πραξιάδου Μιλήσιος Θαλοῦ γενόμενος διάδοχος καὶ μαθητὴς [. . .].

P6 (< A6) Strab. 1.1.11

[. . . cf. **D4**] Ἀναξίμανδρόν τε Θαλοῦ γεγονότα γνώριμον καὶ πολίτην [. . .].

P7 (Ar 23 Wöhrle) *IG* XIV 1464 Frag. V.1–3

Ἀναξίμανδρος Πραξιάδου Μιλήσιος· vacat | ἐγέ[ν]ετο μὲν Θ[αλ]έω . . .

Political Activity (P8)

P8 (A3) Ael. *Var. hist.* 3.17

καὶ Ἀναξίμανδρος δὲ ἡγήσατο τῆς ἐς Ἀπολλωνίαν ἐκ Μιλήτου ἀποικίας.

ANAXIMANDER

Origin and Intellectual Line of Descent (P4–P7)

P4 (< A1) Diogenes Laertius
Anaximander of Miletus, son of Praxiades [. . .].

P5 (< A9) Theophrastus in Simplicius, *Commentary on Aristotle's* Physics
[. . .] Anaximander of Miletus, son of Praxiades, who was the successor and disciple of Thales [. . .].

P6 (< A6) Strabo, *Geography*
[. . .] Anaximander, who had been Thales' friend and fellow citizen [. . .].

P7 (≠ DK) Inscription in the gymnasium of Taormina
Anaximander son of Praxiades, of Miletus. He was [scil. probably: the disciple] of Thales . . . [1]

[1] The inscription, dated by the editor to the second century BC, may have been part of a list of writings available in this gymnasium.

Political Activity (P8)

P8 (A3) Aelian, *Historical Miscellany*
Anaximander headed the foundation at Apollonia[1] of a colony from Miletus.

[1] On the Black Sea.

Prediction (P9)

P9 (A5a) Cic. *Div.* 1.50.112

ab Anaximandro physico moniti Lacedaemonii sunt ut
urbem et tecta linquerent armatique in agro excubarent,
quod terrae motus instaret, tum cum et urbs tota corruit
et monte Taygeto extrema montis quasi puppis avolsa est.

Character (P10)

P10 (A8) Diog. Laert. 8.70

Διόδωρος δὲ ὁ Ἐφέσιος περὶ Ἀναξιμάνδρου[1] γράφων
[*FGrHist* 1102 F1] φησὶν ὅτι τοῦτον ἐζηλώκει, τραγι-
κὸν ἀσκῶν τῦφον καὶ σεμνὴν ἀναλαβὼν ἐσθῆτα.

[1] Ἀναξαγόρου Gigante ex 8.56

Apothegm (P11)

P11 (< A1) Diog. Laert. 2.2

τούτου φασὶν ᾄδοντος καταγελάσαι τὰ παιδάρια, τὸν
δὲ μαθόντα φάναι· "βέλτιον οὖν ἡμῖν ᾀστέον διὰ τὰ
παιδάρια."

Prediction (P9)

P9 (A5a) Cicero, *On Divination*

The Lacedaemonians were warned by the natural philosopher Anaximander to leave their city and houses and to sleep fully armed in the fields because an earthquake was imminent, at the time when the whole city was destroyed and the peak was torn away from Mount Taygetus like the stern of a ship.

Character (P10)

P10 (A8) Diogenes Laertius

Diodorus of Ephesus, writing about Anaximander, says that he [i.e. Empedocles, cf. **EMP. P15**] imitated him in cultivating a theatrical pomp and wearing pretentious clothes.

Apothegm (P11)

P11 (< A1) Diogenes Laertius

They say that while he was singing, children made fun of him; and when he found out, he said, "So I must sing better for the sake of the children."

Iconography (P12)

P12 (cf. vol. 1, p. 90 App., and Nachtrag p. 487.3–4)

Richter I, pp. 78–79 and Figures 299–301; Richter-Smith, p. 86 and Figure 50; Koch, "Ikonographie," in Flashar, Bremer, Rechenauer (2013), I.1, pp. 219, 220.

ANAXIMANDER [12 DK]

D

Anaximander's Book (D1–D3)

D1 (A7) Them. *Orat.* 26 317c

[. . .] ἐθάρρησε πρῶτος ὧν ἴσμεν Ἑλλήνων λόγον ἐξενεγκεῖν περὶ φύσεως ξυγγεγραμμένον.

D2 (< A1) Diog. Laert. 2.2

τῶν δὲ ἀρεσκόντων αὐτῷ πεποίηται κεφαλαιώδη τὴν
ἔκθεσιν, ᾗ[1] που περιέτυχεν καὶ Ἀπολλόδωρος ὁ Ἀθηναῖος [*FGr Hist.* 244 F29].

    [1] ᾗ Cobet: ὥς mss.

D3 (< A2) *Suda* A.1986

ἔγραψε Περὶ φύσεως, Γῆς περίοδον καὶ Περὶ τῶν
ἀπλανῶν καὶ Σφαῖραν καὶ ἄλλα τινά.

ANAXIMANDER

D

Anaximander's Book (D1–D3)

D1 (A7) Themistius, *Orations*

[. . .] he was the first Greek we know of to have ventured to publish a written discourse about nature.

D2 (< A1) Diogenes Laertius

He made a summary exposition of his opinions, which Apollodorus of Athens seems to have come across.

D3 (< A2) *Suda*

He wrote *On Nature, Map of the Earth, On the Fixed Stars, The Sphere,* and some other works.[1]

---

[1] The first three titles at least might refer to different parts of Anaximander's book, but cf. **D5**.

Terrestrial Map and Celestial Globe (D4–D5)

D4 (< A6) Strab. 1.1.11

ὧν τοὺς πρώτους μεθ᾽ Ὅμηρον δύο φησὶν Ἐρατο-
σθένης [Frag. IB5 Berger], Ἀναξίμανδρόν τε [. . . = **P6**]
καὶ Ἑκαταῖον τὸ Μιλήσιον· τὸν μὲν οὖν ἐκδοῦναι
πρῶτον γεωγραφικὸν πίνακα [. . .].

D5 (< A1) Diog. Laert. 2.2

καὶ γῆς καὶ θαλάσσης περίμετρον πρῶτος ἔγραψεν,
ἀλλὰ καὶ σφαῖραν κατεσκεύασε.

*Three Summaries Ultimately Deriving from
Theophrastus (D6–D8)*

D6 (< A9, B1) Simpl. *In Phys.*, p. 24.13–25 (< Theoph.
Frag. 226A FHS&G)

τῶν δὲ ἓν καὶ κινούμενον καὶ ἄπειρον λεγόντων Ἀναξίμανδρος [. . . = **P5**] ἀρχήν τε καὶ στοιχεῖον εἴρηκε τῶν
ὄντων τὸ ἄπειρον, πρῶτος τοῦτο[1] τοὔνομα κομίσας
τῆς ἀρχῆς. λέγει δ᾽ αὐτὴν μήτε ὕδωρ μήτε ἄλλο τι
τῶν καλουμένων εἶναι στοιχείων, ἀλλ᾽ ἑτέραν τινὰ
φύσιν ἄπειρον, ἐξ ἧς ἅπαντας γίνεσθαι τοὺς οὐρανοὺς καὶ τοὺς ἐν αὐτοῖς κόσμους· ἐξ ὧν δὲ ἡ γένεσίς

---

[1] αὐτὸ coni. Usener

Terrestrial Map and Celestial Globe (D4–D5)

D4 (< A6) Strabo, *Geography*

Eratosthenes says that the first two [scil. geographers] after Homer were Anaximander [. . .] and Hecataeus of Miletus; and that the former was the first to publish a map of the earth [. . .].

D5 (< A1) Diogenes Laertius

And he was the first to draw the outline of the earth and sea, and he also constructed a [scil. celestial] sphere.

Three Summaries Ultimately Deriving from Theophrastus (D6–D8)

D6 (< A9, B1) Simplicius, *Commentary on Aristotle's Physics*

Among those who say that it [i.e. the principle] is one, in movement, and unlimited, Anaximander [. . .] said that the principle (*arkhê*) and element of beings is the **unlimited** (*to apeiron*); he was the first to call the principle by this term.[1] He says that it is neither water nor any other of what are called elements, but a certain other unlimited nature from which come about all the heavens and the worlds in them. And the things out of which birth comes about for

---

[1] It is also possible that what Simplicius means is that the term Anaximander was the first to use was not 'unlimited' (*apeiron*) but rather 'principle' (*arkhê*).

ἐστι τοῖς οὖσι, καὶ τὴν φθορὰν εἰς ταῦτα γίνεσθαι
κατὰ τὸ χρεών. διδόναι γὰρ αὐτὰ δίκην καὶ τίσιν
ἀλλήλοις² τῆς ἀδικίας κατὰ τὴν τοῦ χρόνου τάξιν,
ποιητικωτέροις οὕτως³ ὀνόμασιν αὐτὰ λέγων.

² ἀλλήλοις om. A   ³ οὕτως om. F

D7 (< A11, B2) (Ps.-?) Hippol. *Ref.* 1.6.1–7

[1] [. . .] οὗτος ἀρχὴν ἔφη τῶν ὄντων φύσιν τινὰ τοῦ
ἀπείρου, ἐξ ἧς γίνεσθαι τοὺς οὐρανοὺς καὶ τὸν ἐν
αὐτοῖς κόσμον.¹ ταύτην δὲ ἀίδιον εἶναι καὶ ἀγήρω, ἣν
καὶ πάντας περιέχειν τοὺς κόσμους. λέγει δὲ χρόνον,
ὡς ὡρισμένης τῆς γενέσεως καὶ τῆς οὐσίας² καὶ τῆς
φθορᾶς. [2] οὗτος μὲν οὖν³ ἀρχὴν καὶ στοιχεῖον εἴρηκεν τῶν ὄντων τὸ ἄπειρον, πρῶτος τοὔνομα⁴ καλέσας
τῆς ἀρχῆς. πρὸς δὲ τούτῳ κίνησιν ἀίδιον εἶναι, ἐν ᾗ
συμβαίνειν⁵ γίνεσθαι τοὺς οὐρανούς. [3] τὴν δὲ γῆν
εἶναι μετέωρον, ὑπὸ μηδενὸς κρατουμένην, μένουσαν
<δὲ>⁶ διὰ τὴν ὁμοίαν πάντων ἀπόστασιν. τὸ δὲ σχῆμα
αὐτῆς †ὑγρὸν†,⁷ στρογγύλον, κίονι⁸ λίθῳ παραπλή-
σιον· τῶν δὲ ἐπιπέδων ᾧ⁹ μὲν ἐπιβεβήκαμεν, ὃ δὲ
ἀντίθετον ὑπάρχει. [4] τὰ δὲ ἄστρα γίνεσθαι κύκλον
πυρός, ἀποκριθέντα τοῦ κατὰ τὸν κόσμον πυρός,

¹ τοὺς . . . κόσμους Ritter   ² καὶ τῆς γενέσεως τοῖς οὖσι
Marcovich   ³ οὖν T: om. LOB   ⁴ πρῶτος <τοῦτο> τοῦ-
νομα Kirk   ⁵ συμβαίνει mss., corr. Roeper   ⁶ <δὲ>
Diels   ⁷ ὑγρὸν mss.: γυρόν Roeper   ⁸ χίονι mss., corr.
Gronovius: κίονος Teichmüller   ⁹ ὃ mss., corr. Gronovius

beings, into these too their destruction happens, **according to obligation: for they pay the penalty** (*dikê*) **and retribution** (*tisis*) **to each other for their injustice** (*adikia*) according to the order of time[2]—this is how he says these things, with rather poetic words.

[2] Precisely where Simplicius' verbatim citation of Anaximander's sentence ends and his paraphrase or interpretation of it begins is uncertain and controversial.

D7 (< A11, B2) (Ps.-?) Hippolytus, *Refutation of All Heresies*

[1] [. . .] He said that the principle of beings is a certain nature, that of the **unlimited,** from which the heavens come about and the world that is in them. It is eternal and **unaging** and it surrounds all the worlds. He speaks of time, on the idea that generation, subsistence, and destruction are limited. [2] He said that the principle and element of beings is the **unlimited;** he was the first to use this term for the principle.[1] Besides this, there is an eternal motion, in which the birth of the heavens comes about. [3] The earth is suspended; it is not controlled by anything, but remains where it is because it is at the same distance from all things. Its form is †moist†,[2] round, similar to **a stone column;** of its surfaces, one is that upon which we walk, the other is opposite to it. [4] The stars are a **wheel** of fire; they have been separated from the fire in the world and are surrounded by air. There are certain

[1] See note 1 in **D6,** above.   [2] Most editors correct to "curved."

περιληφθέντα δ᾽ ὑπὸ ἀέρος. ἐκπνοὰς δ᾽ ὑπάρξαι, πόρους[10] τινὰς αὐλώδεις,[11] καθ᾽ οὓς φαίνεσθαι[12] τὰ
ἄστρα· διὸ καὶ ἐπιφρασσομένων τῶν ἐκπνοῶν τὰς
ἐκλείψεις γίνεσθαι. [5] τὴν δὲ σελήνην ποτὲ μὲν πλη-
ρουμένην φαίνεσθαι, ποτὲ δὲ μειουμένην κατὰ τὴν
τῶν πόρων ἐπίφραξιν ἢ ἄνοιξιν. εἶναι δὲ τὸν **κύκλον**
τοῦ ἡλίου ἑπτακαιεικοσαπλασίονα[13] τῆς σελήνης, καὶ
ἀνωτάτω μὲν εἶναι τὸν ἥλιον,[14] κατωτάτω δὲ τοὺς τῶν
ἀπλανῶν ἀστέρων κύκλους. [6] τὰ δὲ ζῷα γίνεσθαι
ἐξατμιζόμενα[15] ὑπὸ τοῦ ἡλίου. τὸν δὲ ἄνθρωπον ἑτέρῳ
ζῴῳ γεγονέναι—τούτεστιν ἰχθύι—παραπλήσιον κατ᾽
ἀρχάς. [7] ἀνέμους δὲ γίνεσθαι τῶν λεπτοτάτων ἀτμῶν
τοῦ ἀέρος[16] ἀποκρινομένων καὶ ὅταν ἀθροισθῶσι κι-
νουμένων· ὑετοὺς[17] δὲ ἐκ τῆς ἀτμίδος[18] τῆς ἐκ γῆς ὑφ᾽
ἡλίου ἀναδιδομένης·[19] ἀστραπὰς δέ, ὅταν ἄνεμος ἐμ-
πίπτων διιστᾷ τὰς νεφέλας.

10 πόρους Diels (ex Cedrenus 276.15–277.14 Bekker): τό-
πους mss.   11 αὐλώδεις Diels: ἀερώδεις mss.   12 φαίνεται mss., corr. Usener   13 ‹τῆς γῆς, ἐννεακαιδεκαπλασίονα (ὀκτωκαιδεκαπλασίονα post Tannery maluerunt Frank et
Becker) δὲ τὸν› τῆς σελήνης Diels   14 τὸν ἥλιον ‹μετ᾽
αὐτὸν δὲ τὴν σελήνην› prop. Diels   15 ἐξατμιζόμενα
mss.: ‹ἐξ ὑγροῦ›, ἐξατμιζομένου Diels   16 ‹ἐκ› τοῦ ἀέρος
Marcovich   17 ὑετοὺς Cedrenus: ὑετὸν mss.   18 ἐκ
τῆς ἀτμίδος Cedrenus: om. mss.   19 τῆς ἐκ γῆς ὑφ᾽ ἡλίου
ἀναδιδομένης Diels: τῆς ἐκ τῶν ὑφ᾽ ἥλιον (ἡλίου Par.) ἀναδιδομένης Cedrenus: ἐκ γῆς (τῇς Τ) ἀναδιδομένης ἐκ τῶν ὑφ᾽
ἥλιον mss.

passages serving as orifices as in an *aulos,* through which the stars appear; this is why eclipses happen, when these orifices are obstructed. [5] The moon appears sometimes to increase, sometimes to decrease, because of the obstruction or opening of these passages. The **wheel** of the sun is twenty-seven times that of the moon; and the sun occupies the highest position, the circles of the fixed stars the lowest one.[3] [6] The animals are born by evaporation from the effect of the sun. Human beings were at first similar to a different animal, i.e. to a fish. [7] Winds come about when the finest vapors of the air are detached and when, set into movement, they are agglomerated; and rains from the vapor coming from the earth by the effect of the sun is released; and lightning when the wind falls upon clouds and bursts them.

[3] Diels suggests that this sentence is lacunose and supplemented, "The wheel of the sun is twenty-seven times that of ⟨the earth, nineteen times that of⟩ the moon; and the sun occupies the highest position, ⟨and after it the moon,⟩ and the circles of the fixed stars ⟨and of the planets⟩ the lowest one" (cf. **D22, D24**).

D8 (< A10) Ps.-Plut. *Strom.* 2 (= Eus. *PE* 1.8.2)

μεθ᾽ ὃν Ἀναξίμανδρον [. . .] τὸ ἄπειρον φάναι τὴν
πᾶσαν αἰτίαν ἔχειν τῆς τοῦ παντὸς γενέσεώς τε καὶ
φθορᾶς, ἐξ οὗ δή φησι τούς τε οὐρανοὺς ἀποκεκρί-
σθαι καὶ καθόλου τοὺς ἅπαντας ἀπείρους ὄντας κόσμους. ἀπεφήνατο δὲ τὴν φθορὰν γίνεσθαι, καὶ πολὺ
πρότερον τὴν γένεσιν, ἐξ ἀπείρου αἰῶνος ἀνακυκλου-
μένων πάντων αὐτῶν. ὑπάρχειν δέ φησι τῷ μὲν σχήματι τὴν γῆν κυλινδροειδῆ, ἔχειν δὲ τοσοῦτον βάθος
ὅσον ἂν εἴη τρίτον πρὸς τὸ πλάτος. φησὶ δὲ τὸ ἐκ τοῦ
ἀιδίου γόνιμον θερμοῦ τε καὶ ψυχροῦ κατὰ τὴν γένεσιν τοῦδε τοῦ κόσμου ἀποκριθῆναι καί τινα ἐκ τούτου
φλογὸς σφαῖραν περιφυῆναι τῷ περὶ τὴν γῆν ἀέρι ὡς
τῷ δένδρῳ φλοιόν· ἧστινος ἀπορραγείσης καὶ εἴς τινας ἀποκλεισθείσης κύκλους ὑποστῆναι τὸν ἥλιον
καὶ τὴν σελήνην καὶ τοὺς ἀστέρας. ἔτι φησὶν ὅτι κατ᾽
ἀρχὰς ἐξ ἀλλοειδῶν ζῴων ὁ ἄνθρωπος ἐγεννήθη, ἐκ
τοῦ τὰ μὲν ἄλλα δι᾽ ἑαυτῶν ταχὺ νέμεσθαι, μόνον δὲ
τὸν ἄνθρωπον πολυχρονίου δεῖσθαι τιθηνήσεως· διὸ
καὶ κατ᾽ ἀρχὰς οὐκ ἄν ποτε τοιοῦτον ὄντα διασωθῆ-
ναι.

The Unlimited (D9–D12)

D9 (< A15, B3) Arist. *Phys.* 3.4 203b7–15

ἔτι δὲ καὶ ἀγένητον καὶ ἄφθαρτον ὡς ἀρχή τις οὖσα·
τό τε γὰρ γενόμενον ἀνάγκη τέλος λαβεῖν, καὶ τε-

D8 (A10) Pseudo-Plutarch, *Stromata*

After him [i.e. Thales], Anaximander [. . .] said that the **unlimited** is responsible for the birth and destruction of the whole, and from this he says that the heavens are separated out and in general all the worlds, which are unlimited. He declared that destruction, and much earlier birth, come about after an unlimited eternity, as all of these revolve. He says that the earth is cylindrical in form, and that its depth is one third of its breadth. He says that the seed[1] of the warm and the cold, coming from the eternal, was detached at the birth of this world and that a certain sphere of fire coming from this grew around the air surrounding the earth like the **bark** around a tree. When this was torn away and enclosed within certain circles, the sun, the moon, and the stars were formed. He also says that at the beginning human beings were born from animals of different species, because of the fact that the other animals nourish themselves quickly by themselves, while only human beings are in need of a long period of nursing; that is why, being of this sort, they could not have survived at the beginning.

[1] The term may go back to Anaximander.

The Unlimited (D9–D12)

D9 (< A15, B3) Aristotle, *Physics*

Moreover, it [i.e. the unlimited] is ungenerated and indestructible, inasmuch as it is a principle. For what is gener-

λευτὴ πάσης ἔστιν φθορᾶς. διό, καθάπερ λέγομεν, οὐ
ταύτης ἀρχή, ἀλλ' αὕτη τῶν ἄλλων εἶναι δοκεῖ καὶ
περιέχειν ἅπαντα καὶ πάντα **κυβερνᾶν, ὥς** φασιν ὅσοι
μὴ ποιοῦσι παρὰ τὸ ἄπειρον ἄλλας αἰτίας, [. . .] καὶ
τοῦτ' εἶναι τὸ θεῖον· **ἀθάνατον** γὰρ καὶ **ἀνώλεθρον,**
ὥσπερ φησὶν Ἀναξίμανδρος καὶ οἱ πλεῖστοι τῶν φυ-
σιολόγων.

D10 (< A14) Aët. 1.3.3 (Ps.-Plut.) [περὶ ἀρχῶν]

Ἀναξίμανδρος [. . .] φησι τῶν ὄντων τὴν ἀρχὴν εἶναι
τὸ ἄπειρον· ἐκ γὰρ τούτου πάντα γίνεσθαι καὶ εἰς
τοῦτο πάντα φθείρεσθαι· διὸ καὶ γεννᾶσθαι ἀπείρους
κόσμους, καὶ πάλιν φθείρεσθαι εἰς τὸ ἐξ οὗ γίνονται.[1]
λέγει γοῦν διότι ἄπειρόν ἐστιν, ἵνα μηδὲν ἐλλείπῃ ἡ
γένεσις ἡ ὑφισταμένη [. . . = **R13**].

[1] γίνονται m: γίνεται ΜΠ: γίνεσθαι Diels

D11 (< A1) Diog. Laert. 2.1–2

[. . . = **P4**] οὗτος ἔφασκεν ἀρχὴν καὶ στοιχεῖον τὸ
ἄπειρον, οὐ διορίζων ἀέρα ἢ ὕδωρ ἢ ἄλλο τι. καὶ τὰ
μὲν μέρη μεταβάλλειν, τὸ δὲ πᾶν ἀμετάβλητον εἶναι.

D12 (A16, > A9) Arist. *Phys.* 1.4. 187a12–16, 20–21

ὡς δ' οἱ φυσικοὶ λέγουσι, δύο τρόποι εἰσίν. οἱ μὲν
γὰρ ἓν ποιήσαντες τὸ ὂν[1] σῶμα τὸ ὑποκείμενον, ἢ τῶν

[1] ὂν secl. Ross

ated must necessarily have an end, and there is an ending to every destruction. That is why, as we say, there does not seem to be a principle of this, but it itself is [scil. a principle] for everything else and **surrounds** all things and **steers** all, as is said by all those who do not consider other causes besides the unlimited [. . .] And the divine is this: for it is **deathless** and **imperishable,** as Anaximander says and most of the natural philosophers.

D10 (< A14) Aëtius

Anaximander [. . .] says that the principle of beings is the **unlimited.** For it is from this that all things come about, and into this that all things are destroyed. And that is why worlds unlimited [scil. in number] are generated and are destroyed in turn into what they come from. In any case he says why it is unlimited, so that the existing becoming be lacking in nothing [. . .].

D11 (< A1) Diogenes Laertius

[. . .] He said that the principle and element is the **unlimited,** without defining whether it is air water, or something else. And the parts change, while the whole is changeless.

D12 (A16, > A9) Aristotle, *Physics*

There are two ways in which the natural philosophers speak. For the ones, who posit the existing body, the sub-

τριῶν τι ἢ ἄλλο ὅ ἐστι πυρὸς μὲν πυκνότερον ἀέρος δὲ λεπτότερον, τἆλλα γεννῶσι πυκνότητι καὶ μανότητι πολλὰ ποιοῦντες [. . .] οἱ δ᾽ ἐκ τοῦ ἑνὸς ἐνούσας τὰς ἐναντιότητας ἐκκρίνεσθαι,² ὥσπερ Ἀναξίμανδρός φησι [. . .].

² ἐκκρίνουσιν P et fecit J

The Unlimited Number of Worlds (D13–D14)

D13 (< A17) Aët. 2.1.3 (Stob.; cf. Ps.-Plut.) [περὶ κόσμου]

Ἀναξίμανδρος [. . .] ἀπείρους κόσμους ἐν τῷ ἀπείρῳ κατὰ πᾶσαν περίστασιν.¹

¹ περίστασιν Plut.: περιαγωγήν Stob.

D14 (A17) Aët. 2.1.8 (Stob.) [περὶ κόσμου]

τῶν ἀπείρους ἀποφηναμένων τοὺς κόσμους Ἀναξίμανδρος τὸ ἴσον αὐτοὺς ἀπέχειν ἀλλήλων [. . .].

The Destructibility of the Worlds (D15–D16)

D15 (< A17) Aët. 2.4.6 (Stob.) [εἰ ἄφθαρτος ὁ κόσμος]

Ἀναξίμανδρος [. . .] φθαρτὸν τὸν κόσμον.

strate, as [scil. only] one, whether it is one of the three [scil. elements] or something else, denser than fire but finer than air, make it multiple by generating all other things by condensation and rarefaction. [. . .] The others say that the opposites are present in the one and are separated out from it, as Anaximander says [. . .]. [cf. **R1–R4**]

The Unlimited Number of Worlds (D13–D14)

D13 (< A17) Aëtius

Anaximander [. . .]: worlds unlimited [scil. in number] in the unlimited, throughout the entire surrounding area (*peristasis*).[1]

[1] This statement is probably due to an erroneous extrapolation from the fact that the principle of Anaximander is the 'unlimited.' For similar cases, see Stobaeus 1.22.3b (2) (**DOX. T17**) and **ANAXIMEN. D11**.

D14 (A17) Aëtius

Among those who assert that the worlds are unlimited, Anaximander: they are at an equal distance from one another [. . .].

The Destructibility of the Worlds (D15–D16)

D15 (< A17) Aëtius

Anaximander [. . .]: the world is destructible.

D16 (A17) Simpl. *In Phys.*, p. 1121.5–9

οἱ μὲν γὰρ ἀπείρους τῷ πλήθει τοὺς κόσμους ὑποθέ-
μενοι, ὡς οἱ περὶ Ἀναξίμανδρον [. . .], γινομένους αὐτοὺς καὶ φθειρομένους ὑπέθεντο ἐπ' ἄπειρον, ἄλλων
μὲν ἀεὶ γινομένων ἄλλων δὲ φθειρομένων καὶ τὴν
κίνησιν ἀίδιον ἔλεγον· ἄνευ γὰρ κινήσεως οὐκ ἔστι
γένεσις ἢ φθορά.

The Heavens and Worlds (D17–D19)

D17 (A17) Aët. 1.7.12 (Ps.-Plut.; cf. Stob.) [τίς ἐστιν ὁ
θεός]

Ἀναξίμανδρος τοὺς ἀπείρους οὐρανοὺς[1] θεούς.

   [1] ἀπείρους οὐρανοὺς Stob.: ἀστέρας οὐρανίους Plut.

D18 (< A17) Cic. *Nat. deor.* 1.10.25–26

Anaximandri autem opinio est nativos esse deos longis
intervallis orientis occidentisque, eosque innumerabilis
esse mundos.

D19 (A17a) Aët. 2.11.5 (Stob.) [περὶ τῆς οὐρανοῦ οὐ-
σίας]

Ἀναξίμανδρος ἐκ θερμοῦ καὶ ψυχροῦ μίγματος.

D16 (A17) Simplicius, *Commentary on Aristotle's* Physics

Those who posit that the worlds are unlimited in number, like Anaximander [. . .], posited that they come about and are destroyed in an unlimited way, some always coming to be while others are perishing, and they said that the motion is eternal. For without movement there is not coming to be nor destruction.

The Heavens and Worlds (D17–D19)

D17 (A17) Aëtius

Anaximander declared that the unlimited heavens are gods.

D18 (< A17) Cicero, *On the Nature of the Gods*

The opinion of Anaximander is that the gods are born, that they appear and disappear at long intervals, and that they are innumerable worlds.

D19 (A17a) Aëtius

Anaximander: [scil. the heaven are constituted] out of a mixture of warm and cold.

The Heavenly Bodies (D20–D22)

D20 (A18) Aët. 2.13.7 (Stob.) [περὶ οὐσίας ἀστρῶν]

Ἀναξίμανδρος πιλήματα ἀέρος τροχοειδῆ, πυρὸς ἔμ-πλεα, κατά τι μέρος ἀπὸ στομίων ἐκπνέοντα φλόγας.

D21 (< A20) Plin *Nat. hist.* 18.213

occasum matutinum Vergiliarum [. . .] tradidit fieri [. . .] Anaximander XXXI.[1]

[1] XXXI *Schol. Germ.*: XIXX F[1]E: XXIX d *v.*: XXX F[2] *D.*

D22 (< A18) Aët. 2.15.6 (Ps.-Plut.) [περὶ τάξεως ἀστέ-ρων]

Ἀναξίμανδρος [. . .] ἀνωτάτω μὲν πάντων τὸν ἥλιον τετάχθαι, μετ' αὐτὸν δὲ τὴν σελήνην, ὑπὸ δ' αὐτοὺς τὰ ἀπλανῆ τῶν ἄστρων καὶ τοὺς πλανήτας.

Sun and Moon: Their Nature and Eclipses
(D23–D28)

D23 (A21, B4) Aët. 2.20.1 (Ps.-Plut.) [περὶ οὐσίας ἡλίου]

Ἀναξίμανδρος κύκλον εἶναι ὀκτωκαιεικοσαπλασίονα τῆς γῆς, ἁρματείῳ τροχῷ[1] παραπλήσιον,[2] τὴν ἁψίδα ἔχοντα κοίλην, πλήρη πυρός, κατά[3] τι μέρος ἐκφαί-νουσαν[4] διὰ στομίου τὸ πῦρ ὥσπερ διὰ πρηστῆρος αὐλοῦ. καὶ τοῦτ' εἶναι τὸν ἥλιον.

The Heavenly Bodies (D20–D22)

D20 (A18) Aëtius

Anaximander: [scil. the heavenly bodies are] wheel-shaped compressions of air, full of fire, exhaling flames in a certain part via orifices.

D21 (< A20) Pliny, *Natural History*

Anaximander [. . .] reports that the morning setting of the Pleiades takes place [. . .] thirty-one days [scil. after the autumnal equinox].

D22 (< A18) Aëtius

Anaximander [. . .]: the sun is placed highest of all [scil. the heavenly bodies], after it comes the moon, and under them the fixed stars and the planets.

Sun and Moon: Their Nature and Eclipses (D23–D28)

D23 (A21, B4) Aëtius

Anaximander: [scil. the sun] is a circle twenty-eight times the size of the earth, similar to the **wheel** of a chariot; it has a hollow rim filled with fire, and in a certain place it reveals the fire through an orifice as though through **the nozzle** (*aulos*) **of a bellows** (*prêstêr*). And this is the sun.

---

¹ ἁρματίου τροχῷ Mm: ἁρματείου τροχοῦ Π   ² παρα-πλήσιον post τὴν ἀψίδα mss., transp. Diels   ³ ἧς ante κατά hab. mss., del. Diels   ⁴ ἐκφαινούσης Plut., corr. Diels

D24 (A21) Aët. 2.21.1 (Ps.-Plut.; cf. Eus., Stob.) [περὶ μεγέθους ἡλίου]

Ἀναξίμανδρος τ•ν μὲν ἥλιον ἴσον εἶναι τῇ γῇ, τὸν δὲ κύκλον, ἀφ᾽ οὗ τὴν ἐκπνοὴν ἔχει καὶ ὑφ᾽[1] οὗ περιφέρεται,[2] ἑπτακαιεικοσαπλασίονα τῆς γῆς.

¹ ὑφ᾽ Stob. Eus. (*PE* 15.24.1): ἐφ᾽ Plut.   ² περιφέρεται Stob.: φέρεται Plut. Eus.

D25 (A21) Aët. 2.24.2 (Ps.-Plut.) [περὶ ἐκλείψεως ἡλίου]

Ἀναξίμανδρος τοῦ στομίου τῆς τοῦ πυρὸς διεκπνοῆς ἀποκλειομένου.

D26 (A22) Aët. 2.25.1 (Stob., cf. Ps.-Plut.) [περὶ σελήνης οὐσίας]

Ἀναξίμανδρος κύκλον εἶναι ἐννεακαιδεκαπλασίονα τῆς γῆς, ὅμοιοι ἁρματείῳ **τροχῷ**[1] κοίλην ἔχοντι τὴν ἁψῖδα καὶ πυρὸς πλήρη καθάπερ τὸν τοῦ ἡλίου, κείμενον λοξόν, ὡς κἀκεῖνον, ἔχοντα μίαν ἐκπνοὴν οἷον **πρηστῆρος αὐλόν.** ἐκλείπειν δὲ κατὰ τὰς ἐπιστροφὰς[2] τοῦ τροχοῦ.

¹ τροχῷ Plut., οm. Stob.   ² ἐπιστροφὰς Plut: τροπὰς vel στροφὰς Stob.

D24 (A21) Aëtius

Anaximander: the sun is equal to the earth, but the circle from which it produces its exhalation and by which it is carried in a circle is twenty-seven times the size of the earth.

D25 (A21) Aëtius

Anaximander: [scil. a solar eclipse happens] when the orifice of the exhalation of the fire becomes closed.

D26 (A22) Aëtius

Anaximander: [scil. the moon] is a circle nineteen times the size of the earth, similar to the **wheel** of a chariot; it has a hollow rim filled with fire, like that of the sun; it lies aslant, as does that one, and it has a single place of exhalation like **the nozzle** (*aulos*) **of a bellows** (*prêstêr*). Eclipses happen as a result of the turnings of the wheel.

D27 (> A22) Aë. 2.28.1 (Ps.-Plut.) [περὶ φωτισμῶν σελήνης]

Ἀναξίμανδρος ἴδιον αὐτὴν ἔχειν φῶς, ἀραιότερον δέ πως.

D28 (A22) Aët. 2.29.1 (Ps.-Plut.) [περὶ ἐκλείψεως σελήνης]

Ἀναξίμανδρος[1] τοῦ στομίου τοῦ περὶ τὸν τροχὸν ἐπιφραττομένου.

> [1] Ἀναξίμανδρος m: Ἀναξιμένης ΜΠ

The Shape and Position of the Earth (D29–D32)

D29 (A25) Aët. 3.10.2 (Ps.-Plut.) [περὶ σχήματος γῆς]

Ἀναξίμανδρος λίθῳ κίονι τὴν γῆν[1] προσφερῆ· τῶν ἐπιπέδων <. . .>[2]

> [1] τὴν γῆν Π: τῆ γῆ Mm   [2] lac. ind. Diels

D30 (A26) Arist. *Cael.* 2.13 295b11–16

εἰσὶ δέ τινες οἳ διὰ τὴν ὁμοιότητά φασιν αὐτὴν μένειν, ὥσπερ τῶν ἀρχαίων Ἀναξίμανδρος· μᾶλλον μὲν γὰρ οὐθὲν ἄνω ἢ κάτω ἢ εἰς τὰ πλάγια φέρεσθαι προσήκει τὸ ἐπὶ τοῦ μέσου ἱδρυμένον καὶ ὁμοίως πρὸς τὰ ἔσχατα ἔχον· ἅμα δ᾽ ἀδύνατον εἰς τὸ ἐναντίον[1] ποιεῖσθαι τὴν κίνησιν· ὥστ᾽ ἐξ ἀνάγκης μένειν.

D27 (> A22) Aëtius

Anaximander: it [i.e. the moon] possesses its own light, but it is somewhat weaker.

D28 (A22) Aëtius

Anaximander: [scil. a lunar eclipse happens] when the orifice on the **wheel** is obstructed.

The Shape and Position of the Earth (D29–D32)

D29 (A25) Aëtius

Anaximander: the earth resembles **a stone column.** Of its surfaces . . . [1]

[1] What follows, presumably a reference to the antipodes (cf. **D7 [3]**), is lost.

D30 (A26) Aristotle, *On the Heavens*

There are some who say that it is because of equality (*homoiotês*) that it [i.e. the earth] stays in place, as among the ancients Anaximander. For it is appropriate that what is located in the middle and maintains an equal relation to the extremities should not move at all more up than down or to the sides; and it is impossible to move in opposite directions at the same time. So of necessity it remains in place.

---

[1] τὸ ἐναντίον E: τἀναντία JHE[4]

D31 (< A1) Diog. Laert. 2.1

μέσην τε τὴν γῆν κεῖσθαι, κέντρου τάξιν ἐπέχουσαν, οὖσαν σφαιροειδῆ·

D32 (A26) Theon Sm. *Exp.*, p. 198.18–19 (= Eudem. Frag. 145 Wehrli)

[. . .] Ἀναξίμανδρος δέ ὅτι ἐστὶν ἡ γῆ μετέωρος καὶ κεῖται[1] περὶ τὸ τοῦ κόσμου μέσον.

  [1] κινεῖται mss., corr. Montucla

Meteorological Phenomena (D33–D34)

D33 (A23)

a Aët. 3.3.1 (Ps.-Plut.) [περὶ βροντῶν ἀστραπῶν κεραυνῶν πρηστήρων τε καὶ τυφώνων]

Ἀναξίμανδρος ἐκ τοῦ πνεύματος ταυτὶ πάντα συμβαίνειν· ὅταν γὰρ περιληφθὲν νέφει παχεῖ βιασάμενον ἐκπέσῃ τῇ λεπτομερείᾳ καὶ κουφότητι, τόθ᾽ ἡ μὲν ῥῆξις τὸν ψόφον, ἡ δὲ διαστολὴ παρὰ τὴν μελανίαν τοῦ νέφους τὸν διαυγασμὸν ἀποτελεῖ.

b Sen. *Quaest. nat.* 2.18

Anaximandrus omnia[1] ad spiritum retulit. tonitrua, inquit, sunt nubis ictae sonus. quare inaequalia sunt? quia et ipse

  [1] omnia <ista> Hine

D31 (< A1) Diogenes Laertius

The earth is in the middle, occupying the position of the center, and it is spherical.[1]

[1] This last indication, which contradicts **D20** (cf. **D7[3]**), is doubtless influenced by Plato, *Phaedo* 108e–109a.

D32 (A26) Eudemus in Theon of Smyrna, *Mathematics Useful for Understanding Plato*

Anaximander [scil. discovered] that the earth is suspended and that it rests at the center of the world.

Meteorological Phenomena (D33–D34)

D33 (A23)

a Aëtius

Anaximander: all of these phenomena [scil. thunder, lightning, thunderbolts, whirlwinds, and typhoons] come about from wind. For when this has been caught in a thick cloud but then breaks out violently by reason of its fineness and lightness, the tearing causes the noise, and the crack, against the blackness of the cloud, causes the flash.

b Seneca, *Natural Questions*

Anaximander relates all these phenomena [scil. those connected with thunder] to wind. Thunder, he says, is the noise produced by a cloud when it is struck. Why are they unequal [scil. in intensity]? Because ⟨the wind⟩ itself [scil.

303

‹spiritus›.[2] quare et sereno tonat? quia tunc quoque per crassum et scissum aëra spiritus prosilit. at quare aliquando non fulgurat, et tonat? quia spiritus infirmior non valuit in flammam, in sonum valuit. quid est ergo ipsa fulguratio? aëris diducentis se corruentisque iactatio, languidum ignem nec exiturum aperiens. quid est fulmen? acrioris densiorisque spiritus cursus.

[2] ‹spiritus› Hine: ictus inaequalis est δ (om. ζθπ): ‹spiritus inaequalis est› Diels

D34 (A24) Aët. 3.7.1 (Ps.-Plut.) [περὶ ἀνέμων]

Ἀναξίμανδρος ἄνεμον εἶναι ῥύσιν ἀέρος τῶν λεπτοτάτων ἐν αὐτῷ καὶ ὑγροτάτων ὑπὸ τοῦ ἡλίου κινουμένων ἢ τηκομένων.

The Formation and History of the Sea (D35–D36)

D35 (A27)

a Arist. *Meteor.* 2.1 353b6–11

εἶναι γὰρ τὸ πρῶτον ὑγρὸν ἅπαντα τὸν περὶ τὴν γῆν
τόπον, ὑπὸ δὲ τοῦ ἡλίου ξηραινόμενον τὸ μὲν διατμί-
σαν πνεύματα καὶ τροπὰς ἡλίου καὶ σελήνης φασὶ
ποιεῖν, τὸ δὲ λειφθὲν θάλατταν εἶναι· διὸ καὶ ἐλάττω
γίνεσθαι ξηραινομένην οἴονται καὶ τέλος ἔσεσθαί
ποτε πᾶσαν ξηράν.

is unequal]. Why is there thunder even in a cloudless sky? Because at this moment too the wind rushes through the crack in thick air. And why is there sometimes no lightning but there is thunder? Because the air is too weak to produce a flame, but not too weak [scil. to produce] a sound. Then what is lightning? The agitation of air which, extending and retracting itself, reveals fire that is weak and cannot escape. What is the lightning bolt? The passage of air that is sharper and denser.

D34 (A24) Aëtius

Anaximander: wind is a current of air, when the most fine and moist parts in it are set in motion or melted by the sun.

The Formation and History of the Sea (D38–D39)

D35 (A27)

a Aristotle, *Meteorology*

For they [i.e. the thinkers whose wisdom is human, by contrast with the theologians] say that the terrestrial region was at first entirely moist, but that, while it was being dried out by the sun, the part that evaporated produced the winds and the returns of the sun [i.e. the solstices] and moon, and what remained formed the sea; and this is why they think that it diminishes while it dries out and that one day it will be completely dry.

b Alex. *In Meteor.*, p. 67.1–12

οὗτοι δὲ γένεσιν ποιοῦσι τῆς θαλάσσης, ἀλλ᾽ οὐκ
ἀγένητον αὐτὴν λέγουσιν ἰδίας πηγὰς ἔχουσαν, ὡς οἱ
θεολόγοι. οἱ μὲν γὰρ αὐτῶν ὑπόλειμμα λέγουσιν εἶναι
τὴν θάλασσαν τῆς πρώτης ὑγρότητος. ὑγροῦ γὰρ
ὄντος τοῦ περὶ τὴν γῆν τόπου κἄπειτα τὸ μέν τι[1] τῆς
ὑγρότητος ὑπὸ τοῦ ἡλίου ἐξατμίζεσθαι καὶ γίνεσθαι
πνεύματά τε ἐξ αὐτοῦ καὶ τροπὰς ἡλίου τε καὶ
σελήνης, ὡς διὰ τὰς ἀτμίδας ταύτας καὶ τὰς ἀναθυ-
μιάσεις κἀκείνω τὰς τροπὰς ποιουμένων, ἔνθα[2] ἡ
ταύτης αὐτοῖς χορηγία γίνεται, περὶ ταῦτα τρεπο-
μένων· τὸ δέ τι αὐτῆς ὑπολειφθὲν ἐν τοῖς κοίλοις τῆς
γῆς[3] τόποις θάλασσαν εἶναι· διὸ καὶ ἐλάττω γίνεσθαι
ξηραινομένην ἑκάστοτε ὑπὸ τοῦ ἡλίου καὶ τέλος ἔσεσθαί ποτε ξηράν. ταύτης τῆς δόξης ἐγένετο, ὡς ἱστορεῖ Θεόφραστος Fr. 221 FHS&G], Ἀναξίμανδρός τε
καὶ Διογένης [. . = **DIOG. D24**].

[1] κἄπειτα τὸ μέν τι] τὰ πρῶτα Awa   [2] ἔνθεν
Usener   [3] τῆς —ῆς om. AWa

D36 (A27) Aët. 3.16.1 (Ps.-Plut.) [περὶ θαλάσσης πῶς
συνέστη καὶ πῶς ἐστι πικρά]

Ἀναξίμανδρος τὴν θάλασσάν φησιν εἶναι τῆς πρώτης
ὑγρασίας λείψανον, ἧς τὸ μὲν πλεῖον[1] μέρος ἀνεξή-
ρανε τὸ πῦρ, τὸ δὲ ὑπολειφθὲν διὰ τὴν ἔκκαυσιν μετέβαλεν.

306

b Alexander of Aphrodisias, *Commentary on Aristotle's* Meteorology

These authors [scil. the ones Aristotle is discussing] attribute a birth to the sea, instead of saying as the theologians do, that it is ungenerated and provided with its own sources [cf. **COSM. T10**].[1] For some of them say that the sea is a residue of the original moisture. For at first the region around the earth was moist, but then part of the moisture evaporated by the effect of the sun, and this is why the winds and the turnings of the sun [i.e. the solstices] and moon came about, for these [scil. heavenly bodies] too make their turnings as a result of these vapors and exhalations, returning to the place where they find an abundant supply of these. But the part of it [i.e. the original moisture] that remained in the hollows of the earth forms the sea; and that is why it is diminishing, since it is being constantly dried out by the sun, and will end up one day becoming dry. As Theophrastus reports, Anaximander and Diogenes [scil. of Apollonia] were of this opinion [. . .].

[1] Alexander, who is referring to the theologians (i.e. Homer and Hesiod), interprets Ocean as the sea.

D36 (A27) Aëtius

Anaximander says that the sea is a residue of the original moisture, of which the fire dried up the greater part, while what remained was transformed by the heat.

---

[1] πλεῖον ΜΠ: πλεῖστον m

The Nature of the Soul (D37)

D37 (< A29) Aët. 4.3.2 (Theod. *Cur.* 5.18) [εἰ σῶμα ἡ ψυχὴ καὶ τίς ἡ οὐσία αὐτῆς]

Ἀναξίμανδρος [. . .] ἀερώδη τῆς ψυχῆς τὴν φύσιν εἰρήκασιν.

The Origin of Animals (D38–D40)

D38 (A30) Aët. 5.19.4 (Ps.-Plut.) [περὶ ζῴων γενέσεως, πῶς ἐγένοντο ζῷα καὶ εἰ φθαρτά]

Ἀναξίμανδρος ἐν ὑγρῷ γεννηθῆναι τὰ πρῶτα ζῷα φλοιοῖς περιεχόμενα ἀκανθώδεσι, προβαινούσης δὲ τῆς ἡλικίας ἀποβαίνειν ἐπὶ τὸ ξηρότερον καὶ περιρρηγνυμένου τοῦ φλοιοῦ ἐπ᾽ ὀλίγον χρόνον μεταβιῶναι.

D39 (A30) Cens. *Die nat.* 4.7

Anaximander Milesius videri sibi ex aqua terraque calefactis[1] exortos esse sive pisces seu piscibus simillima animalia; in his homines concrevisse fetusque[2] ad pubertatem intus retentos, tunc demum ruptis illis[3] viros mulieresque, qui iam se alere possent, processisse.

[1] coalefactis *corr. Meursius*   [2] et usque *coni. Meursius*
[3] iliis *coni. Meursius*

ANAXIMANDER

The Nature of the Soul (D37)

D37 (< A29) Aëtius

[. . .] Anaximander [. . .] said that the nature of the soul is air-like.

The Origin of Animals (D38–D40)

D38 (A30) Aëtius

Anaximander: the first animals were born n moisture, surrounded by thorny bark, but as they increased in age they moved to where it was drier, and when the bark burst open they changed their way of life in a short t me.

D39 (A30) Censorinus, *The Birthday*

Anaximander of Miletus thought that when the water and earth were heated, there arose from them either fish or animals very similar to fish; human beings developed in these and remained inside as embryos until they reached puberty; then finally they [i.e. these animals] burst open, and men and women came forth who were already capable of nourishing themselves.

D40 (< A30) Plut. *Quaest. conv.* 8.8.4 730E–F

[. . . cf. **R18**] οὐ γὰρ ἐν τοῖς αὐτοῖς ἐκεῖνος ἰχθῦς καὶ ἀνθρώπους, ἀλλ᾽ ἐν ἰχθύσιν ἐγγενέσθαι τὸ πρῶτον ἀνθρώπους ἀποφαίνεται καὶ τραφέντας ὥσπερ οἱ γαλεοὶ[1] καὶ γενομένους ἱκανοὺς ἑαυτοῖς βοηθεῖν ἐκβῆναι τηνικαῦτα καὶ γῆς λαβέσθαι [. . .].

---

[1] γαλεοὶ Doehner, Emperius: παλαιοὶ mss.

D40 (< A30) Plutarch, *Table Talk*

[. . .] For he does not think that fish and humans [scil. developed] in the same circumstances, but he declares that at first humans developed and were nourished inside fishes, like sharks, and that they went out and reached land when they had become capable of protecting themselves [. . .].

ANAXIMANDER [12 DK]

R

The Unlimited of Anaximander (R1–R6)
As Intermediary Substance (R1–R5)

R1 (≠ DK) Arist. *Phys.* 3.4 203a16–18

οἱ δὲ περὶ φύσεως πάντες[1] ὑποτιθέασιν ἑτέραν τινὰ
φύσιν τῷ ἀπείρῳ τῶν λεγομένων στοιχείων, οἷον
ὕδωρ ἢ ἀέρα ἢ τὸ μεταξὺ τούτων.

---

[1] πάντες Philop. *In Phys.*, p. 395.8, Simpl. *In Phys.*, p. 458.17:
ἅπαντες ἀεὶ FHIJ: ἀεὶ πάντες E

R2 (< A9) Simpl. *In Phys.*, p. 24.21–22

δῆλον δὲ ὅτι τὴν εἰς ἄλληλα μεταβολὴν τῶν τεττάρων
στοιχείων οὗτος θεασάμενος οὐκ ἠξίωσεν ἕν τι τούτων
ὑποκείμενον ποιῆσαι, ἀλλά τι ἄλλο παρὰ ταῦτα [. . .
= **R9**].

ANAXIMANDER

R

The Unlimited of Anaximander (R1–R6)
As Intermediary Substance (R1–R5)

R1 (≠ DK) Aristotle, *Physics*

All those who study nature assign to the unlimited a certain other nature belonging to what are called the elements, like water, air, or what is intermediary between these.[1]

[1] For other passages in which Aristotle mentions a doctrine of the intermediary element and seems to be alluding to Anaximander (without ever naming him), cf. *Physics* 1.6 189b1–8, 205a25–29; *Generation and Corruption* 2.1 328b35, 2.5 332a19–25; *Metaphysics* A7 988a29–32, 989a14. The identification derives from the commentators on Aristotle (cf. e.g. **R2, R4**). In **D12,** Aristotle explicitly distinguishes Anaximander from those who posited an intermediary.

R2 (< A9) Simplicius, *Commentary on Aristotle's* Physics

It is clear that, having observed the transformation of the four elements into one another, he thought that he should not make one of these the substrate, but some other thing besides them [. . .].

R3 (A16) Arist. *Ceel.* 3.5 303b10–13

ἔνιοι γὰρ ἓν μόνον ὑποτίθενται, καὶ τοῦτο[1] οἱ μὲν
ὕδωρ, οἱ δ' ἀέρα, οἱ δὲ πῦρ, οἱ δ' ὕδατος μὲν λεπτότερον, ἀέρος δὲ πυκνότερον, ὃ **περιέχειν** φασὶ πάντας
τοὺς οὐρανοὺς **ἄπειρον** ὄν.

[1] τοῦτο EH: τούτων J

R4 (A16) Alex. *In Metaph.*, p. 60.8–10

προσέθηκε δὲ τῇ ἱστορίᾳ καὶ τὴν Ἀναξιμάνδρου
δόξαν, ὃς ἀρχὴν ἔθετο τὴν μεταξὺ φύσιν ἀέρος τε καὶ
πυρός, ἢ ἀέρος τε καὶ ὕδατος· λέγεται γὰρ ἀμφο-
τέρως.

R5 (≠ DK) Simpl *In Cael.*, p. 615.13–15

Ἀναξίμανδρος [. . .] ἀόριστόν τι ὕδατος μὲν λεπτότερον ἀέρος δὲ πυκνότερον, διότι τὸ ὑποκείμενον εὐφυὲς
ἐχρῆν εἶναι πρὸς τὴν ἐφ' ἑκάτερα μετάβασιν [. . . =
R6].

As Reservoir (R6)

R6 (< A17) Simpl. *In Cael.*, p. 615.15–18

ἄπειρον δὲ πρῶτος[1] ὑπέθετο, ἵνα ἔχῃ χρῆσθαι πρὸς
τὰς γενέσεις ἀφθόνως· καὶ κόσμους δὲ ἀπείρους οὗτος
καὶ ἕκαστον τῶν κόσμων ἐξ ἀπείρου τοῦ τοιούτου
στοιχείου ὑπέθετο, ὡς δοκεῖ.

[1] πρῶτος A: πρώ-ως DEF

R3 (A16) Aristotle, *On the Heavens*

For some people posit only one [scil. element], and the
ones [scil. posit] that this is water, others air, others fire,
others something finer than water and denser than air; and
they say that this, being **unlimited, surrounds** all the
heavens.

R4 (A16) Alexander of Aphrodisias, *Commentary on Aristotle's* Metaphysics

He [i.e. Aristotle] has added to his historical presentation
the opinion of Anaximander, who posited as principle a
nature intermediary between air and fire, or between air
and water—for it is reported in both ways.

R5 (≠ DK) Simplicius, *Commentary on Aristotle's* On
the Heavens

Anaximander [. . .] [scil. posed as element] something
undefined (*aoristos*), finer than water but denser than air,
since the substrate had to be well suited for transformation
into both of these [. . .].

As Reservoir (R6)

R6 (< A17) Simplicius, *Commentary on Aristotle's* On the
Heavens

He was the first to posit an **unlimited**, so that he would
have something he could make use of unstintingly for gen-
eratings; and he said that the worlds are unlimited [scil. in
number] and that each one of the worlds comes from this
sort of unlimited element, as it seems.

EARLY GREEK PHILOSOPHY II

A Comparison with Empedocles
and Anaxagoras (R7–R9)

R7 (A9) Arist. *Phys.* 1.4 187a20–23

οἱ δ᾽ ἐκ τοῦ ἑνὸς ἐνούσας τὰς ἐναντιότητας ἐκκρίνεσθαι, ὥσπερ Ἀναξίμανδρός φησι καὶ ὅσοι δ᾽ ἓν καὶ
πολλά φασιν εἶναι, ὥσπερ Ἐμπεδοκλῆς καὶ Ἀναξ-
αγόρας· ἐκ τοῦ μείγματος γὰρ καὶ οὗτοι ἐκκρίνουσι
τἆλλα.

R8 (A9a, 59 A41) Simpl. *In Phys.*, p. 154.14–23 (= Theophr. Frag. 228B FHS&G)

καὶ Θεόφραστος δὲ τὸν Ἀναξαγόραν εἰς τὸν Ἀναξίμανδρον συνωθῶν καὶ οὕτως ἐκλαμβάνει τὰ ὑπὸ
Ἀναξαγόρου λεγόμενα, ὡς δύνασθαι μίαν αὐτὸν φύσιν λέγειν τὸ ὑποκείμενον. γράφει δὲ οὕτως ἐν τῇ
Φυσικῇ ἱστορίᾳ· "οὕτω μὲν οὖν λαμβανόντων δόξειεν
ἂν ποιεῖν τὰς μὲν ὑλικὰς ἀρχὰς ἀπείρους, ὥσπερ
εἴρηται, τὴν δὲ τῆς κινήσεως καὶ τῆς γενέσεως αἰτίαν
μίαν. εἰ δέ τις τὴν μῖξιν τῶν ἁπάντων ὑπολάβοι μίαν
εἶναι φύσιν ἀόριστον καὶ κατ᾽ εἶδος καὶ κατὰ μέγεθος, ὅπερ ἂν δόξειε βούλεσθαι λέγειν, συμβαίνει δύο
τὰς ἀρχὰς αὐτῷ λέγειν τήν τε τοῦ ἀπείρου φύσιν καὶ
τὸν νοῦν, ὥστε πάντως φαίνεται τὰ σωματικὰ στοιχεῖα παραπλησίως ποιῶν Ἀναξιμάνδρῳ."

A Comparison with Empedocles
and Anaxagoras (R7–R9)

R7 (A9) Aristotle, *Physics*

The other ones [scil. than those who posit a single sub-
strate] say that the contraries are present in the One and
are separated out from it, as Anaximander says and all
those who assert the existence of both the one and the
many, like Empedocles and Anaxagoras; for these too
think that all other things separate out from the mixture
[cf. **EMP. D81; ANAXAG. D20**].

R8 (A9a, 59 A41) Theophrastus in Simplicius, *Commentary on Aristotle's* Physics

And Theophrastus, pushing Anaxagoras toward Anaximander, understands in this way too what Anaxagoras says,
i.e. that it is possible that he is saying that the substrate is
a single nature. He writes as follows in his *Natural History:*
"If we take things in this way, he would seem to posit
material principles that are unlimited [scil. in number], as
we have said, and a single cause of motion and of generation. But if one supposed that the mixture of all things is
a single nature, undefined both in form and in size, which
is what he would seem to have meant then the result is
that he is saying that there are two principles, the nature
of the unlimited and mind, so that he seems absolutely to
conceive corporeal elements in the same way as Anaximander" [= **ANAXAG. R19**].

R9 (< A9) Simpl. *In Phys.*, p. 24.23–25

[. . . = **R2**] οὗτος δὲ οὐκ ἀλλοιουμένου τοῦ στοιχείου τὴν γένεσιν ποιεῖ, ἀλλ᾽ ἀποκρινομένων τῶν ἐναντίων διὰ τῆς ἀιδίου κινήσεως· διὸ καὶ τοῖς περὶ Ἀναξαγόραν τοῦτον ὁ Ἀριστοτέλης συνέταξεν.

Four Peripatetic Criticisms (R10–R13)

R10 (Ar 12 Wöhrle) Arist. *GC* 2.5 332a19–25

[. . .] οὐκ ἔστιν ἓν τούτων ἐξ οὗ τὰ πάντα. οὐ μὴν οὐδ᾽ ἄλλο τί γε παρὰ ταῦτα, οἷον μέσον τι ἀέρος καὶ ὕδατος ἢ ἀέρος καὶ πυρός, ἀέρος μὲν παχύτερον ἢ πυρός, τῶν δὲ λεπτότερον· ἔσται γὰρ ἀὴρ καὶ πῦρ ἐκεῖνο μετ᾽ ἐναντιότητος· ἀλλὰ στέρησις τὸ ἕτερον τῶν ἐναντίων· ὥστ᾽ οὐκ ἐνδέχεται μονοῦσθαι ἐκεῖνο οὐδέποτε, ὥσπερ φασί τινες τὸ ἄπειρον καὶ τὸ περιέχον.

R11 (A16) Arist. *Phys.* 3.5 204b22–29

ἀλλὰ μὴν οὐδὲ ἓν καὶ ἁπλοῦν εἶναι σῶμα ἄπειρον ἐνδέχεται, οὔτε ὡς λέγουσί τινες τὸ παρὰ τὰ στοιχεῖα, ἐξ οὗ ταῦτα γεννῶσιν, οὔθ᾽ ἁπλῶς. εἰσὶν γάρ τινες οἳ τοῦτο ποιοῦσι τὸ ἄπειρον, ἀλλ᾽ οὐκ ἀέρα ἢ ὕδωρ, ὅπως μὴ τἆλλα φθείρηται ὑπὸ τοῦ ἀπείρου αὐτῶν· ἔχουσι γὰρ πρὸς ἄλληλα ἐναντίωσιν, οἷον ὁ μὲν ἀὴρ ψυχρός, τὸ δ᾽ ὕδωρ ὑγρόν, τὸ δὲ πῦρ θερμόν· ὧν εἰ ἦν

318

R9 (< A9) Simplicius, *Commentary on Aristotle's* Physics

[. . .] He does not explain birth by the alteration of the element but by the separation of the contraries because of the eternal motion. And that is why Aristotle has placed him together with Anaxagoras and his followers [cf. **ANAXAG. D2**].

Four Peripatetic Criticisms (R10–R13)

R10 (≠ DK) Aristotle, *On Generation and Corruption*

[. . .] not one of these things [i.e. fire, air, earth, water] is something from which all things could derive. But certainly neither is anything else besides these, such as something intermediary between air and water or between air and fire, denser than air or fire, and finer than the others. For that air or that fire will include a contrariety; but one of the contraries is a privation, so that it is not possible that that [scil. intermediary] ever exist alone, as some say is the case of the unlimited and of what surrounds.

R11 (A16) Aristotle, *Physics*

But neither is it possible for an unlimited body to be one and simple, whether it is, as some say, something beside the elements from which they generate these, or absolutely speaking. For there are some who identify the unlimited with this, and not with air or water, so that the other things are not destroyed by their being unlimited. For they stand in contrariety to one another, for example air is cold, water moist, fire hot; and if one of them were

ἓν ἄπειρον, ἔφθαρτο ἂν ἤδη τἆλλα· νῦν δ᾽ ἕτερον εἶναί
φασιν ἐξ οὗ ταῦτα.

R12 (< A14) Arist. *Phys.* 3.7 208a 2–4

φαίνονται δὲ πάντες καὶ οἱ ἄλλοι ὡς ὕλη χρώμενοι τῷ
ἀπείρῳ· διὸ καὶ ἄτοπον τὸ **περιέχον** ποιεῖν αὐτὸ ἀλλὰ
μὴ περιεχόμενον.

R13 (< A14) Aët. 1.3.3 (Ps.-Plut.) [περὶ ἀρχῶν]

[. . . = **D10**] ἁμαρτάνει δὲ οὗτος μὴ λέγων τί ἐστι τὸ
ἄπειρον, πότερον ἀήρ ἐστιν ἢ ὕδωρ ἢ γῆ ἢ ἄλλα τινὰ
σώματα. ἁμαρτάνει οὖν τὴν μὲν ὕλην ἀποφαινόμενος,
τὸ δὲ ποιοῦν αἴτιον ἀναιρῶν. τὸ γὰρ ἄπειρον οὐδὲν
ἄλλο ἢ ὕλη ἐστίν· οὐ δύναται δὲ ἡ ὕλη εἶναι ἐνεργείᾳ,
ἐὰν μὴ τὸ ποιοῦν ὑποκέηται.

Astronomical Discoveries and Inventions
Attributed to Anaximander (R14–R17)

R14 (< A1) Diog. Laert. 2.1

εὗρε δὲ καὶ γνώμονα πρῶτος καὶ ἔστησεν ἐπὶ τῶν
σκιοθήρων ἐν Λακεδαίμονι, καθά φησι Φαβωρῖνος ἐν
Παντοδαπῇ ἱστορίᾳ [Frag. 65 Amato], τροπάς τε καὶ
ἰσημερίας σημαίνοντα· καὶ ὡροσκόπια κατεσκεύασε.

unlimited, then the others would already have been destroyed. But as it is, they say that what these latter come from is different.

R12 (< A14) Aristotle, *Physics*

It is evident that all the others make use of the unlimited as matter. And for this reason it is absurd to say that it **surrounds** and not that it is surrounded.

R13 (< A14) Aëtius

[. . .] He errs in not saying what the unlimited is, whether it is air or water, or earth or some other bodies. Thus he errs in declaring the matter but in suppressing the efficient cause. For the unlimited is nothing else than matter. But matter cannot be in activity if one does not posit the efficient [scil. cause].

Astronomical Discoveries and Inventions
Attributed to Anaximander (R14–R17)

R14 (< A1) Diogenes Laertius

He was also the first to discover the *gnomon* and he placed it on the sundials in Sparta, as Favorinus says in his *Miscellaneous History,* to indicate the solstices and the equinoxes, and he constructed clocks.

R15 (< A4) Eus. *PE* 10.14.11

οὗτος πρῶτος γνώμονας κατεσκεύασε πρὸς διάγνω-
σιν τροπῶν τε ἡλίου καὶ χρόνων καὶ ὡρῶν καὶ ἰσημερίας.

R16 (< A5) Plin. *Nat. hist.* 2.31

obliquitatem eius intellexisse, hoc est rerum fores[1] aper-
uisse, Anaximander Milesius traditur primus [. . . = **P3**].

   [1] fortissimi *vel* -mas *ante* fores *hab.* FEaz., *del.* R

R17 (< A19) Simpl. *In Cael.*, p. 471.4–9

[. . .] Ἀναξιμάνδρου πρώτου τὸν περὶ μεγεθῶν καὶ
ἀποστημάτων λόγον εὑρηκότος, ὡς Εὔδημος ἱστορεῖ
[Frag. 146 Wehrli] [. . . = **PYTHS. ANON. D39**]. τὰ δὲ
μεγέθη καὶ τὰ ἀποστήματα ἡλίου καὶ σελήνης [. . .]
εἰκὸς ἦν ταῦτα καὶ τὸν Ἀναξίμανδρον εὑρηκέναι [. . .].

An Ironic Allusion to a Notorious Doctrine (R18)

R18 (< A30) Plut. *Quaest. conv.* 8.8.4 730D–E

οἱ δ' ἀφ' Ἕλληνος τοῦ παλαιοῦ καὶ πατρογενείῳ Πο-
σειδῶνι θύουσιν, ἐκ τῆς ὑγρᾶς τὸν ἄνθρωπον οὐσίας
φῦναι δόξαντες[1] ὡς καὶ Σύροι· διὸ καὶ σέβονται τὸν
ἰχθῦν, ὡς ὁμογενῆ καὶ σύντροφον, ἐπιεικέστερον

   [1] δοξάζοντες Turnebus

322

R15 (< A4) Eusebius, *Evangelical Preparation*

He was the first to construct *gnomons* to distinguish the solstices of the sun, the periods of time, the seasons, and the equinox.

R16 (< A5) Pliny, *Natural History*

Anaximander of Miletus is reported to have been the first person [. . .] to have understood its [i.e. the zodiac's] inclination, that is to have opened up the gates of these matters [. . .].

R17 (< A19) Simplicius, *Commentary on Aristotle's* On the Heavens

[. . .] Anaximander was the first to discover the explanation for the sizes and distances [scil. of the planets], as is reported by Eudemus [. . .]. As for the sizes and distances of the sun and moon [. . .], it is probable that Anaximander discovered them too [. . .].

An Ironic Allusion to a Notorious Doctrine (R18)

R18 (< A30) Plutarch, *Table Talk*

The descendants of ancient Hellen sacrifice to their ancestor Poseidon too, since they believe, as the Syrians do, that human beings were born from the moist substance. And

Ἀναξιμάνδρου φιλοσοφοῦντες· [. . . = **D40**] καθάπερ
οὖν τὸ πῦρ τὴν ὕλην, ἐξ ἧς ἀνήφθη, μητέρα καὶ πα-
τέρ᾽ οὖσαν ἤσθιεν [. . .] οὕτως ὁ Ἀναξίμανδρος τῶν
ἀνθρώπων πατέρα καὶ μητέρα κοινὸν ἀποφήνας τὸν
ἰχθῦν διέβαλεν πρὸς τὴν βρῶσιν.

A Christian Polemic (R19)

R19 (Ar 52 Wöhle) Iren. *Adv. haer.* 2.14.2

Anaximander autem hoc quod immensum est omnium
initium subiecit, seminaliter habens in semetipso omnium
genesim, ex quo immensos mundos constare ait: et hoc
autem in Bythum et in Aeonas ipsorum transfiguraverunt.

A Greek Alchemical Adaptation (R20)

R20 (Ar 216 Wöhle) Ps.-Olymp. *Ars sacra* 25

Ἀναξίμανδρος δὲ τὸ μεταξὺ ἔλεγεν ἀρχὴν εἶναι·
μεταξὺ δὲ λέγω τῶν ἀτμῶν ἢ τῶν καπνῶν· ὁ μὲν γὰρ
ἀτμὸς μεταξὺ ἐστιν πυρὸς καὶ γῆς, καὶ καθόλου δὲ
εἰπεῖν, πᾶν το μεταξὺ θερμῶν καὶ ὑγρῶν ἀτμός ἐστιν·
τὰ δὲ μεταξὺ θερμῶν καὶ ξηρῶν καπνός.

324

that is why they revere the fish as belonging to the same line of descent as they do and as having been raised together with them—philosophizing thereby more plausibly than Anaximander [. . .]. So just as fire devours the wood from which it was kindled and which is its father and mother [. . .], so too Anaximander, having declared that fish is the common father and mother of all human beings, criticized its use for eating.[1]

[1] The discussion bears upon the Pythagoreans' prohibitions (cf. **PYTH. c D20[83]**).

A Christian Polemic (R19)

R19 (≠ DK) Irenaeus, *Against the Heresies*

Anaximander posited as the origin of all things the unlimited, which contains within itself in the form of seeds the generation of all things, and from which, he said, the infinite worlds come. And this is what they [i.e. the Valentinian Gnostics] transformed into their own Bythus and Eons.

A Greek Alchemical Adaptation (R20)

R20 (≠ DK) Ps.-Olympiodorus, *On the Sacred Art*

Anaximander said that the intermediary is the principle; I say that the intermediary belongs to vapor or smoke. For vapor is intermediary between fire and earth, and to speak generally everything that is intermediary between what is hot and what is moist is vapor; and what is intermediary between what is hot and what is dry is smoke.

Anaximander in The Assembly of Philosophers (R21)

R21 (≠ DK) *Turba Phil.* Sermo I

a p. 109.15–16 Ruska; 38.1–6 Plessner

iussit autem, ut Eximedrus prius loqueretur, qui optimi erat consilii.

incipiens ait omnium initium esse naturam quandam et eam esse perpetuam ac omnia coquentem et quidem videtur naturas eorumque nativitates et corruptiones esse tempora, quibus termini, ad quos pervenire videntur et noscuntur. doceo autem vos stellas esse igneas et aera ipsas continere et quod si aeris humiditas et spissitudo non esset, quae solis flammam separaret a creaturis, omnia subsistentia sol combureret. Deus autem aerem separantem constituit ne combureret quod in terra creavit.

b (Ar 242 Wöhrle) Muḥammad ibn Umayl al-Tamīmī, *Kitāb al-māʾ al-waraqī wa al-arḍ al-naǧmiyya* (cf. p. 39.15–40.24 Plessner)

قال أكسميدوس الجرعاني [. . .] فالماء والنار عدوان ليست بينهما قرابة واشجة لأن النار حارّة يابسة والماء بارد رطب فأمّا الهواء فحدِّ رطب فأصلح ما بينهما برطوبته مع حرارته فصار الهواء مصلحا بين الماء والنار. والأرواح كلهم من لطيف بخار الهواء تكون لأنه إذا اجتمعت السخونة مع الرطوبة فليس لهما بد من أن يخرج من بينهما لطيف يصير بخارا أو ريحا لأن حرارة الشمس تُخرج

Anaximander in The Assembly of
Philosophers *(R21)*

R21 (≠ DK) *The Assembly of Philosophers*

a in Latin translation

He [i.e. Pythagoras] ordered that Eximedrus [i.e. Anaximander] speak first, since he was the best in counsel.

Beginning, he said that the beginning of all things is a certain nature and that this is eternal and concocts all things, and indeed it seems that their natures, generations, and destructions are times that have limits that they reach, as is seen and known. But I teach you that the stars are fiery and that air surrounds these and that, if there did not exist the moisture and density of the air, which keeps the sun's flame separate from the creatures, the sun would burn up everything that exists. But God created the air as a separation, so that it would not burn up what He had created on the earth.

b in Arabic translation in Muḥammad ibn Umayl al-Tamīmī, *Book of the Silvery Water and the Starry Earth*

Aksimīdūs al-Ǧurʿānī [i.e. Anaximander] said, "[. . .] Water and Fire are two enemies and there is between them no affinity and close connection, because Fire is hot and dry while Water is cold and moist; as for Air, it is hot and moist, and it has been established between the two due to its humidity accompanied by heat; thus Air became the reconciler between Water and Fire. All the spiritual realities that derive from the refined exhalation of Air come to be because, when warmth mixes with humidity, it is inevita-

من الهواء لطيفا يصير روحا وحيوة لكل مخلوق وكلِ هذا إنما هو من تقدير الله تعالى. والهواء إنما يستمدّ الرطوبة من الماء ولولا أ ٮ يستمدّ من رطوبة الماء ما يقوى به على حرارة الشمس لقهرت اٮشمس الهواء ٮحرّها ولو لا تنفس الهواء حينئذ بالأرواح التي تتولد منها الخلائق لأُهْلِكَتِ الشمسَ ما من تحتها من الخلائق بحرّها وإنما قوى عليها الهواء لائتلاف حرارته بٮحرارتها وائتلاف رطوبته برطوبة الماء.

ble for them to have something refined proceeding from them both, which becomes an exhalation or a breath, because the sun's heat extracts from air something refined, which becomes breath and life for all the creatures, and all this depends upon the design of God Almighty. Air, in its turn, acquires humidity from water; if it did not acquire something of the water's humidity, by means of which it can counter the sun's heat, the sun would dry the air by its heat; and if air did not blow through the spiritual realities out of which all the creatures come, then the sun would annihilate all the creatures below it, because of its heat; but air overcomes the latter by means of the connection it establishes between its own heat and that heat, and between its own humidity and the humidity of water."[1]

[1] Translated by Germana Chemi.

7. ANAXIMENES [ANAXIMEN.]

The data provided by the ancient sources for the dates of Anaximenes' birth and death are confused, but his activity can be situated toward the middle of the sixth century BC, a little after Anaximander's. Of his original writings only a few isolated terms survive. Diogenes Laertius reports that his mode of expression was "simple and plain" (**R2**): this is surely to be understood by contrast with the poetically charged style of Anaximander, to whose thought he is certainly responding. The evanescent character of his person—despite the fact that his name seems to have remained famous for a long time (cf. **R10, P5**)—contrasts with the importance to be assigned philosophically to his monism, which is founded on the properties of air.

BIBLIOGRAPHY

Editions

G. Wöhrle, ed. *Anaximenes aus Milet. Die Fragmente zu seiner Lehre* (Stuttgart, 1993).

G. Wöhrle et al., ed. *Die Milesier: Anaximander und Anaximenes.* Coll. Traditio Praesocratica vol. 1 (Berlin, 2012).

Studies

D. Graham. *Explaining the Cosmos. The Ionian Tradition
of Scientific Philosophy* (Princeton, 2006), Chapter 3.

OUTLINE OF THE CHAPTER

ANAXIMENES

R

ANAXIMENES [13 DK]

P

Chronology (P1–P4)

P1 (< A1) Diog. Laert. 2.3

Ἀναξιμένης Εὐρυστράτου, Μιλήσιος, ἤκουσεν Ἀναξιμάνδρου. ἔνιοι δὲ καὶ Παρμενίδου φασὶν ἀκοῦσαι αὐτὸν[1] [. . .]. καὶ γεγένηται μέν, καθά φησιν Ἀπολλόδωρος [*FGrHist* 244 F66], <. . .>[2] περὶ τὴν Σάρδεων ἅλωσιν, ἐτελεύτησε δὲ τῇ ἑξηκοστῇ τρίτῃ Ὀλυμπιάδι.[3]

  [1] Παρμενίδην . . . αὐτοῦ Volkmann: ἔνιοι . . . αὐτοῦ secl. Marcovich   [2] <. . .> lac. posuimus   [3] τῇ ἑξηκοστῇ τρίτῃ ὀλυμπιάδι, ἐτελεύτησε δὲ περὶ τὴν σάρδεων ἅλωσιν mss., transp. Simson

P2 (< A7) (Ps.- ?) Hippol. *Ref.* 1.7.8

οὗτος ἤκμασεν περὶ ἔτος πρῶτον τῆς πεντηκοστῆς ὀγδόης Ὀλυμπιάδος.

ANAXIMENES

P

Chronology (P1–P4)

P1 (< A1) Diogenes Laertius

Anaximenes, son of Eurystratus, of Miletus, studied with Anaximander; some people say that he also studied with Parmenides [. . .].[1] And as Apollodorus says, he was <. . .>[2] around the time of the capture of Sardis [= 546/5 BC], and he died during the 63rd Olympiad [= 528/4].

> [1] Editors usually correct in order to reestablish the only possible chronology: "Some people say that Parmenides studied with him." But perhaps the fiction is meaningful, emphasizing that Anaximenes is a 'monist.'   [2] The transmitted text says that Anaximenes was born at the time of the capture of Sardis, but this is incompatible with the date given for his death. We suggest that an adjective indicating a particular age or meaning "famous" [cf. **P3**] or "mature" [cf. **P2**] has dropped out of the text.

P2 (< A7) (Ps.-?) Hippolytus, *Refutation of All Heresies*

He reached full maturity around the first year of the 58th Olympiad [= 548/7].

P3 (A3) Eus. *Chron.* (Hier.), p. 102b

[ad Ol. 55] Anaximenes physicus agnoscitur.

P4 (< A2) *Suda* A 1988

γέγονεν ἐν τῇ νεʹ Ὀλυμπιάδι ἐν τῇ Σάρδεων ἁλώσει,
ὅτε Κῦρος ὁ Πέρσης Κροῖσον καθεῖλεν.

Statue (P5)

P5 (As 176 Wöhrle) Christod. *Ecphr.* 50–51

ἦν μὲν Ἀναξιμένης νοερὸς σοφός, ἐν δὲ μενοινῇ
δαιμονίης ἐλέλιζε νοήματα ποικίλα βουλῆς.

336

P3 (A3) Eusebius, *Chronicle*

55th Olympiad [= 560/56]: The natural philosopher Anaximenes is well known.

P4 (< A2) *Suda*

He was born in the 55th Olympiad [= 560/56] during the capture of Sardis, when Cyrus the Persian destroyed Croesus [= 546/5].[1]

---

[1] The indication is erroneous or the text corrupt (cf. the uncertainties involved in **P1**).

Statue (P5)

P5 (≠ DK) Christodorus, *Description of the Statues in the Gymnasium of Zeuxippus at Constantinople*

Anaximenes was there, the intellectual sage; in his
    enthusiasm
He brandished multifarious thoughts of a divine
    intention.

Iconography (P6)

P6 (≠ DK) Richter I, p. 79; Koch, "Ikonographie," in Flashar, Bremer, Rechenauer (2013), I.1, pp. 219–20.

ANAXIMENES [13 DK]

D

Three Summaries Deriving Ultimately from
Theophrastus (D1–D3)

D1 (< A5) Simp. *In Phys.*, p. 24.26–25.1 (= Theophr. Frag. 226A FHSEG)

Ἀναξιμένης δὲ [. . .] μίαν μὲν καὶ αὐτὸς[1] τὴν ὑποκειμένην φύσιν καὶ ἄπειρόν φησιν ὥσπερ ἐκεῖνος,[2] οὐκ ἀόριστον δὲ ὥσπερ ἐκεῖνος, ἀλλὰ[3] ὡρισμένην, ἀέρα λέγων αὐτήν· διαφέρειν δὲ μανότητι καὶ πυκνότητι κατὰ τὰς οὐσίας, καὶ ἀραιούμενον[4] μὲν πῦρ γίνεσθαι, πυκνούμενον δὲ ἄνεμον, εἶτα νέφος, ἔτι δὲ μᾶλλον ὕδωρ, εἶτα γῆν, εἶτα λίθους, τὰ δὲ ἄλλα ἐκ τούτων· κίνησιν δὲ καὶ οὗτος ἀίδιον ποιεῖ, δι᾽ ἣν καὶ τὴν μεταβολὴν γίνεσθαι.

[1] καὶ αὐτὸς om A [2] ὥσπερ ἐκεῖνος del. Usener
[3] ἀλλὰ καὶ F [4] διαρούμενον mss., corr. Diels

D2 (A6) Ps.-Plut. *Strom.* 3 (= Eus. *PE* 1.8.3)

Ἀναξιμένην δέ φασι τὴν τῶν ὅλων ἀρχὴν τὸν ἀέρα

ANAXIMENES

D

Three Summaries Deriving Ultimately from Theophrastus (D1–D3)

D1 (< A5) Simplicius, *Commentary on Aristotle's* Physics

Anaximenes [. . .] says too, as he [i.e. Anaximander] does, that the underlying nature is [scil. only] one and unlimited, but not that it is indeterminate, as he [i.e. Anaximander] does, but rather that it is determinate, for he says that it is air. It differs by its rarefaction or density according to the substances: rarefied, it becomes fire; condensed, wind, then cloud; even more, water, then earth, then stones; and everything else comes from these last. As for motion, he too considers it to be eternal; and it is because of it that change too comes about

D2 (A6) Ps.-Plutarch, *Stromata*

They say that Anaximenes affirms that the principle of all things is air and that this is unlimited in kind but limited

εἰπεῖν καὶ τοῦτο· εἶναι τῷ μὲν γένει ἄπειρον, ταῖς δὲ
περὶ αὐτὸν ποιότησιν ὡρισμένον· γεννᾶσθαί τε πάντα
κατά τινα πύκνωσιν τούτου καὶ πάλιν ἀραίωσιν. τήν
γε μὴν κίνησιν ἐξ αἰῶνος ὑπάρχειν· πιλουμένου[1] δὲ
τοῦ ἀέρος πρώτην γεγενῆσθαι λέγει τὴν γῆν, πλατεῖαν μάλα·[2] διὸ καὶ κατὰ λόγον αὐτὴν ἐποχεῖσθαι τῷ
ἀέρι· καὶ τὸν ἥλιον καὶ τὴν σελήνην καὶ τὰ λοιπὰ
ἄστρα τὴν ἀρχὴν τῆς γενέσεως ἔχειν ἐκ γῆς. ἀποφαίνεται γοῦν τὸν ἥλιον γῆν, διὰ δὲ τὴν ὀξεῖαν κίνησιν
καὶ μάλ' ἱκανῶς θερμότητα[3] λαβεῖν.[4]

[1] πιλουμένου BCDV: -μένην N: ἀπλουμένου A   [2] μάλα
ANDV: μᾶλλον BCN (in marg.)   [3] θερμότητα D (ος
superscr. prima manus): θερμότητος Usener: θερμοτάτην
ABONV   [4] κίνησιν λαβεῖν ABOND (in marg., prima
manus) V: κίνησιν om. D

D3 (< A7) (Ps.-?) Hippol. Ref. 1.7.1–8

[1] Ἀναξιμένης δε [. . .] ἀέρα ἄπειρον ἔφη τὴν ἀρχὴν
εἶναι, ἐξ οὗ τὰ γινόμενα καὶ[1] τὰ γεγονότα καὶ τὰ ἐσόμενα
καὶ[2] θεοὺς καὶ θεῖα γίνεσθαι,[3] τὰ δὲ λοιπὰ ἐκ τῶν τούτου
ἀπογόνων. [2] τὸ δὲ εἶδος τοῦ ἀέρος τοιοῦτον· ὅταν μὲν
ὁμαλώτατος ᾖ, ὄψει ἄδηλον, δηλοῦσθαι δὲ τῷ ψυχρῷ
καὶ τῷ θερμῷ καὶ τῷ νοτερῷ καὶ τῷ κινουμένῳ. κινεῖσθαι
δὲ ἀεί· οὐ γὰρ <ἂν> μεταβάλλειν ὅσα μεταβάλλει, εἰ μὴ
κινοῖτο. [3] πυκνούμενον γὰρ καὶ ἀραιούμενον διάφορον
φαίνεσθαι· ὅταν γὰρ[5] εἰς τὸ ἀραιότερον διαχυθῇ, πῦρ
γίνεσθαι· ἄνεμους[6] δὲ πάλιν εἶναι[7] ἀέρα πυκνούμενον·

340

by the qualities it possesses; and that all things are generated according to a certain condensation and, in turn, rarefaction on its part; but that motion is present from eternity. He says that when the air is compressed the first thing
to come about is the earth, which is extremely flat. That is
why it is appropriate that it **rides** upon the air. And the
sun, the moon, and the other heavenly bodies have the
principle of their generation from the earth. In any case
he states that the sun is of earth, but that it is strongly
heated by reason of the swiftness of its motion.

D3 (< A7) (Ps.-?) Hippolytus, *Refutation of All Heresies*

[1] Anaximenes [. . .] said that the principle is unlimited
air, from which comes about what is, what has been, and
what will be, the gods and divine things, while everything
else comes from its descendants. [2] The form of air is the
following: when it is perfectly homogeneous, it is invisible
to the eye, but it becomes visible by cold, heat, moisture,
and motion. It is moved incessantly: for whatever is transformed would not be transformed if there were no motion.
[3] For its appearance is different when it is condensed or
rarefied. For whenever it expands and becomes more rarefied, it becomes fire, and in turn winds are air that has
become condensed; and from the air, a cloud is created by

---

¹ καὶ Cedrenus (cf. p. 277.15–24 Bekker), om. mss.
² τὰ γινόμενα . . . τὰ ἐσόμενα καὶ secl. Marcovich   ³ ἐξ οὗ
. . . γίνεσθαι damn. Heidel   ⁴ ‹ἂν› Th. Gomperz
⁵ γὰρ Roeper: δὲ mss.   ⁶ ἀνέμους Zeller: μέσως mss.
⁷ πάλιν Roeper, εἶναι Diels: ἐπὰν εἰς mss.

ἐξ ἀέρος ⟨δὲ⟩[8] νέφος ἀποτελεῖσθαι[9] κατὰ τὴν πίλησιν·
ἔτι δὲ μᾶλλον ὕδωρ, ἐπὶ πλεῖον ⟨δὲ⟩[10] πυκνωθέντα γῆν
καὶ εἰς τὸ μάλιστα πυκνότατον[11] λίθους. ὥστε τὰ
κυριώτατα τῆς γενέσεως ἐναντία εἶναι, θερμόν τε καὶ
ψυχρόν.

[4] τὴν δὲ γῆν πλατεῖαν εἶναι ἐπ᾽ ἀέρος ὀχουμένην·
ὁμοίως δὲ καὶ ἥλιον καὶ σελήνην καὶ τὰ ἄλλα ἄστρα
πάντα[12] πύρινα ὄντα ἐποχεῖσθαι τῷ ἀέρι διὰ πλάτος.
[5] γεγονέναι δὲ τὰ ἄστρα ἐκ γῆς διὰ τὸ τὴν ἰκμάδα ἐκ
ταύτης ἀνίστασθαι· ἧς ἀραιουμένης τὸ πῦρ γίνεσθαι,
ἐκ δὲ τοῦ πυρὸς μετεωριζομένου τοὺς ἀστέρας συνίστασθαι. εἶναι δὲ καὶ γεώδεις φύσεις ἐν τῷ τόπῳ τῶν
ἀστέρων συμ⟨πε ι⟩φερομένας[13] ἐκείνοις. [6] οὐ κινεῖσθαι δὲ ὑπὸ γῆν τὰ ἄστρα λέγει, καθὼς ἕτεροι ὑπει-
λήφασιν, ἀλλὰ περὶ γῆν, ὡσπερεὶ περὶ τὴν ἡμετέραν
κεφαλὴν στρέφεται τὸ πιλίον.[14] κρύπτεσθαι δὲ[15] τὸν
ἥλιον οὐχ ὑπὸ γῆν γενόμενον, ἀλλ᾽ ὑπὸ τῶν τῆς γῆς
ὑψηλοτέρων μερῶν σκεπόμενον, καὶ διὰ τὴν πλείονα
ἡμῶν αὐτοῦ γενομένην ἀπόστασιν. τὰ δὲ ἄστρα μὴ
θερμαίνειν διὰ τὸ μῆκος τῆς ἀποστάσεως.

[7] ἀνέμους δὲ γεννᾶσθαι, ὅταν ἐκπεπυκνωμένος[16] ὁ
ἀὴρ ἀραιωθεὶς[17] φέρηται· συνελθόντα δὲ καὶ ἐπὶ πλεῖον
παχυνθέντα[18] νέφη γεννᾶσθαι, καὶ οὕτως εἰς ὕδωρ

---

8 ⟨δὲ⟩ Diels   9 ἀποτελεσθῇ mss., corr. Roeper
10 ⟨δὲ⟩ Diels   11 πυκνότατον secl. Diels
12 γὰρ post πάντα hab. LOB: om. Cedrenus, del. Diels
13 συμφερομένας mss., corr. Diels ex Cedrenus

342

compression, water when this increases, earth when it is condensed even more, and stones when it has reached the maximum condensation. So that the principal factors responsible for generation are contraries, heat and cold.

[4] The earth is flat, borne upon the air; similarly, the sun, the moon, and the other heavenly bodies, which are all fiery, **ride** upon the air because of their flatness. [5] The heavenly bodies have come about from the earth because moisture rises up and leaves it; from its rarefaction, fire comes about; and from fire that rises aloft, the stars are composed. There are also earthy natures in the region of the heavenly bodies that accompany them in their revolution. [6] He says that the heavenly bodies do not move below the earth, as the others supposed, but around the earth, just as a **felt cap** turns around our head. And the sun is hidden not because it comes to be located below the earth, but because it is covered by the higher parts of the earth and because of the greater distance between it and us. The heavenly bodies do not cause heat because of the size of their distance.

[7] The winds are created when air that has become very condensed becomes rarefied and is set in motion. When it collects together and is condensed even more, clouds are created and in this way are transformed into water. Hail comes about when water coming from the

---

14 πιλεῖον mss., corr. Menagius   15 δὲ L in marg.: τε LOT: om. B   16 ἐκπεπυκνωμένος LOE, -μένης T: εἰς πεπυ-κνωμένον Usener: ἢ πεπυκνωμένος Diels   17 ἀραιωθεὶς mss.: ἀρθεὶς Zeller: καὶ ὠσθεὶς Diels   18 παχύθεντα mss., corr. Salvin: συνελθόντος . . . παχυνθέντος Zeller

μεταβάλλειν. χάλαζαν δὲ γίνεσθαι, ὅταν ἀπὸ τῶν νεφῶν τὸ ὕδωρ καταφερόμενον παγῇ· χιόνα δέ, ὅταν αὐτὰ
ταῦτα ἐνυγρότερα ὄντα πῆξιν λάβῃ. [8] ἀστραπὴν δ᾿,
ὅταν τὰ νέφη διιστῆται βίᾳ πνευμάτων· τούτων γὰρ
διισταμένων λαμπρὰν καὶ πυρώδη γίνεσθαι τὴν αὐγήν.
ἶριν δὲ γεννᾶσθα τῶν ἡλιακῶν αὐγῶν εἰς ἀέρα συν-
εστῶτα πιπτουσᾶν· σεισμὸν δὲ τῆς γῆς ἐπὶ πλεῖον
ἀλλοιουμένης ὑπὸ θερμασίας καὶ ψύξεως.

Air as Principle (D4)

D4 (A4) Arist. *Metaph.* A3 984a5–6

Ἀναξιμένης δὲ ἀέρα καὶ Διογένης πρότερον ὕδατος
καὶ μάλιστ᾿ ἀρχὴν τιθέασι τῶν ἁπλῶν σωμάτων [. . .].

Air as God (D5–D6)

D5 (< A10) Aët. 1.7.13 (Stob.) [περὶ θεοῦ]

Ἀναξιμένης τὸν ἀέρα [. . . = **R6**].

D6 (< A10) Cic. *Nat. deor.* 1.10.26

[. . .] Anaximenes aera deum statuit eumque gigni esseque
inmensum et infinitum et semper in motu [. . . = **R7**].

clouds freezes while it descends; snow, when these same [scil. drops] possess more moisture and become frozen; [8] lightning, when the clouds burst by the violence of the winds—for when these burst, the bright and fiery flash is produced. The rainbow is born when the rays of the sun fall upon an accumulation of air; the earthquake, when the earth is transformed more by the effect of heat and cold.

Air as Principle (D4)

D4 (A4) Aristotle, *Metaphysics*

Anaximenes as well as Diogenes [cf. **DIOG. D7**] posit air as being anterior to water and as most of all principle among the simple bodies [. . .].

Air as God (D5–D6)

D5 (< A10) Aëtius

Anaximenes: air [scil. is god] [. . .].

D6 (< A10) Cicero, *On the Nature of the Gods*

[. . .] Anaximenes declared that air is god, that it is born, and that it is immense and unlimited and always in motion [. . .].

The Transformations of Air (D7–D8)

D7 (< A5) Simpl. *In Phys.*, p. 149.32–150.2 (= Theophr. Frag. 226B FHS&G)

ἐπὶ γὰρ τούτου μόνου Θεόφραστος ἐν τῇ Ἱστορίᾳ τὴν μάνωσιν εἴρηκε καὶ πύκνωσιν.

D8 (< B1) Plut. *Prim. frig.* 7 947F

[. . . cf. **R4**] τὸ γὰρ συστελλόμενον αὐτῆς καὶ πυκνού-μενον ψυχρὸν εἶναί φησι, τὸ δ᾽ ἀραιὸν καὶ τὸ χα-λαρὸν (οὕτω πως ὀνομάσας καὶ τῷ ῥήματι) θερμόν. ὅθεν οὐκ ἀπεικότως λέγεσθαι τὸ καὶ θερμὰ τὸν ἄν-θρωπον ἐκ τοῦ στόματος καὶ ψυχρὰ μεθιέναι· ψύχεται γὰρ ἡ πνοὴ πιεσθεῖσα καὶ πυκνωθεῖσα τοῖς χείλεσιν, ἀνειμένου δὲ τοῦ στόματος ἐκπίπτουσα γίνεται θερ-μὸν ὑπὸ μανότητος [. . .].

*Is There Only One World or an Unlimited
Number of Worlds? (D9–D11)*

D9 (< 59 A65) Aët. 2.4.6 (Stob.) [εἰ ἄφθαρτος ὁ κόσμος]

[. . .] Ἀναξιμένης [. . .] φθαρτὸν τὸν κόσμον.

D10 (< A11) Simpl. *In Phys.*, p. 1121.12–15

γενητὸν δὲ καὶ φθαρτὸν τὸν ἕνα κόσμον ποιοῦσιν, ὅσοι ἀεὶ μέν φασιν εἶναι κόσμον, οὐ μὴν τὸν αὐτὸν

The Transformations of Air (D7–D8)

D7 (< A5) Simplicius, *Commentary on Aristotle's* Physics

It is only about him [i.e. Anaximenes] that Theophrastus in his *History* has spoken of **rarefaction** and **condensation**.

D8 (< B1) Plutarch, *On the Principle of Cold*

[. . .] For he [i.e. "ancient Anaximenes," cf. **R4**] says that the contraction and concentration of this [i.e. matter] is cold, while what is loose in texture and **slack** (calling it this very way in his own words) is hot. And that is why it is said, not implausibly, that a man emits both heat and cold from his mouth: for the breath is cooled when it is pressed together and condensed by the lips, whereas when the mouth is distended it comes out of it heated by the effect of its rarefaction [. . .].

Is There Only One World or an Unlimited Number of Worlds? (D9–D11)

D9 (< 59 A65) Aëtius

[. . .] Anaximenes [. . .]: the world is perishable.

D10 (< A11) Simplicius, *Commentary on Aristotle's* Physics

All those who state that the world is eternal, but that it is not eternally the same but is generated successively in different forms according to certain periods of time, like

ἀεί, ἀλλὰ ἄλλοτε ἄλλον γινόμενον κατά τινας χρόνων περιόδους, ὡς Ἀναξιμένης [. . .].

D11 (< 12 A17) Aët. 2.1.3 (Stob.; cf. Ps.-Plut.) [περὶ κόσμου]

[. . .] Ἀναξιμένης [. . .] ἀπείρους κόσμους ἐν τῷ ἀπείρῳ κατὰ πᾶσαν περίστασιν.[1]

¹ περίστασιν Plut.: περιαγωγήν Stob.

Astronomy (D12–D20)
Heavens and Heavenly Bodies (D12–D14)

D12 (< A13) Aët. 2.11.1 (Stob.) [περὶ τῆς οὐρανοῦ οὐσίας]

Ἀναξιμένης [. . .] τὴν περιφορὰν τὴν ἐξωτάτω τῆς γῆς εἶναι τὸν οὐρανόν.

D13 (A14) Aët. 2.13.10 (Stob.) [περὶ οὐσίας ἄστρων]

Ἀναξιμένης πυρίνην μὲν τὴν φύσιν τῶν ἄστρων, περιέχειν[1] δέ τινα καὶ γεώδη σώματα συμπεριφερό-μενα τούτοις ἀόρατα.

¹ περιέχειν F: παρέχειν C

Anaximenes, posit that the one world is subject to generation and destruction and that it is generated successively
in different forms according to certain periods of time,
like Anaximenes [. . .].

D11 (< 12 A17) Aëtius

[. . .] Anaximenes [. . .]: worlds unlimited [scil. in number]
in the unlimited, throughout the entire surrounding area
(*peristasis*).

Astronomy (D12–D20)
Heavens and Heavenly Bodies (D12–D14)

D12 (< A13) Aëtius

Anaximenes [. . .]: the revolution farthest from the earth
is the heavens.

D13 (A14) Aëtius

Anaximenes: the nature of the heavenly bodies is fiery, but
they also comprise certain invisible earthy bodies that accompany them in their revolution.

D14 (A14) Aët. 2.14.3–4 (Ps.-Plut.; cf. Stob.) [περὶ σχημάτων ἀστέρων]

[3] Ἀναξιμένης ἥλων δίκην καταπεπηγέναι[1] τῷ κρυσταλλοειδεῖ.
[4] ἔνιοι δὲ[2] **πέταλα**[3] εἶναι πύρινα ὥσπερ ζωγραφήματα.

¹ καταπεπηγέναι ΛΠ: -πληγέναι m   ² ἔνιοι δὲ ΜΠ:
om. m: ἐνίους δὲ Heath   ³ καθάπερ ante πέταλα add. m

The Sun (D15–D18)

D15 (A15) Aët. 2.22.1 (Ps.-Plut.) [περὶ σχήματος ἡλίου]

Ἀναξιμένης πλατὺν ὡς **πέταλον** τὸν ἥλιον.

D16 (A14) Arist. Meteor. 2.1 354a28–32

[. . .] πολλοὺς πεισθῆναι τῶν ἀρχαίων μετεωρολόγων τὸν ἥλιον μὴ φέρεσθαι ὑπὸ γῆν ἀλλὰ περὶ τὴν γῆν καὶ τὸν τόπον τοῦτον, ἀφανίζεσθαι δὲ καὶ ποιεῖν νύκτα διὰ τὸ ὑψηλὴν εἶναι πρὸς ἄρκτον τὴν γῆν.

D17 (A14) Aët. 2.19.2 (Ps.-Plut.) [περὶ ἐπισημασίας ἀστέρων καὶ πῶς γίνεται χειμὼν καὶ θέρος]

Ἀναξιμένης δὲ διὰ μὲν ταῦτα[1] μηδὲν τούτων, διὰ δὲ τὸν ἥλιον μόνον.

¹ ταῦτα m: ταύτην ΜΠ

D14 (A14) Aëtius

[3] Anaximenes: the stars are stuck into the crystalline [scil. sphere] like **nails.**
[4] Some people say that they are fiery **leaves** like paintings.[1]

---

[1] "Some people" might refer to sources that present Anaximenes' doctrine in a different way, rather than to other philosophers (cf. the term "leaf" in **D15**).

The Sun (D15–D18)

D15 (A15) Aëtius

Anaximenes: the sun is flat like **a leaf**

D16 (A14) Aristotle, *Meteorology*

[. . .] many of the ancients who spoke about heavenly phenomena (*meteôrologoi*) were convinced that the sun goes not below the earth but around the earth and this region, and that it disappears and causes night because the earth is elevated in the north [cf. **D3[6]**].

D17 (A14) Aëtius

Anaximenes: none of these phenomena [scil. the signs of the change from summer to winter and from winter to summer] occurs because of this [scil. the risings and settings of the various heavenly bodies], but because of the sun alone.

D18 (A15) Aët. 2.23.1 (Ps.-Plut.) [περὶ τροπῶν ἡλίου]

Ἀναξιμένης ὑπὸ πεπυκνωμένου ἀέρος καὶ ἀντιτύπου
ἐξωθεῖσθαι τὰ ἄστρα.

The Shape and Position of the Earth (D19–D20)

D19 (< A20) Arist. *Cael.* 2.13 294b13–23

Ἀναξιμένης δὲ καὶ [. . **ANAXAG. D58; ATOM. D110**]
τὸ πλάτος αἴτιον εἶναί φασι τοῦ μένειν αὐτήν. οὐ γὰρ
τέμνειν ἀλλ᾽ ἐπιπωμάζειν τὸν ἀέρα τὸν κάτωθεν, ὅπερ
φαίνεται τὰ πλάτος ἔχοντα τῶν σωμάτων ποιεῖν·
ταῦτα γὰρ καὶ πρὸς τοὺς ἀνέμους ἔχει δυσκινήτως
διὰ τὴν ἀντέρεισιν. ταὐτὸ δὴ τοῦτο ποιεῖν τῷ πλάτει
φασὶ τὴν γῆν πρὸς τὸν ὑποκείμενον ἀέρα (τὸν δ᾽ οὐκ
ἔχοντα[1] μεταστῆναι τόπον ἱκανὸν[2] ἀθρόως[3] κάτωθεν
ἠρεμεῖν), ὥσπερ τὸ ἐν ταῖς κλεψύδρας ὕδωρ. ὅτι δὲ
δύναται πολὺ βάρος φέρειν ἀπολαμβανόμενος καὶ
μένων ὁ ἀήρ, τεκμήρια πολλὰ λέγουσιν.

---

[1] ἔχοντα ‹τοῦ› Diels   [2] an τόπον ἱκανὸν μεταστῆναι?   [3] τῷ post ἀθρόως utrum delendum an ante ἀθρόως
ponendum dub. Moraux

D20 (A20) Aët.

a 3.10.3 (Ps.-Plut.) [περὶ σχήματος γῆς]

Ἀναξιμένης τραπεζοειδῆ.

D18 (A15) Aëtius

Anaximenes: the heavenly bodies [scil. retrograde] because they are pushed back by the condensed air that opposes them.

The Shape and Position of the Earth (D19–D20)

D19 (A20) Aristotle, *On the Heavens*

Anaximenes and [. . .] say that [scil. the earth's] flatness is the cause for its stationary position. For it does not cut the air beneath it but covers it like a lid, which is what bodies possessing flatness are seen to do; for winds too have difficulty moving these bodies, because of their resistance. And [scil. they say] that the earth acts in the same way with regard to the air underlying it because of its flatness, and that since it [i.e. the air] does not have sufficient room to move, it remains motionless below [scil. the earth] in a dense mass, just like the water in clepsydras. And for the fact that air that is enclosed and stationary can bear a great weight, they provide many proofs.

D20 (A20) Aëtius

a

Anaximenes: it [i.e. the earth] is table-shaped.

b 3.15.8 (Ps.-Plut.) [περὶ σεισμῶν γῆς]

Ἀναξιμένης διὰ τὸ πλάτος ἐποχεῖσθαι τῷ ἀέρι.

Meteorological Phenomena (D21–D26)
Clouds, Thunder, Lightning (D21–D23)

D21 (A17) Aët. 3.4.1 (Ps.-Plut.) [περὶ νεφῶν ὑετῶν χιόνων χαλαζῶν]

Ἀναξιμένης νέφη μὲν γίνεσθαι παχυνθέντος ἐπὶ πλεῖστον τοῦ ἀέρος, μᾶλλον δ᾽ ἐπισυναχθέντος ἐκθλίβε-
σθαι τοὺς ὄμβρους, χιόνα δέ, ἐπειδὰν τὸ καταφερόμενον ὕδωρ παγῇ· χάλαζαν[1] δ᾽ ὅταν συμπεριληφθῇ
τῷ ὑγρῷ πνεῦμά τι.[2]

[1] χιόνα . . . χάλαζαν mss. (-ζα M): χάλαζαν . . .
χιόνα Diels   [2] τῷ ὑγρῷ πνεῦμά τι m: τι ὑγρῷ πνεύματι
MII

D22 (As 24 Wöhrle) Sen. *Quaest. nat.* 2.17

quidam existimant igneum[1] spiritum per frigida atque
umida meantem[2] sonum reddere, nam ne ferrum quidem
ardens silentio tingitur[3] sed, si in aquam fervens massa
descendit, cum multo murmure extinguitur. ita, ut Anaximenes ait, spiritus incidens nubibus tonitrua edit et, dum
luctatur per obstantia atque interscissa[4] vadere, ipsa ignem fuga accendit.

b

Anaximenes: because of its [i.e. the earth's] flatness it **rides** upon the air.

Meteorological Phenomena (D21–D26)
Clouds, Thunder, Lightning (D21–D23)

D21 (A17) Aëtius

Anaximenes: clouds are formed when the air becomes extremely condensed, and if it becomes even more concentrated rains are squeezed out; snow when the water freezes while it descends; and hail when some air is enclosed together with the moisture.

D22 (≠ DK) Seneca, *Natural Questions*

Some people think that a current of fiery air passing through what is cold and moist produces a sound, for neither is a blazing piece of iron dipped in silence, but if a burning lump of metal is plunged into water its quenching is accompanied by a great noise. So too, as Anaximenes says, a current of air that falls upon clouds produces a thunderclap and, while it struggles to find a passage through obstacles and fissures, it ignites a fire by its very escape.

---

¹ igneum Z: in eum Φ: eum ET: ipsum Δ: istum B   ² ineuntem ΔP   ³ tinguitur δJ¹KZ: tingitur Φ: extinguitur A²ε
⁴ interscissa HTZ²: intercissa LOPZ¹: intercisa ΔE (-cisam) JK

D23 (A17) Aët. 3.3.2 (Stob.) [περὶ βροντῶν ἀστραπῶν κεραυνῶν πρηστήρων τε καὶ τυφώνων]

Ἀναξιμένης ταῦτα τούτῳ[1] προστιθεὶς τὸ ἐπὶ τῆς θαλάσσης, ἥτις σχιζομένη ταῖς κώπαις παραστίλβει.

¹ ταῦτα τοῦτο ms, corr. Heeren

Rainbow (D24–D25)

D24 (A18) Aët. 3.5.10 (Ps.-Plut.) [περὶ ἴριδος]

Ἀναξιμένης ἶριν γίνεσθαι κατ᾽ αὐγασμὸν ἡλίου πρὸς νέφει πυκνῷ καὶ παχεῖ καὶ μέλανι παρὰ τὸ μὴ δύνασθαι τὰς ἀκτῖνας εἰς τὸ πέραν διακόπτειν ἐπισυνισταμένας αὐτῷ.

D25 (A18) Schol. in Arat., p. 515.27

τὴν ἶριν Ἀναξιμένης φησὶ γίνεσθαι, ἡνίκα ἂν ἐπιπέσωσιν αἱ τοῦ ἡλίου αὐγαὶ εἰς παχὺν καὶ πυκνὸν τὸν ἀέρα. ὅθεν τὸ μὲν πρότερον αὐτοῦ[1] τοῦ ἡλίου φοινικοῦν φαίνεται, διακαιόμενον ὑπὸ τῶν ἀκτίνων, τὸ δὲ μέλαν, κατακρατούμενον[2] ὑπὸ τῆς ὑγρότητος. καὶ νυκτὸς δέ φησι γίνεσθαι τὴν ἶριν ἀπὸ τῆς σελήνης, ἀλλ᾽ οὐ πολλάκις διὰ τὸ μὴ πανσέληνον εἶναι διὰ παντὸς καὶ ἀσθενέστερον αὐτὴν φῶς ἔχειν τοῦ ἡλίου.

¹ αὐτῆς M   ² κρατούμενον A

356

D23 (A17) Aëtius

Anaximenes: the same as he [i.e. Anaximander about thunder, lightning, and other related phenomena, cf. **ANAXIMAND. D33a**], adding what happens on the sea, which flashes when it is broken by oars.

Rainbow (D24–D25)

D24 (A18) Aëtius

Anaximenes: the rainbow is produced because of the shining of the sun upon a dense, thick, and dark cloud, since the rays cannot penetrate through it and therefore accumulate against it.

D25 (A18) Scholia on Aratus' *Phaenomena*

Anaximenes says that the rainbow is produced when the rays of the sun fall upon thick and dense air. That is why the part of it that is closest to the sun appears purple, since it is completely burned by the rays, while the other part appears dark, since it is dominated by the moisture. And he says that at night too the rainbow is produced because of the moon, but that this does not happen often, because there is not always a full moon and its light is weaker than the sun's.

Winds (D26)

D26 (A19) Ps.-Gal. *In Hipp. Hum.* 3

Ἀναξιμένης δὲ ἐξ ὕδατος καὶ ἀέρος γίνεσθαι τοὺς ἀνέμους βούλεται καὶ[1] ῥύμῃ τινὶ ἀγνώστῳ βιαίως φέρεσθαι καὶ τάχιστα ὡς τὰ πτηνὰ πέτεσθαι.[2]

[1] τῇ post καὶ mss., secl. Kaibel   [2] πέτασθαι mss., corr. Kaibel

Earthquakes (D27–D29)

D27 (A21) Arist. *Meteor.* 2.7 365b6–12

Ἀναξιμένης δέ φησι βρεχομένην τὴν γῆν καὶ ξηραινομένην ῥήγνυσθαι, καὶ ὑπὸ τούτων τῶν ἀπορρηγνυμένων κολωνῶν ἐμπιπτόντων σείεσθαι· διὸ καὶ γίγνεσθαι τοὺς σεισμοὺς ἔν τε τοῖς αὐχμοῖς καὶ πάλιν ἐν ταῖς ἐπομβρίαις·[1] ἔν τε γὰρ τοῖς αὐχμοῖς, ὥσπερ εἴρηται, ξηραινομένην ῥήγνυσθαι καὶ ὑπὸ τῶν ὑδάτων ὑπερυγραινομένην διαπίπτειν.

[1] ὑπερομβρίαις duc mss.

D28 (> A21) Sen. *Quaest. nat.* 6.10.1–2

[1] Anaximenes ait terram ipsam sibi causam esse motus, nec extrinsecus incurrere quod illam impellat, sed intra ipsam[1] et ex ipsa: quasdam enim partes eius decidere, quas aut umor resolverit aut ignis exederit aut spiritus violentia

Winds (D26)

D26 (A19) Ps.-Galen, *Commentary on Hippocrates'* On Humors

Anaximenes supposes that the winds are produced out of water and air, and move violently with an unknown rush, and fly with great speed like birds.

Earthquakes (D27–D29)

D27 (A21) Aristotle, *Meteorology*

Anaximenes says that when the earth is moistened and dries out, it breaks apart and is shaken by the collapse of its supports by the effect of this breaking. And that is why earthquakes occur both when there is a drought and also in periods of rainstorms. For when there is a drought, as has been said, it is dried out and breaks apart, and when it is moistened too much by the rains it collapses.

D28 (> A21) Seneca, *Natural Questions*

[1] Anaximenes says that the earth itself is the cause of earthquakes and that nothing happens to it from outside that would shake it, but rather [scil. the cause] is located in itself and comes from itself: for some of its parts, which either water has dissolved, or fire has consumed, or a strong wind has shaken, collapse. But when these factors

---

[1] sibi . . . ipsam *om.* Δ

excusserit. sed his quoque cessantibus non deesse, propter
quod aliquid abscedat[2] aut[3] revellatur;[4] nam primum
omnia vetustate labuntur nec quicquam tutum a senectute
est; haec solida quoque et magni roboris[5] carpit: [2] itaque
quemadmodum in aedificiis veteribus quaedam non per-
cussa tamen decidunt, cum plus ponderis habuere quam
virium, ita in hoc universo terrae corpore evenit ut partes
eius vetustate solvantur, solutae cadant et tremorem su-
perioribus afferant, primum, dum abscedunt (nihil enim
utique magnum sine motu eius, cui haesit, absciditur[6]);
deinde, cum deciderunt, solido exceptae resiliunt pilae
more (quae cum cecidit, exultat ac saepius pellitur, totiens
a solo in novum impetum missa); si vero in stagnantibus
aquis delatae[7] sunt, hic ipse casus vicina concutit fluctu,
quem subitum vastumque illisum ex alto pondus eiecit.

----

[2] accedat δ   [3] ac ρZ   [4] relevetur δ   [5] corporis δ
[6] abscinditur *BT*: abscond. *O*: absorb. *P*   [7] delatae
Gertz: delata AΦ: demissa g²ρ: delapsa *B*

D29 (< 12 A28) Amm. Marc. 17.7.12

Anaximenes[1] ait arescentem nimia aestuum siccitate aut
post madores imbrium terram rimas pandere grandiores,
quas penetrat supernus[2] aer violentus et nimius, ac per eas
vehementi spiritu quassatam cieri propriis sedibus. qua de

----

[1] Anaximenes *ed. Accursii:* Anaximander *mss.*   [2] supernus
EAG: supernos *V*: super nos *B*

too are lacking, there is always some reason for something to be detached or torn away. For first of all, all things decay as they age and nothing is free from old age; this weakens even solid things and ones of considerable sturdiness. [2] And so, just as in old buildings some things fall down even without having been struck hard, since they have more weight than strength, so too in the whole body of the earth it happens that parts of it are dissolved by age, and when they are dissolved they fall down and shake what is above them—first, at the moment they are detached (for nothing, whatever its size, is detached without causing a jolt to what it is attached to); then, at the moment they fall, for when they hit something solid they rebound like a ball (which, when it falls, bounces up and springs many times, as many as it rebounds from the ground at every bounce): but if they fall into stagnant waters, this fall itself shakes the nearby areas by causing a sudden, huge wave, which is produced by the weight crashing down into them from above.[1]

[1] It is difficult to distinguish Seneca's elaboration from what belongs to Anaximenes.

D29 (< 12 A28) Ammianus Marcellinus, *Histories*

Anaximenes says that when the earth is dried out by an excessive drought caused by heat or after it has been drenched by rainstorms, very large cracks open up, which a violent and excessive current of air penetrates from above, and that when it is shaken by the forceful wind passing through these it quakes in its very foundations.

causa tremores[3] huiusmodi vaporatis temporibus aut nimia aquarum caelestium superfusione contingunt.

[3] tremores *Lind.* in *adn. Btl.*: terrores *mss.*

The Soul (D30–D31)

D30 (cf. A23) Aët. 4.3.2 (Stob.) [περὶ ψυχῆς]

Ἀναξιμένης [. . .] ἀερώδη.

D31 (< B2) Aët. 1.3.4 (Ps.-Plut.) [περὶ ἀρχῶν]

Ἀναξιμένης [. . .] ἀρχὴν τῶν ὄντων ἀέρα ἀπεφήνατο· ἐκ γὰρ τούτου τὰ[1] πάντα γίγνεσθαι καὶ εἰς αὐτὸν πάλιν ἀναλύεσθαι, "οἷον ἡ ψυχή," φησίν, "ἡ ἡμετέρα ἀὴρ οὖσα συγκρατεῖ ἡμᾶς, καὶ ὅλον τὸν κόσμον πνεῦμα καὶ ἀὴρ περιέχει"· λέγεται δὲ συνωνύμως ἀὴρ καὶ πνεῦμα [. . . = **R5**].

[1] τὰ del. Diels

This is why tremors of this sort happen in warm seasons or when there is excessive precipitation of water falling from the sky.

The Soul (D30–D31)

D30 (cf. A23) Aëtius

Anaximenes [. . .]: [scil. the soul is] of air.

D31 (< B2) Aëtius

Anaximenes [. . .] asserted that the principle of beings is air. For it is out of this that all things come about and it is into this that they are dissolved in turn. He says, "Just as our soul, which is air, dominates us, so too breath and air surround the whole world."[1] ('Air' and 'breath' are being used synonymously) [. . .].

[1] Diels considers this sentence to be a direct quotation from Anaximenes, but it is more likely to be a paraphrase reflecting later terminology.

ANAXIMENES [13 DK]

R

Ancient Treatises on Anaximenes (R1)

R1 Diog. Laert.

a (As 7 Wöhrle) 5.42 (Theophr.)

Περὶ τῶν Ἀναξιμένους αʹ

b (As 14 Wöhrle) 10.28 (Epicur.)

Ἀναξιμένης

Style (R2)

R2 (< A1) Diog. Laert. 2.3

κέχρηταί τε λέξει[1] Ἰάδι ἁπλῇ καὶ ἀπερίττῳ.

> [1] λέξει B et P[1] in marg.: γλώσσῃ P[1] in textu

ANAXIMENES

Ancient Treatises on Anaximenes (R1)

R1 (≠ DK) Diogenes Laertius
a From the catalog of books written by Theophrastus
On the Doctrines of Anaximenes, one book

b From the catalog of books written by Epicurus
Anaximenes

Style (R2)

R2 (< A1) Diogenes Laertius
He makes use of an Ionic style that is simple and plain.

A Probable Criticism in Plato (R3)

R3 (As 1 Wöhrle) Plat. *Tim.* 49b–d

πρῶτον μέν, ὃ δὴ νῦν ὕδωρ ὠνομάκαμεν, πηγνύμενον
ὡς δοκοῦμεν λίθους καὶ γῆν γιγνόμενον ὁρῶμεν, τη-
κόμενον δὲ καὶ διακρινόμενον αὖ ταὐτὸν τοῦτο πνεῦμα
καὶ ἀέρα, συγκαυθέντα δὲ ἀέρα πῦρ, ἀνάπαλιν δὲ
συγκριθὲν καὶ κατασβεσθὲν εἰς ἰδέαν τε ἀπιὸν αὖθις
ἀέρος πῦρ, καὶ πάλιν ἀέρα συνιόντα καὶ πυκνούμενον
νέφος καὶ ὁμίχλην· ἐκ δὲ τούτων ἔτι μᾶλλον συμπι-
λουμένων ῥέον ὕδωρ, ἐξ ὕδατος δὲ γῆν καὶ λίθους
αὖθις, κύκλον τε οὕτω διαδιδόντα εἰς ἄλληλα, ὡς φαίνεται, τὴν γένεσιν. οὕτω δὴ τούτων οὐδέποτε τῶν αὐτῶν ἑκάστων φαντζομένων, ποῖον αὐτῶν ὡς ὂν ὁτι-
οῦν τοῦτο καὶ οὐκ ἄλλο παγίως διισχυριζόμενος οὐκ
αἰσχυνεῖταί τις ἑαυτόν;

Two Peripatetic Criticisms (R4–R5)

R4 (< B1) Plut. *Prim. frig.* 7 948A

[. . .] ἢ, καθάπερ Ἀναξιμένης ὁ παλαιὸς ᾤετο, μήτε τὸ
ψυχρὸν ἐν οὐσίᾳ μήτε τὸ θερμὸν ἀπολείπωμεν, ἀλλὰ
πάθη κοινὰ τῆς ὕλης ἐπιγινόμενα ταῖς μεταβολαῖς·
[. . . = **D8**] τοῦτο μὲν οὖν ἀγνόημα ποιεῖται τοῦ ἀνδρὸς
ὁ Ἀριστοτέλης· ἀνειμένου γὰρ τοῦ στόματος ἐκπνεῖ-
σθαι τὸ θερμὸν ἐξ ἡμῶν αὐτῶν, ὅταν δὲ συστρέψα-
ντες τὰ χείλη φυσήσωμεν, οὐ τὸν ἐξ ἡμῶν ἀλλὰ τὸν

A Probable Criticism in Plato (R3)

R3 (≠ DK) Plato, *Timaeus*

First, we see that what we now call water, when it solidifies, becomes, as we think, stones and earth, but then again the same thing, when it liquefies and becomes dissolved, [scil. becomes] wind and air, and when air is strongly heated [scil. it becomes] fire, and conversely when fire is brought together and extinguished it returns once again into the form of air, and again air, coming together and condensing, [scil. becomes] cloud and mist, and that out of these, when they are compressed together even more, water flows, and out of water earth and stones once again, and that in a circle they pass on generation to one another in this way, as it appears [cf. **D1, D3[3]**]. But since none of these things ever manifests itself as being the same, which of them is there about which one could claim with confidence and without embarrassment that it really is this and not something else?

Two Peripatetic Criticisms (R4–R5)

R4 (< B1) Plutarch, *On the Principle of Cold*

[. . .] or else, as ancient Anaximenes thought, let us accept neither cold nor hear as substance, but consider them to be common affections of matter supervening during its transformations. Aristotle attributes this [cf. **D8**] to ignorance on the part of that man. For when the mouth is distended, we breathe out the heat that comes from ourselves, but when we draw our lips together and blow out,

ἀέρα τὸν πρὸ τοῦ στόματος ὠθεῖσθαι ψυχρὸν ὄντα καὶ προσπίπτειν.[1]

[1] προσπίπτειν gX (et BE teste Wyttenbach): προσεμπίπτειν O

R5 (< B2) Aët. 1.3.4 (Ps.-Plut.) [περὶ ἀρχῶν]

[. . . = **D31**] ἁμαρτάνει δὲ καὶ οὗτος ἐξ ἁπλοῦ καὶ μονοειδοῦς ἀέρος καὶ πνεύματος δοκῶν συνεστάναι τὰ ζῷα· ἀδύνατον γὰρ ἀρχὴν μίαν τὴν ὕλην τῶν ὄντων ἐξ ἧς τὰ πάντα ὑποστῆναι· ἀλλὰ καὶ τὸ ποιοῦν αἴτιον χρὴ ὑποτιθέναι· οἶον ἄργυρος οὐκ ἀρκεῖ πρὸς τὸ ἔκπωμα γενέσθαι, ἂν μὴ καὶ τὸ ποιοῦν ᾖ, τουτέστιν ὁ ἀργυροκόπος· ὁμοίως καὶ ἐπὶ τοῦ χαλκοῦ καὶ τοῦ ξύλου καὶ τῆς ἄλλης ὕλης.

A Stoicizing Scholastic Interpretation (R6)

R6 (< A10) Aët. 1.7.13 (Stob.) [τίς ἐστιν ὁ θεός]

[. . . = **D5**] δεῖ δ᾽ ὑπακούειν ἐπὶ τῶν οὕτως λεγομένων τὰς ἐνδιηκούσας[1] τοῖς στοιχείοις ἢ τοῖς σώμασι δυνάμεις.

[1] ἐνδιηκούσας P: ἐνδϵικούσας F

then it is not the air that comes from us but cold air in front of the mouth that is pushed and ejected.

R5 (< B2) Aëtius

[. . .] he too [scil. like Anaximander, **ANAXIMAND. R13**] is mistaken in thinking that animals are composed out of simple and uniform air and breath. For it is impossible to posit the matter of the beings from which all things come as the sole principle: it is also necessary to posit the efficient cause—for example, the silver is not enough for the cup to come about, if there is not what makes it, that is the silversmith; and so too for bronze, wood, and all other kinds of matter.

A Stoicizing Scholastic Interpretation (R6)

R6 (< A10) Aëtius

[. . .] With regard to what is said in this way [scil. that air is god], one must understand the powers that traverse the elements or the bodies.

An Epicurean Criticism (R7)

R7 (< A10) Cic. *Nat. deor.* 1.10.26

[. . . = **D6**] quasi aut aer sine ulla forma deus esse possit, cum praesertim deum non modo aliqua, sed pulcherrima specie deceat esse, aut non omne quod ortum sit mortalitas consequatur.

Discoveries Attributed to Anaximenes (R8–R9)

R8 (< A14a) Plin. *Nat. hist.* 2.187

umbrarum hanc rationem et quam vocant gnomonicen invenit Anaximenes Milesius [. . .] primusque horologium quod appellant sciothericon Lacedaemone ostendit.

R9 (< A16) Theon Sm. *Exp.* 3.10, pp. 198.19–99.2

Εὔδημος ἱστορεῖ ἐν ταῖς Ἀστρολογίαις [Frag. 145 Wehrli] [. . .] Ἀναξιμένης δὲ ὅτι ἡ σελήνη ἐκ τοῦ ἡλίου ἔχει τὸ φῶς καὶ τίνα ἐκλείπει τρόπον.

An Epicurean Criticism (R7)

R7 (< A10) Cicero, *On the Nature of the Gods*

[. . .] as though air without any form could be a god—whereas it is fitting especially for a god to have not just some appearance, but the most beautiful appearance possible; or as though everything that comes into being were not subject to mortality.

Discoveries Attributed to Anaximenes (R8–R9)

R8 (< A14a) Pliny, *Natural History*

Anaximenes of Miletus [. . .] discovered this calculation of shadows, which they call "gnomic," and he was the first to exhibit in Sparta the clock they call *skiotherikon*.[1]

[1] Probable confusion with Anaximander, cf. **ANAXIMAND. R14.** The *skiotherikon* is a kind of sundial

R9 (< A16) Theon of Smyrna, *Mathematics Useful for Understanding Plato*

Eudemus reports in his *Astronomy* [. . .]: Anaximenes [scil. was the first to discover] that the moon gets its light from the sun and in what way it is eclipsed.[1]

[1] Probable confusion with Parmenides, cf. **PARM. D27–D29.**

A Fictional Scene from a Fragmentary
Greek Novel: The Philosopher at the
Court of Polycrates (R10)

R10 (As 18 Wöhrle) P. Berol. 7927, 9588, 21179 Col.
1.24–33; Col. 2.34–36, 53–57, 62–68 (Stephens-Winkler,
pp. 82–89)

[1.24] . . . πάντωι δὲ τῶ[ν] ε[.] | θαυ]μασάντων τὸ
εὐθαρσὲς καὶ | τῶν λόγων ὁ Πολυκράτης ὑπερ |]ν,"
ἔφη, "τέκνον, πότο꞉ καιρὸς |]χειν χρὴ τὰ λυποῦντα
μέθη |]υτωνομεια σχολάζομεν | [30] [ ] . ων εἰς τὸν
Ἀναξιμένην οι |] . . . ς ἡμῖν," ἔφη, "σήμερον α|]τ[ο]υ
παιδὸς ἥκοντος ενω]μαντεύομαι μοῦσαν, προτι|[2.34]
[θεὶς τ]ὴν φ[ιλ]οσόφου ζήτησιν κατὰ τύχην τ[. . . .]."|
[35] [καὶ ἐταράχθ ησαν οἱ δύο τὰς ψυχὰς λα-
β[όν]|[τες. . . . . . .]ου πάθους ἀνάμνησιν ἐφο[. . .]
|[. . .]

[2.53] [εἴη] δ' ἂν ϝἀκεῖνο παντελῶς ἀπίθανο[ν, εἰ] |
[βρέφ]ος ἐστὶν ὁ Ἔρως, περινοστεῖν αὐτ[ὸ]ν ὅ[λη]ν
τὴν | [55] [οἰκου]μένη꜄, τοξεύειν μὲν τῶν ὑπαντών|των,
οὓς ἂν αὐτὸς ἐθέλῃ, καὶ πυρπ[ο]λεῖν | [ὥστ' ἐ]ν μὲν
ταῖς τῶν ἐρώντων ψυχαῖς ἐγγίγνε|[σθαι] ἱερὸν πνεῦμά
τι οἷον θε[ο]φορ. . .·

[2.62] ἐβου-|[. . . .]ϝ λόγον περαίνειν καὶ ὁ [Ἀ]ν[α]-
ξιμένης δι[ελέγ]ετο πρὸς τὴν Παρθενόπην ἀντιλαβέ-
σθαι | [65] [τῆς ζ]ητήσεως· κἀκείνη | δ[ι' ὀ]ργῆς
ἔχουσα τὸν Μητίοχοϝ διὰ τὸ μὴ ὁμολογῆσαι μήπω
οὐδεμιᾶς ἐρασ|θῆναι (καὶ εὔξατο μηδὲ μέλλειν·)
". . . . ." ἔφη, [. . .]

ANAXIMENES

*A Fictional Scene from a Fragmentary
Greek Novel: The Philosopher at the
Court of Polycrates (R10)*

R10 (≠ DK) *Metiochus and Parthenope*[1]

While all of the . . . marveled at the courage and . . . of the
words, Polycrates . . . said, "Child, it is time to drink . . .
inebriation must . . . what causes grief . . we are at leisure
. . ." . . . [scil. looking?] at Anaximenes . . . for us," he said,
"today . . . since the boy has arrived . . . I predict a . . .
Muse, as I have proposed . . . the philosopher's inquiry by
chance . . . " [And] the two [scil. were thrown into a tur-
moil?] in their souls when they heard . . . the recollection
of suffering.

[scil. Metiochus said,] "[. . .] And that too would be
entirely implausible, if Eros is a child, that he wanders
about the whole inhabited world, shoots arrows at whomever he wishes among the people he encounters, and sets
them ablaze, so that in the lovers' souls some kind of holy
breath (*hieron pneuma ti*) is produced, as it is in people
who are inspired (?). [. . .]"

. . . He wanted to finish his speech, but Anaximenes
told Parthenope to take part in her turn in the inquiry. And
she, being angry with Metiochus because he refused to
admit that he had ever loved any woman (and he prayed
that he never would), said . . .

[1] This anonymous novel, which may date to the first century
BC, illustrates the cultural role of Polycrates, the tyrant of Samos.
Metiochus is the son of Polycrates and Hegesipyle. The poet
Ibycus is present too.

An Apocryphal Correspondence between
Anaximenes and Pythagoras (R11)

R11 Diog. Laert.

a (As 73 Wöhrle) 2.4

Θαλῆς Ἐξαμύου[1] ἐπὶ γήρως οὐκ εὔποτμος οἴχεται· εὐ-
φρόνης, ὥσπερ ἐώθει,[2] ἅμα τῇ ἀμφιπόλῳ προϊὼν ἐκ
τοῦ αὐλίου τὰ ἄστρα ἐθηεῖτο· καὶ (οὐ γὰρ ἐς μνήμην
ἔθετο) θηεύμενος ἐς τὸ κρημνῶδες ἐκβὰς καταπίπτει.
Μιλησίοισι μέν νυν[3] ὁ αἰθερολόγος ἐν τοιῷδε κεῖται
τέλει. ἡμέες δὲ οἱ λεσχηνῶται αὐτοί τε μεμνώμεθα τοῦ
ἀνδρός, οἵ τε ἡμέων παῖδές τε καὶ λεσχηνῶται, ἐπι-
δεξιοίμεθα[4] δ' ἔτι τοῖς ἐκείνου λόγοις. ἀρχὴ μέντοι
παντὸς τοῦ λόγου Θαλῇ ἀνακείσθω.

[1] ἐκ καλοῦ mss., corr. M. Gudius ap. Menagium
[2] ἔωθεν mss., corr. Cobet   [3] νῦν mss., corr. Casaubon
[4] ἐπιδεξιούμεθα prop. dub. Von der Mühll

b (As 74 Wöhrle) 2.5

εὐβουλότατος ἦς ἡμέων, μεταναστὰς ἐκ Σάμου ἐς
Κρότωνα, ἐνθάδε εἰρηνέεις. οἱ δὲ Αἰακέος παῖδες ἄλαστα[1] κακὰ ἔρδουσι καὶ Μιλησίους οὐκ ἐπιλείπουσι
αἰσυμνῆται. δεινὸς δὲ ἡμῖν καὶ ὁ Μήδων βασιλεύς,
οὐκ ἤν γε ἐθέλωμεν δασμοφορέειν· ἀλλὰ μέλλουσι δὴ
ἀμφὶ τῆς ἐλευθερίης ἁπάντων Ἴωνες Μήδοις κατ-

[1] ἄλαστα Porson: ἄλλοι τὰ mss.

ANAXIMENES

An Apocryphal Correspondence between
Anaximenes and Pythagoras (R11)

R11 (≠ DK) Diogenes Laertius

a [Anaximenes to Pythagoras:]

Thales, the son of Examyas, in his old age was not fortunate in his passing. At night, as was his custom, he went forth from the courtyard with his serving-maid to observe the stars. And forgetting where he was he came to a cliff while he was observing and fell over. This is how the Milesians lost their student of the heavens [cf. **THAL. P12**]. But let us, his pupils, cherish this man's memory, and so too our children and our pupils; and let us continue to enjoy (?) his discourses. May the starting point of our every discourse be dedicated to Thales.

b [Anaximenes to Pythagoras:]

You were the best advised of us all: for now that you have moved away from Samos to Croton, you live in peace there. Aeaces' sons [i.e. the tyrant Polycrates and his brothers] commit dreadful evils, and tyrants continue to rule the Milesians. The king of the Medes too is terrifying for us, unless indeed we are willing to pay him tribute. But the Ionians are about to start a war against the Medes for

375

ἵστασθαι ἐς πόλεμον· καταστᾶσι δὲ οὐκέτι ἐλπὶς ἡμῖν
σωτηρίης. κῶς ἂν οὖν Ἀναξιμένης ἐν θυμῷ ἔτι ἔχοι
αἰθερολογέειν, ἐν δείματι ἐὼν ὀλέθρου ἢ δουλοσύνης;
σὺ δὲ εἶ καταθύμιος μὲν Κροτωνιήτῃσι, καταθύμιος
δὲ καὶ τοῖσι ἄλλοισι Ἰταλιώτῃσι· φοιτέουσι δέ τοι
λεσχηνῶται καὶ ἐκ Σικελίης.

c (As 77 Wöhrle) 8.49–50

καὶ σύ, ὦ λῷστε, εἰ μηδὲν ἀμείνων ἧς Πυθαγόρεω
γενεήν τε καὶ κλέος, μεταναστὰς ἂν οἴχεο ἐκ Μιλή-
του· νῦν δὲ κατερύκει σε ἡ πατρόθεν εὔκλεια, καὶ ἐμέ
γε[1] ἂν κατείρυκεν Ἀναξιμένει ἐοικότα. εἰ δὲ ὑμεῖς οἱ
ὀνήιστοι τὰς πόλιας ἐκλείψετε, ἀπὸ μὲν αὐτέων ὁ κό-
σμος αἱρεθήσεται, ἐπὶ δὲ κινδυνότερα αὐτῇσι τὰ ἐκ
Μήδων. [50] οὔτε δὲ αἰεὶ καλὸν αἰθερολογίη[2] μελεδω-
νόν τε εἶναι τῇ πατρίδι κάλλιον. καὶ ἐγὼ δὲ οὐ πάντα
περὶ τοὺς ἐμεωυτοῦ μύθους, ἀλλὰ καὶ ἐν πολέμοις οὓς
διαφέρουσιν ἐς ἀλλήλους Ἰταλιῶται.

[1] τε mss., corr. Von der Mühll   [2] αἰθερολογίη PF: -γεῖν
B

Anaximenes Among the Christians (R12–R13)

R12 (As 59 Wöhrle) Min. Fel. *Octav.* 19.5

Anaximenes deinceps et post Apolloniates Diogenes aera
deum statuunt infinitum et inmensum; horum quoque
similis de divinitate consensio est.

the sake of everyone's freedom.[1] But if this happens, we shall lose any hope of being saved. How then could Anaximenes still think to study the heavens, living as he does in fear of death or slavery? But you find favor with the Crotonians and also the other Greeks in southern Italy [cf. **PYTH. a P24–P26**]; and pupils come to you even from Sicily.

[1] An allusion to the Ionian revolt against Cyrus.

c [Pythagoras to Anaximenes:]

You too, worthy friend, if you had not been superior to Pythagoras in family and fame, would have moved away and left Miletus. But as it is your ancestral renown detains you, as mine would have detained me had I been the equal of Anaximenes. But if you, the best of men, abandon the cities, then their fine order will be destroyed and the Medes' schemes will become more dangerous for them. [50] To study the heavens is not always a fine thing: it is finer to be concerned for your fatherland. I too am not completely occupied by my discourses, but I am also engaged in the wars that the Greeks in Italy fight against one another.

Anaximenes Among the Christians (R12–R13)

R12 (≠ DK) Minucius Felix, *Octavius*

Then Anaximenes and later Diogenes of Apollonia declare that air is an infinite and immense god; the view they too share regarding divinity is similar [scil. to ours].

R13 August.

a (< A10) *Civ. Dei* 8.2

[. . .] non tamen ab ipsis aerem factum, sed ipsos ex aere
ortos credidit.

b (< As 101 Wöhrle) *Conf.* 10.6

et quid est hoc? interrogavi terram, et dixit: "non sum"; et
quaecumque in eadem sunt, idem confessa sunt. interrogavi mare et abyssos et reptilia animarum vivarum, et
responderunt: "non sumus deus tuus; quaere super nos."
interrogavi auras flabiles, et inquit universus aer cum
incolis suis: "fallitur Anaximenes: non sum deus."

A Greek Alchemical Adaptation (R14)

R14 (B3) Ps.-Olymp. *Ars sacra* 25

μίαν δὲ κινουμένην ἄπειρον ἀρχὴν πάντων τῶν ὄντων
δοξάζει Ἀναξιμένης τὸν ἀέρα. λέγει γὰρ οὕτως· "ἐγ-
γύς ἐστιν ὁ ἀὴρ τοῦ ἀσωμάτου· καὶ ὅτι κατ᾽ ἔκροιαν
τούτου γινόμεθα, ἀνάγκη αὐτὸν καὶ ἄπειρον εἶναι καὶ
πλούσιον διὰ τὸ μηδέποτε ἐκλείπειν."

R13 Augustine

a (< A10) *City of God*

[. . .] however he believed not that air was made by them [i.e. the gods] but that they came to be out of air.

b (≠ DK) *Confessions*

And what is this [i.e. God]? I asked the earth, and it said, "I am not He"; and all the things that are in it admitted the same thing. I asked the sea and the abysses and, among the animate creatures, the ones that walk the earth; and they replied, "We are not your God seek above us." I asked the blowing winds, and the whole air together with its inhabitants said, "Anaximenes is mistaken: I am not God."

A Greek Alchemical Adaptation (R14)

R14 (B3) Ps.-Olympiodorus, *On the Sacred Art*

Anaximenes is of the opinion that air is the one principle, moved and unlimited, of all beings. For he speaks as follows: "Air is near to the incorporeal. And since we are born from an outflow of this, it is necessary that it be infinite and rich, because it never fails."[1]

[1] This citation is inauthentic.

Anaximenes in The Assembly of Philosophers (R15)

R15 (As 232 Wöhle) *Turba Phil.* Sermo II, p. 45.1–9 Plessner

ait Exumdrus: magnifico aera et honorifico—ut Eximedri roborem sermonem[1]—eo quod per ipsum opus emendatur, et spissatur et rarescit et calefit et frigescit. eius autem spissitudo fit, quando disiungitur propter solis elongationem; eius vero raritas fit, quando in coelo[2] exaltato sole calescit aer et rarescit. similiter vero fit in veris complexione,[3] in temporis nec calidi nec frigidi distinctione. nam secundum alterationem dispositionis constitutae ad distinctiones anni alterandas hyems alteratur. aer igitur spissatur, cum ab eo sol elongatur, et tunc hominibus frigus pervenit; aere vero rarescente prope fit sol, quo propinquo et aere rarescente calor pervenit hominibus.

[1] ut . . . sermonem *secl. Ruska*   [2] in coelo *solus M, om. cett.*   [3] complexione *BM*: compilatione *E*: copulatione *N*

Anaximenes in The Assembly of Philosophers (R15)

R15 (≠ DK) *The Assembly of Philosophers*

Exumdrus [i.e. Anaximenes[1]] said: "I exalt the air and honor it—so that I might corroborate Eximedrus' [i.e. Anaximander's] discourse—because by its means the work [scil. of alchemy] is rectified, and it becomes dense and rarefied, and hot and cold. Its condensation comes about when it is separated [scil. from the sun] because of the increase in the distance of the sun; but its rarefaction comes about when because of the height of the sun in the sky the air becomes warm and rarefed. But it becomes homogeneous in the mixture of the spring, in the season of the year that is neither hot nor cold. For according to the alteration of the arrangement that is constituted for altering the seasons of the year, the winter is altered. Thus the air becomes condensed when the distance of the sun from it is increased, and at that time coldness reaches humans; but when the air becomes rarefied the sun comes near, and when it is near and the air becomes rarefied warmth reaches humans."

---

[1] Identified as Anaximenes by Plessner, as Anaximander by Ruska.